SHAPING
OUR
NATION

ALSO BY MICHAEL BARONE

OUR FIRST REVOLUTION
*The Remarkable British Upheaval That Inspired
America's Founding Fathers*

HARD AMERICA, SOFT AMERICA
*Competition vs. Coddling and the Battle for the
Nation's Future*

THE NEW AMERICANS
How the Melting Pot Can Work Again

OUR COUNTRY
The Shaping of America from Roosevelt to Reagan

THE ALMANAC OF AMERICAN POLITICS
(as coauthor)

HOW SURGES OF

MIGRATION

TRANSFORMED AMERICA

AND ITS POLITICS

SHAPING

OUR

NATION

MICHAEL
BARONE

CROWN
FORUM
NEW YORK

Copyright © 2013 by Michael Barone

All rights reserved.
Published in the United States by Crown Forum,
an imprint of the Crown Publishing Group,
a division of Random House LLC,
a Penguin Random House Company, New York.
www.crownpublishing.com

CROWN FORUM with colophon is a registered trademark
of Random House LLC.

Library of Congress Cataloging-in-Publication Data
is available upon request.

ISBN 978-0-307-46151-3
eISBN 978-0-307-46153-7

Printed in the United States of America

Book design by Barbara Sturman
Maps by David Lindroth
Jacket design by Jess Morphew
Jacket photograph: WIN-Initiative/Getty Images
Author photograph: Andrew Harnik, Washington Examiner

10 9 8 7 6 5 4 3 2 1

First Edition

To Alex P.

CONTENTS

Preface: A Story for Our Time   1

1. THE FIGHTING SCOTS-IRISH   15

2. YANKEES AND GRANDEES   51

3. THE IRISH AND GERMANS 105

4. INCOMPLETE CONQUEST 147

5. PROMISED LANDS 183

6. MIGRATIONS OF CHOICE 227

Notes 273

Acknowledgments 287

Index 289

Maps

Areas of Major Scots-Irish Settlement Up to the American
Revolution 32
Moving Against the National Trend, 2004 to 2008 49
Southern Grandees: Cotton Production in 1859 62
Southern Grandees: Slaves as a Percent of Total Population in 1860 . 79
Southern Counties Favoring Barack Obama in 2008. 93
New England Yankees: Counties Carried by John C. Fremont
in 1856. 98
New England Yankees, 1924: Counties Carried by Calvin Coolidge
by 60% or More 99
Irish Population, 1870: Counties with the Highest Percentage
of Irish-Born 113
German Population, 1870: Counties with the Highest Percentage
of German-Born 128
Migration That Didn't Happen: Percentages of Northerners Born
in the South and Southerners Born in the North in 1930 153
Ellis Islanders: Percentage of Foreign-Born in Each State in 1930,
Just Six Years After the End of the Ellis Island Migration. . . . 167
Blacks Move Northward: In 1940 a Large Majority of American
Blacks Lived in the South 189
Blacks Move Northward: Between 1940 and 1970 Black
Population Had Shifted Dramatically. 212
Volitional Movement: High and Low Growth Rates, 1930–1970. . . 228
Volitional Movement: High and Low Growth Rates, 1970–2010. . . 229
Asian Population: Percentage Per State, 1970 248
Asian Population: Percentage Per State, 2010 249
Hispanic Population: Percentage Per State, 1970. 256
Hispanic Population: Percentage Per State, 2010. 257

SHAPING
OUR
NATION

Preface: A Story for Our Time

L OOKING back on four decades of published writings, I can discern a common theme: I have been trying in different ways to understand American politics and the course of American history, starting with the twenty-two editions of *The Almanac of American Politics* of which I have been coauthor since the first edition was published in 1971. The *Almanac* describes every state and congressional district and its members of Congress, and over the years I have been able in its pages to follow political and policy developments in granular detail. My 1990 book, *Our Country: The Shaping of America from Roosevelt to Reagan*,[1] was a narrative history of American politics from 1930 to 1988, buttressed by demographic and electoral analysis intended as an alternative to the prevailing analyses of the New Deal historians. In *The New Americans*[2] I argued that the minority groups of today resembled, up to a point, the immigrant groups of a hundred years ago: blacks resembled Irish, Latinos resembled Italians, Asians resembled Jews. My thesis implied a certain continuity in the American experience, with of course some contrasts and differences. In *Hard America, Soft America*[3] I contrasted the zones of American life where you have competition and accountability (Hard America) and those where you don't (Soft America). This was an attempt to view various developments in the twentieth century through a different and mostly nonpartisan lens, with an understanding that we don't want every part of American life to be too Hard or too many parts to be too Soft. In *Our First Revolution*[4] I went far back in time with a narrative of the events generally known as the Glorious Revolution of 1688–89, the ouster of King James II and the installation of King William III and Queen Mary II, the Catholic James's Protestant daughter and son-in-law and nephew. These events, I argued, greatly advanced the causes of representative government in Britain and in its North American seaboard colonies as well as guaranteed liberties, global capitalism, and an anti-hegemonic foreign policy. The Glorious Revolution was a very chancy and close-run thing, with strong reverberations to this day; it not only inspired but made possible the American Revolution and put first Britain and then America on their ways to be a leading force for liberty and the rule of law throughout the world.

For my next book, I sought a way to look at the American experience through a new prism, and my editor, having heard me riff on this theme, suggested a book on American migrations, internal as well as immigrant. In examining the data, it became apparent that to a great extent the United States was in large part peopled—a word I borrow from historian David Hackett Fischer, author of the superb *Albion's Seed*[5]—by surges of migration, large mass movements across the oceans or within the nation, which typically lasted only one or two generations but in that time reshaped the nation . . . and created lasting tensions difficult to resolve. None of these surges of migration was widely anticipated, and most of them ceased rather suddenly and contrary to expectations.

I was inspired as well by the picture painted by historian Walter McDougall in the first pages of his magisterial history of the United States from 1829 to 1877:[6] He described that if you could be transported back in time four hundred years and view the world in 1600, you would find most of the concentrations of population very similar to today's. There were great population masses in Ming China and Mogul India, a Muslim world of many varieties and schisms, a western Europe of fertile farms and trading ports, and a Russia expanding from its Muscovite base. In the Western Hemisphere there were the vast populations of Aztecs and Incas in the Mesoamerican and South American cordillera ruled by a thin layer of Spanish soldiers and priests. But North America then was very different from today. It was not vacant, as the writer Charles C. Mann has informed us in his wonderful books *1491*[7] and *1493*;[8] Indian farming and hunting civilizations of various degrees of advancement had developed there over centuries. But these civilizations had only the slightest of connections to the more advanced societies of Europe and Asia, and their peoples were soon to suffer from enormous depopulation due to diseases for which they had no immunity.

In their place today, in vivid contrast with the years around 1600, is a nation with 5 percent of the world's population that produces 25 percent of its economic product and deploys more than 50 percent of its military capacity, a nation in which only 1 percent of its current population claims ancestry from the peoples variously called American Indians or Native Americans. The peopling of the United States is one of the most important stories of the last five hundred years, a story of successive surges of migration, across the oceans and across the continent.

It is often said that in the past quarter century America has become culturally diverse. But it was culturally diverse from its colonial beginnings, and each successive surge of migration has changed the cultural and ethnic and political balance of the country. Americans have learned not only to cope but even to prosper as a nation with cultural variety, but that diversity has also led to grave and seemingly irrepressible conflict.

The history of American migrations is a story of surprises: few anticipated when these surges of migration would begin and even fewer predicted that they would abruptly end, as most did. That may be especially relevant, as this is written, for the vast Latino migration of the quarter century from 1982 to 2007 seems to have tapered off sharply, with net migration from Mexico apparently below zero, while internal migration sharply slowed with the onset of recession in 2007, as it did even more sharply in the economic depression of the 1930s. This apparent pause in American migrations, immigrant and internal, may provide an unusually good vantage point for looking back on the migrations of the past and trying to imagine the character and magnitude of the American migrations of the future.

⁓

IN *Albion's Seed* Fischer shows how the initial major migrations to Britain's North American colonies came primarily from four different and distinct parts of the British Isles and how they brought their "folkways," ranging from religious beliefs and political attitudes to sexual mores and food preferences, with them. These first four migrations up through 1760 were motivated not by economics but by religion and politics. The New England colonies were largely peopled by 21,000 settlers primarily from East Anglia, the easternmost part of England, most of whom arrived in the single decade of the 1630s. They were members of various Puritan sects that were out of favor with the government of King Charles I and the Church of England headed by Archbishop William Laud.

There was almost no migration to or migration out of New England in the next 150 years; the moralistic and intolerant Yankees repelled new settlers and were not much welcomed elsewhere. Starting earlier but accelerating later was the migration of about 30,000 from the royalist West Country of England to the Chesapeake colonies, Virginia and Maryland, in the 1640s and 1650s, when Charles was opposed by Parliament and its army and then beheaded and replaced by a republic headed by Oliver Cromwell. Starting in the 1680s there was a major migration of about 40,000 Quakers and others primarily from the North Midlands of England to the Delaware Valley colonies, Pennsylvania, Delaware, and West Jersey. Pennsylvania's pacifist founder and proprietor William Penn also recruited colonists from pacifist and pietist sects in Germany.

These migrants increased rapidly in numbers. Though deaths from disease were numerous in the Chesapeake colonies—migrants were considered "seasoned" after they survived their first year—the colonies to the north proved far healthier. Their numbers were augmented by those arriving in some form of servitude—slaves forcibly imported from Africa and indentured servants from England obliged to work a term of years in return for payment of their passage, plus a few convicts sent to the new colony of Georgia. So these colonies, starting off as narrow patches of land on coasts and bays, grew lustily because of very high birth rates and what was probably the highest protein diet for the masses of any in the world. By the middle of the eighteenth century, the population of these colonies was vastly increased to some 1.2 million. They included about 360,000 in New England, where the cold climate proved unhealthy for slaves; 220,000 in the Delaware River colonies—Pennsylvania, Delaware, New Jersey—with another 75,000 in Dutch-settled and ethnically diverse New York along the Hudson; and about 370,000 in the Chesapeake colonies, about 30 percent of whom were slaves. In addition there were about 140,000 in the colonies to the south, sparsely settled North Carolina, slave-majority South Carolina, and tiny Georgia. Small handfuls of colonists three and four centuries before did much to determine the culture and character of a nation of 310 million.

The subject of this book is the much larger surges of migration, internal and immigrant, that came next, starting with the mass movement from 1763 to 1775 of the Scots-Irish from Northern Ireland and Lowland Scotland to the Appalachian frontier, the fourth of the British folkways in Fischer's *Albion's Seed*. This was an international migration in the sense that people sailed across the Atlantic Ocean to a land that would soon become a separate and independent nation. But it was also an internal migration in the sense that the Scots-Irish were moving from one unruly fringe of the British Empire to another, motivated not just to seek a better living but even more to establish a community where they could live as they pleased. Unlike previous colonial migrations, it was not organized by profit-minded proprietors like the leaders of the Virginia Company or by community leaders motivated by religious or political views such as John Winthrop or William Penn; nor was it a migration of indentured servants or exiled convicts of slaves. And it was a migration different in kind from those that came before.

It was, like surges of migration over the next two centuries and more, a seemingly spontaneous movement of large numbers of like-minded people, motivated in part by the desire to make a better living, but also and more important determined to create a new community in which they could thrive and live as they wanted. American migrants were not just seeking more money; they were pursuing dreams or escaping nightmares.

Voluntary mass migrations—settler migrations, as historian James Belich calls them—are a relatively late phenomenon in world history and could not occur without the right combination of technological, political, and economic factors. Migrants need available and affordable transportation and must not be prevented from moving by government action. Economic historians have disagreed on when these conditions have been met; some say after the conclusion of the world war between Britain and France in 1815,[9] others, after Britain recognized the independence of the United States in the Treaty of Paris of 1783.[10] But the Scots-Irish migrated to North America in significant numbers after the Treaty of Utrecht ended a British-French war in 1713 and, in mass numbers encouraged by those who came earlier, after the Treaty of Paris ended another war in 1763. They came in numbers that no one seems to have predicted and stopped coming suddenly in a way that almost no one foresaw. In these respects the Scots-Irish migration was a prototype of later, post-Independence American migrations, both immigrant and internal. They sought a new place to establish their way of life, where they could flourish and perhaps be an inspiration to others as well.

THIS account will start off with the Scots-Irish migration and show how these migrants continued to move in a *drang nach* southwest to occupy and Americanize the Indian lands of the Southeast and much of the Mississippi Valley and how their emblematic leader, Andrew Jackson, successfully promoted the acquisition of Florida, Texas, and California—our first, second, and soon-to-be third most populous states—to the young republic. Having accomplished this enterprise, the Scots-Irish seemed to stop in their tracks and occupy the same swath of the nation today. But their achievement presented the nation's political leaders with the difficult issue of whether slavery should be allowed in the new territories, an issue that could not be peaceably settled but resulted in a bloody and hugely divisive civil war, one in which the Scots-Irish fought on both sides.

The next section of the book will look at two surges of internal migration in the first half of the nineteenth century: the Yankee diaspora spreading from New England across Upstate New York and the Great Lakes states and across the Mississippi, and the southern grandees' extension of plantation slavery from the Atlantic coast to the Mississippi Valley. These migrations were motivated not only by a desire to establish safe havens for each of these two colonial American cultures but were increasingly aimed at extending their cultural influence beyond their regional bases, to shape the national character in their own image. The collision this produced was the Civil War, in which the Yankee vision was not only the cultural but the military victor, and in which the defeated southern culture—or rather cultures, white and black—subsequently lived apart from the rest of the nation for three-quarters of a century.

The second pair of migrations were the two immigrations—of Irish Catholics and of mainly Protestant Germans—that began suddenly in great numbers in the middle 1840s and continued, with scarcely a pause during the Civil War, until the middle 1890s. Irish came over in vast numbers—1.3 million in the first decade, 1846–55, and about half a million in each of the next four decades. Germans came over in even larger numbers—about 1 million for five successive decades, except for half a million in the decade that included the Civil War. These 3 million Irish and 4.6 million Germans made a major impact in a nation with 38 million people at the beginning of the Civil War. Irish Catholics established communities in major cities and factory towns, which did much to determine the character of politics and popular culture in urban America; they built an American Catholic Church that for a century was very much an Irish institution. Germans started off settling in rural areas as well as in New York City and in large cities in the interior. They ended up establishing a Germano-Scandinavian zone in the Old Northwest, north of the Yankee diaspora settlements—in Wisconsin, Iowa, Minnesota, the Dakotas. That zone has always had a distinctive politics, hospitable to bureaucratizing reforms and cooperative enterprises and hostile to military involvement abroad—the most pacifist, isolationist, and dovish part of the nation for more than a century.

The third pair of migrations consists of one very large surge of migration and one potential surge of migration that never happened at all. In the three-quarters of a century between the Civil War and World War II there was a vast movement from rural to urban America, as the economy grew robustly though unevenly. From the 1890s through the 1930s, the development of mass production techniques created a demand in labor markets for mass production workers, and wages in the industrial Northeast and Midwest drew workers from farms. But not evenly. From the American South, where wage levels were less than half those in the North, very few migrants ventured northward during these decades—only about 1 million whites and 1 million blacks. The enormous impact of the Civil War and the continuing bitterness it engendered created a psychological barrier between North and South, as if a wall had been built along the Mason-Dixon Line and the Ohio River.

Immigration from traditional sources—Britain, Ireland, and Germany—dropped off as those nations' economies developed roughly in tandem with America's. Instead there was a vast and unanticipated Ellis Islander immigration to the northern states from regions of Europe that had produced few immigrants before the 1890s. These were largely peoples who were in some sense second-caste citizens in the multiethnic empires and kingdoms of eastern and southern

Europe—Jews and Poles from tsarist Russia; Poles, Czechs, and other Slavs from the Hapsburg Empire; and southern Italians from the northern-dominated kingdom of Italy. While American Southerners found the culture of Northern America unwelcoming, second-caste peoples from the far sides of Europe found it more attractive than their native lands. The Ellis Islander migration halted during World War I and was ended by the restrictive Immigration Act of 1924, which allocated immigration quotas according to the national origins of the nation's population in the pre–Ellis Island year of 1890.

If the Civil War was a divisive conflict, leaving the southern culture alienated from the northern one, and vice versa, World War II was an annealing event, bringing Americans together, putting them in uniform and sending them around the country and around the world. Altogether 16 million Americans served at one time or another in the military, in a nation of 131 million; the proportionate number in 2010 would be 38 million. The unity of the war effort also fostered cultural uniformity, promoted already by mass media with universal appeal, the radio of the 1920s and 1930s, and the movies of the 1930s. The demands of war industries brought Southerners, black and white, to the great cities and factory towns of the North. The war in the Pacific drew for the first time millions of the 90 percent of Americans who lived east of the Rockies to the West Coast. These wartime movements introduced many Americans to what they came to regard as a promised land and stimulated two surges of migration, which continued for the first postwar generation and which are the subject of the next section of the book, the movement of mostly white Midwesterners to California and the movement of one-third of American blacks from the rural South to the urban North. Those surges of migration lost momentum when the destination no longer seemed to be a promised land—the black northward migration waning in the middle 1960s as effective national civil rights legislation was passed, and the California migration, in the early 1980s when its coastal climate lost its comparative advantage in a country where air-conditioning and comfortable winter clothing became near-universal.

The final chapter concerns the two unpredicted and vast surges of migration over the four decades from 1970 to 2010. One was the vast migration from Latin America and Asia first to major metropolitan areas, especially in California, Texas, and Florida, plus New York City and Chicago, then dispersing over time to smaller but rapidly growing metropolitan areas in other states. The other was volitional migration, primarily from high-tax states to low-tax states, but also for many liberals' and conservatives' movement to culturally congenial surroundings.

The turning points here came at the end of the first postwar generation, in the years on either side of 1970. Formerly immigration was minimal, thanks to the Immigration Law of 1924 and the postwar economic recovery in European nations with large immigrant quotas. When the immigration law was rewritten in 1965, little thought was given to potential immigration from other sources. In fact immigration from Latin America was theoretically restricted more by the 1965 law than previously. But country quotas proved beside the point as millions immigrated legally using family unification provisions and millions more immigrated illegally by crossing the border clandestinely or overstaying visas.

As for volitional immigration, the generation from 1945 to 1970 saw the conclusion of longtime farm-to-factory internal migration. Growth concentrated in major metropolitan areas including the corridor from New York City to Washington, D.C., and in the industrial factory cities of the Midwest, where auto and other manufacturers were siting new plants. From 1970 to 2010 the picture is very different. The population of the major metropolitan areas of the Northeast and the Midwest (with the conspicuous exception of Washington) stagnated, as millions fled increasingly high state and local taxes. The major northern immigrant destinations, including Los Angeles and the San Francisco Bay Area, starting around 1990 saw internal outmigration for similar reasons. Domestic inflow was channeled largely to the South Atlantic states, from Virginia to Florida, to Texas, and to the smaller states of the West, almost all of them low-tax territory.

The rule-proving exceptions were inflow into tax havens in the Northeast and Midwest, including New Hampshire, Delaware, and South Dakota.

By 1970 the cultural uniformity of World War II and early post-war America was being replaced by a cultural diversity more typical of the nation in the long run of its history. As a result many Americans in deciding where to live their adult lives or where to retire sought out places compatible with their lifestyle. This was particularly true of professionals and others in a position to choose where to live. Liberals gravitate to New York, Los Angeles, and San Francisco, university towns, and ski resorts, while conservatives gravitate to Dallas, Houston, and Atlanta and retirement towns in the Smokies or the Ozarks. The result is what journalist Bill Bishop has called "the big sort," with liberal areas becoming more liberal and conservative areas, more conservative.

The surges of migration in these four decades have produced an America that seems to be flying apart. It may not be headed to a collision as dramatic as the Civil War, which was the result of the surges of migration in the first sixty years of the nineteenth century—though culture-wars political rhetoric sometimes gives that impression—but it can seem sorely in need of some less-than-total-war equivalent of the annealing experience of World War II. Just when the centripetal forces seemed at their maximum, the recession and financial crisis of the late 2000s produced a sudden halt to the surges of migration that had been occurring for at least a quarter century. Immigration from Asia fell and immigration from Latin America plummeted, with more reverse migration back to Mexico, particularly of illegal immigrants, than migration from Mexico to the United States. It seems at least possible that immigration from Mexico and perhaps from all of Latin America will never again reach the levels of the almost entirely prosperous years from 1983 to 2007. The surge of Latin immigration may have stopped as abruptly as the surge from Ireland and Germany did in the 1890s or as the northward migration of southern blacks stopped in the middle 1960s. In addition, domestic migration also was sharply reduced, though not to the very low levels of the 1930s.

The post-1970 surges of migration, like surges of migration in the past, have led many to question whether and how Americans with diverse cultural, religious, and political beliefs can live together. This is a question Americans have always had to grapple with, not one that has suddenly and for the first time been posed by the transformation of a long-homogeneous country to one with cultural and racial diversity. The Framers of the Constitution and the Bill of Rights had to deal with similar problems. They were well aware of the different religious and cultural backgrounds of the different states. They had seen that the colonies were unable to come together in response to a proposed plan of union at the Albany Conference in 1754. They learned to their dismay that the federal government set up by the Articles of Confederation lacked the power to effectively tax and protect its citizens. They were determined to create a stronger federal government but one whose powers would be limited in order to reduce cultural conflict and preserve zones of autonomy. And they were careful in their grants of power to the president and the Congress; they were vague about the powers of a supreme court; they required in a religiously diverse nation that there would be no religious test for federal office (although religious tests for state office persisted through the late nineteenth century). This was a revolutionary doctrine, adopted when England required public officials to be members of the established Church of England and when in all European nations Jews were subject to civic disabilities, including prohibitions on holding public office.

The First Amendment, ratified in 1790, provided that Congress "shall make no law . . . regarding an establishment of religion, nor prohibiting the free exercise thereof." They acted knowing that different colonies had had different established churches and as several states, notably Virginia, were amid controversy regarding disestablishing their established churches, while other states were determined to keep theirs, as Connecticut did until 1818 and Massachusetts, until

1831. The Framers' formula—limited government and individual rights—has not always been applied faithfully in American history, and it was not enough to prevent the outbreak of a civil war. But it has provided a ready and useful template for the accommodation of diverse peoples, even as the nation has been peopled by successive and culturally diverse surges of migration.

1. THE FIGHTING SCOTS-IRISH

THE Scots-Irish migration to North America was a movement of people who did not call themselves Scots-Irish and who did not consider themselves immigrants. And certainly they did not think that their migration would be a template for American migrations, internal and immigrant, over the next two centuries. Yet it has been, for it was both an internal migration in a move from one fringe of the British Empire to another and also an international migration across an ocean and between what would soon be two separate nations. This was an enormous migration for the times, from the cramped lands of northern Ireland and Lowland Scotland facing the Irish Sea west across the Atlantic, down the Appalachians, and eventually stretching far west to the Rio Grande. The Scots-Irish came primarily from Ulster, the province that covers the northeast corner of Ireland, from the Lowlands of Scotland, and from the northernmost counties of England.

This migration, beginning before the Revolutionary War, was a sharp departure from the patterns of settlement of previous migrations to the American colonies. By numbers, most colonial migrants were either black slaves transported from Africa or indentured servants from England, almost all of them male, who in return for free passage were bound to work for those who paid for them on their arrival. Few of the Scots-Irish were indentured servants and most immigrated as members of families, with women and children, not as single men.

Most of the previous free colonial migrants arrived as followers of movements seeking refuge from religious or political persecution—the Puritans of New England, the Cavaliers of the Chesapeake country, the Quakers and pietists attracted to William Penn's Pennsylvania—and settled in colonies established or developed for that purpose. The Scots-Irish migration, in contrast, was not the product of organized religious or political leaders and the migrants made no effort to establish a colony of their own. The earlier migrants came from cultures characterized by deference to those regarded as occupying a higher place in society. The Scots-Irish, though varying widely in economic status, were a proud people unaccustomed to doffing their hats to others.

The Scots-Irish seemed to be fleeing places where market capitalism—the need to produce flax and cattle for the English linen, meat, and butter trades—was encroaching on what had been fighting fields, limiting personal freedom and autonomy and enmeshing people in commercial relationships. They set out for another extreme of the British Empire, new fighting fields where they could make their way independent of overbearing bureaucracies and not be forced to submit to the seemingly random and unpredictable discipline of the market. Religious diversity was not so important to them; they were used to fighting for their religious assertion and for following chieftains more than faiths.

The initial movement came after the War of Spanish Succession (Queen Anne's War in North America), ending in 1713, and prepared the way for the surge that began after the war, ending with the Treaty of Paris in 1763. The British Empire in the years just afterward had a population of about 13 million people, of which 6 million were in England and Wales, including 750,000 in the giant metropolis of London. From this central core the population spread out to peripheral lands. One was Scotland, joined with England to form the United Kingdom in the Act of Union of 1707 but the scene of armed rebellion as recently as 1745, which had about 1.3 million people. Another was Ireland, technically a second kingdom but one whose parliament's acts required approval from the British Parliament in Westminster, with about 3 million people, the majority Catholic, but with about 750,000, mostly Presbyterians of Scots origin, in the northeastern province of Ulster. Across the ocean Canada, just acquired from France, had 300,000 residents, almost all French-speaking. To the south, Jamaica had 170,000 people, the various British Caribbean islands 100,000, and Barbados, to the east in the Atlantic Ocean, 80,000—at least 90 percent of them black slaves. Finally, the seaboard North American colonies that would become the United States had nearly 2 million residents, of whom one-fifth were black slaves.

OVERALL this empire, headed by a monarch who was required by the Act of Settlement of 1701 to be Protestant and to be married to a Protestant, had a population that was about 20 percent Catholic. Although slavery was not legally recognized in England, about 5 percent of the empire's people were black slaves. The Church of England was the established church in England and the similarly Anglican Church of Ireland was established in Ireland, but the established Church of Scotland was Presbyterian, the established churches of the New England colonies were Calvinist, and the colonies of Pennsylvania, New Jersey, and Delaware had no established church at all. Although religious denomination does not seem to have been too important for the Scots-Irish, it was anyway a continual source of dispute—the various arguments within and against the Church of Scotland, the anomalous position of Presbyterians in Ireland with its Catholic majority and its Anglican-established church. In North America the Scots-Irish were quite ready to switch denominations and weren't fussy about established churches.

They were very concerned about their unwritten code of behavior, priding themselves on their independence and ever ready to uphold personal honor and retaliate against attacks on family or community; they were punctilious about being rambunctious. The point was personal independence, natural liberty; Presbyterianism tended to be in line with this, but other denominations would do.

The Scots-Irish came from borderlands within this empire: from the Lowlands of Scotland, the scenes of fighting and religious disorder for generations, and from Ulster, where Presbyterians had moved from Scotland in the 1690s and lived in uncomfortable proximity with Irish Catholics and under the governance of English landlords and the Anglican bishops of the Church of Ireland—lands of "endemic violence" in the words of historian David Hackett Fischer.[1] Here, and in the northern counties of England, great landholders had commanded the loyalty of their tenants and on occasion led them into battle. Yet these were also lands that in the eighteenth century had been tied in with England in trade in a growing capitalist economy. Scotland produced sheep, and Ireland, cattle; in Ulster flax was raised and woven in country cottages into the linen cloth used in most clothing; and the linen, wool, and cattle trades connected these areas at the fringes of the British Isles with the growing English economy. Market fluctuations produced windfall gains in some years and economic distress in others; land values could vary widely and when the typical thirty-one–year lease expired, landlords often raised rents sharply— "rack renting," as protesters said. Some Scottish landlords, calculating that they could make more money from raising sheep and cattle than from subsistence tenant farmers, simply evicted all their tenants. This was not a stable, somnolent society, but a zone that had recently been the scene of almost constant fighting to become the scene of rapid and dizzying economic change.[2] Once isolated and distant from commercial centers, it came to be connected by dozens of ships constantly crossing the Irish Sea, at one point only 16 miles wide between Ulster and the Galloway country of Scotland, tying together disparate British lands but also suggesting the possibility of flight to the British world beyond the Atlantic.

These people didn't much like commerce or commercial society, which depends on peace and in which fluctuations in worth depend not on fighting but on the operations of markets that are often far outside the control of the individual or even the clan.

In North America they certainly seemed more set on self-sufficiency and tended to avoid engagement in the market economy. Initially, high transportation costs kept them mostly separate from the coastal market economy. The southern grandees wanted free trade to sell their export crops abroad; the Scots-Irish didn't seem to care so much—though they certainly didn't want their whiskey taxed.

They wanted to conquer territory—oust the British, expel the Indians, take over vast lands from Mexico, and, if possible, other Latins; they wanted lordship rather than economic cultivation.

DURING the course of the eighteenth century some 250,000 Scots-Irish migrated from the British Isles to the North American colonies, about 125,000 in the decades between 1717 and 1763, and another 125,000 in the dozen years from 1763 to 1775. This was a significant outflow from islands with a population of some 10 million and an enormous inflow into colonies with about 300,000 at the beginning of the migration and close to 2 million at the end. One political obstacle to migration was removed with the Act of Union of 1707, which united England and Scotland; before that, Scots had been barred from the North American colonies. So, starting in 1717, shortly after the end of the war, some combination of economic, religious, and political insecurity motivated large numbers of Scots-Irish to move from the fringes of Western civilization in the British Isles to the fringes of civilization in British North America. The Irish Sea had been a wide-open road from Scotland to Ireland for one hundred years; now the Atlantic Ocean suddenly became a wide-open road from Ireland and Scotland to North America.

The way was not led by any single leader, such as John Winthrop of Massachusetts. Nor does it appear that any colonial proprietor, such

as William Penn of Pennsylvania, sought out these migrants. They
were self-starters. The typical Scots-Irish migrants were not single
men or indentured servants, but married couples and entire families with enough resources to pay for their passage; the very poorest,
in this as in other migrations, simply could not afford to move, and
indentured servitude was becoming increasingly uncommon in these
years.[3] Many were, in Fischer's words, "independent yeomen who had
achieved a measure of independence," not landowners but tenants and
subtenant farmers and skilled craftsmen and small traders.[4] But they
also included a small minority of gentry, significant landowners with
some military renown, including ancestors of Patrick Henry, John C.
Calhoun, James K. Polk, and Sam Houston. To some extent they
appear to have been acting in response to economic distress. Northern Ireland and Lowland Scotland produced flax for linen and cattle
for the English beef and butter trade. The Scots-Irish were increasingly participants or (as some saw it) prisoners of market capitalism,
forced to submit to the laws of supply and demand. Scots-Irish migration seems to have increased during recessionary times in 1725–29,
1740–41, and 1754–55.[5] And many may have been prompted to move
by a sense that they were running out of space; the practice of partible inheritances, dividing properties equally among heirs, resulted
in the splintering of landholdings and tenancies. But the chief motive
seems to have been to maintain their accustomed patterns of life and
the natural liberty they cherished in a British world being continually
transformed by the workings of economic markets in a time of uneven
and unanticipated growth. The vast lands of North America seemed
an open place where they could enjoy the practical liberty to which
they were accustomed and where they could forge their own livings
relatively free of the restrictions of landlords and hostile churchmen.
To British authorities their flight raised the specter of depopulation.
"The humour has spread like a contagious distemper," one wrote,
"and the people will hardly hear anybody that tries to cure them of
their madness."[6]

THE Scots-Irish certainly made a distinct impression when, in the summer and fall of 1717, some five thousand began arriving in Philadelphia in ships from ports on the Irish Sea, from Belfast, Londonderry, and Carrickfergus in Ulster, from Kirkcudbright and Wigtown in southwestern Scotland, and from Liverpool in northwestern England.[7] They were proud, hard, undeferential men and women, ready to defend their honor and unwilling to doff their hats. They chose Philadelphia, in tolerant and multiethnic Pennsylvania, rather than other ports. New England Yankees with their narrow Calvinism did not welcome outsiders, and had almost no immigrants in the colonial period; the Scots-Irish founded a few towns there, like Londonderry, New Hampshire, but they mostly stayed away. New York had an established Anglican church and little land available for settlers. Most of the territory along the Hudson River was owned by Dutch patrons and other great landowners; north and west of Albany was Iroquois territory. The Chesapeake colonies of Virginia and Maryland had no great ports, and most new entrants there were indentured servants from England.

But Philadelphia was not the ultimate destination of the Scots-Irish. These proud, pugnacious people did not fit in well with the pacifist mercantile Quakers of Pennsylvania or with the pietist Germans whom William Penn recruited to settle his colony. The first Scots-Irish tended to move inland to the frontier, 30 or 40 miles from Philadelphia, early in the eighteenth century. The colony's provincial secretary, James Logan, himself born in Ulster, invited Ulstermen to Pennsylvania in 1720 and urged them to settle inland "as a frontier in case of disturbance," but soon found them "troublesome settlers to the government and hard neighbors to the Indians."[8] Penn and other colonial officials sought only to purchase lands from the Indians and to recognize their rights; the Ulster migrants, used to defending lands from the claims of hostile Irish Catholic neighbors, had no such scruples. These squatters asserted their claims self-righteously: it was "against the Laws of God & Nature that so much land should lie idle, while so many Christians wanted it to labour on and raise their Bread."[9] They were used to fighting hostile and what they believed were primitive peoples, like the Catholics in Ireland and Highlanders in Scotland, and they were ready or even eager for such fights in their new homeland.

These people with a natural tendency to wandering and adventure were not inclined to stay in one place long. They built stockade forts and rude log cabins, with notched logs and mud chinking, not lumber or stone-clad houses like the Quakers and Germans, and they were ever ready to leave them behind for better opportunities.[10] They worked with neighbors to cut trees and at house-raisings, house-warmings, and quiltings; they kept flintlock rifles to shoot deer, bear, and small game—wild turkeys, pigeons, squirrels—and fend off wolves. They raised corn and potatoes and kept cattle and horses and sometimes sheep. Tables and stools as well as kitchen utensils and bowls were carved from wood, with iron spits and pots to roast meat. They were careful to seek springs or dig wells to obtain potable water (thus giving them a considerable health advantage over many coastal settlers); in their cabins they always kept a fire going. They built churches and attracted ministers, who also taught their children.[11] They resisted becoming tenants of a large landholder, as so many of their ancestors had been in Ireland and Britain, but in a frontier region where land claims were anything but firmly established they were not eager to risk everything on their claim to the land they occupied. So while they were ready to litigate land titles as soon as a court was available, they developed no strong attachment to specific plots of ground.[12] Some order was provided by Presbyterian churches, where the minister might teach school, and from the seemingly spontaneous organization of local militias, whose leaders were often from families that had been prominent in Ulster before the emigration.[13]

Over the next sixty years these migrants, confined so long to the valleys and hills of Ulster and Lowland Scotland, spread out in the American backcountry, up to and just beyond the first Appalachian chains, filling a broad expanse of land 700 miles long—twice the distance from the northwest tip of Ulster to the southwest tip of County Cork, as far as the distance from the northern tip of Scotland to the southwest tip of Cornwall—from Pennsylvania to South Carolina. From Philadelphia they headed west on the Great Philadelphia Wagon Road into Lancaster County, then farther west across the Susquehanna River at Harris's Ferry (now Harrisburg) to York and Cumberland Counties, a land of fertile, gentle hills sheltered by the first Appalachian chain, then south between the Blue Ridge, the first Appalachian chain, and the second, through the narrow neck of Maryland and, in the early 1730s, into the Shenandoah Valley of Virginia.[14] This was wild country, once burned over by Indians to provide fertilizer for crops and now grazing land for plentiful buffalo and deer, while wolves, bears, and bobcats roamed the nearby forests. This route down the Shenandoah was used for communication by the Iroquois in the north seeking to dominate the Cherokee and the Creek in the south, and it was the path used by the Tuscarora to move from North Carolina to Upstate New York after they agreed to become the Sixth Nation of the Iroquois in 1726,[15] but it had little permanent Indian population and so was open to the Scots-Irish. It was a frontier buzzing with movement and activity, with trees felled to form trails or build rude houses, with sun coming through the leaves during the day and fires burning at night.

THIS was not empty land, but it was only lightly populated. Maps show the Indian tribes occupying far larger areas than the colonial settlers, though this is highly misleading. The Indians suffered huge disease kill off,[16] and in the seventeenth century the Iroquois, eager to monopolize the beaver-for-arms trade with first the Dutch and then the British, made war on other tribes and drove them westward.[17]

As a result, the number of Indians east of the Mississippi and south of the Great Lakes in the eighteenth century was probably only about one-tenth the population of the seaboard colonies. Historian J. H. Elliott's estimates for the population east of the Mississippi are 1,816,000 whites (75 percent of the total), 467,000 blacks (19 percent), and only 150,000 Indians (6 percent).[18]

The Iroquois were the dominant force among the Indians not only in Upstate New York but far to the south. By following a course of neutrality between the British and the French—with some warriors fighting alongside the British and others betraying British plans to the French—they were recognized in the eighteenth century as the negotiators for other tribes. Their sale of lands occupied by the Delaware in eastern Pennsylvania in 1737 resulted in the move of that tribe west beyond the Appalachians.[19] The low density of Indian populations reflected their continuing reliance on hunting, but they were not simple hunter-gatherers; they raised corn, beans, and squash as well as cattle and pigs, and traded with whites, selling furs and hides and buying guns, ammunition, cloth, and other manufactured goods, usually by barter (the colonies always were short of metal coins). The Indians were regarded as savages by many colonists, but the freedom accorded to individuals within tribal units evidently persuaded many whites kidnapped from colonial settlements to remain voluntarily in the Indian society, and the fighting tactics and woodcraft of the Indians were imitated by colonial soldiers. In the seventeenth century they had massacred some white settlements, and as late as 1704 plundered Deerfield, Massachusetts, in the Connecticut River Valley. But their dependence on whites for guns and ammunition and, even more important, their much smaller numbers put them at a severe disadvantage against the British settlers whose vast increase in numbers and hunger for more land as their soil wore out made them seek to expand in lands only lightly populated by Indians.

Thus the Scots-Irish migrants heading out to valleys amid the Appalachians and south along the Great Wagon Road in the Shenandoah Valley found plentiful land—a vivid contrast with what they had known in Ulster and Scotland. "They launched into a new World," as one contemporary described them, "breathing a Spirit of Liberty and a Desire of every individual becoming a Proprietor, where they imagine they can still obtain land for themselves, and their flocks of Cattle at a trifling Rent, or of conquering it from the Indian with the Sword,"[20] as many of their ancestors had obtained land in Ulster from the Catholic Irish. They did not seek to create a colony of their own but met with encouragement from colonial authorities. Virginia governor William Gooch issued enormous land grants to them in the 1730s with the proviso that they attract more settlers.[21] The news of these settlements traveled throughout the trans-Atlantic British Empire. Many, perhaps most, of the Scots-Irish were literate (the Presbyterian Church encouraged women as well as men to learn to read and write), but like all Anglophones of the time they were eccentric spellers; in any case they sent letters back to Ulster and Scotland with glowing reports. They had found land of their own with plenty more available, they enjoyed a hearty diet with plenty of meat as well as corn and whiskey, and they could practice their Presbyterian religion unmolested. These reports encouraged others to cross the ocean, particularly when conditions in Ulster and Scotland deteriorated, and the newcomers sent back similar messages to others.

They continued moving south along the Great Wagon Road and, where it met mountain barriers south of Roanoke, they headed directly south to more open lands east of the Appalachian chains in the Yadkin and Catawba River valleys in the Piedmont of North Carolina around 1740 and reached the up-country of South Carolina around 1760. Here they were less hemmed in by mountains and spread out over the Yadkin and Catawba River valleys. The interior of the Carolinas was mostly empty: North Carolina was a very lightly settled colony, with most settlers near the inlets off the Atlantic Ocean, and South Carolina in the middle eighteenth century was a colony of slave plantations and the small port city of Charleston. The Scots-Irish were encouraged to settle on these mostly empty lands of Lord Granville, one of the original proprietors of the colony who held title to vast areas, and were welcomed by successive royal governors of North Carolina, Gabriel Johnston, a native of Scotland, and Matthew

Rowan and Arthur Dobbs, who were from Ulster,[22] and enjoyed friendly relations with the local Catawba Indians.[23]

These were relatively peaceful times in the colonies. Britain and France, almost constantly at war from 1689 to 1713, were at peace from 1713 to 1740, and the War of Austrian Succession (King George's War in North America) over the next eight years did not have much impact on the colonial frontier. The major British initiative was the capture of the French fortress of Louisbourg, considered the key to its control of the St. Lawrence River, by New England colonials who were frustrated when it was handed back in the treaty ending the war in 1748. The picture was very different in the 1750s. Fighting between Britain and France broke out first not in Europe but in North America. The initial focus was the Forks of the Ohio, where the Allegheny and Monongahela Rivers join to form the Ohio. There the French with Indian allies who had been driven west by collusion of the Iroquois and the Pennsylvania proprietors built Fort Duquesne, in an attempt to preserve their hold on the Ohio Valley, which connected lightly populated French Canada on the St. Lawrence River with the even more lightly populated Louisiana near the mouth of the Mississippi. This brought to a sudden stop the Scots-Irish movement down the Great Wagon Road[24] and prompted Virginia governor Robert Dinwiddie in November 1753 to send a twenty-one-year-old lieutenant colonel named George Washington to assert the colony's interest in the Forks country.[25] Washington and his few troops clashed with French troops in spring 1754, resulting in the death of a captured French officer, and then retreated. He returned in 1755 under the command of Gen. Edward Braddock, where their forces were defeated in July; three of Washington's horses were shot out from under him and Braddock was killed.[26]

Thus began what was known in Europe as the Seven Years' War and in North America as the French and Indian War. Warfare broke out in much of British North America. The British avenged Braddock's defeat when Washington and Gen. John Forbes led their men to capture a largely abandoned Fort Duquesne. The pacific Quakers withdrew from the Pennsylvania Assembly and let the more belligerent Scots-Irish and Germans take charge of the defense of the colony against the Indians.[27] The French attempt to attack New York through the Hudson River was foiled in large part by the efforts of Robert Rogers, descendant of Scots-Irish settlers of Londonderry, New Hampshire. Rangers helped capture Crown Point and Fort Ticonderoga from the French and became the model of American special forces from the eighteenth to the twenty-first centuries.[28] In 1762, anticipating a peace treaty, the French off-loaded their Louisiana colony on their ally Spain. In 1763 they signed the Treaty of Paris, which recognized British sovereignty over North America east of the Mississippi.

Scots-Irish migration to North America, which ceased suddenly with the outbreak of war in 1754, resumed in far greater numbers than ever after the Treaty of Paris and the suppression of the Cherokee Uprising and Pontiac's rebellion. The attractiveness of the new land had become well known; the way seemed suddenly open after the British victory; the linen industry of Ulster faced sharply declining prices in the 1770s; and rents were raised sharply by Ulster and Scottish landlords, like the Marquis of Donegal, who had hundreds of his tenants evicted.[29] The British government attempted to shield Indians from settlers with the Proclamation of 1763, which banned settlement west of a line running roughly along the Appalachian crest. But that ban seemed beyond the capacity of the Crown to enforce. From 1763 to 1775, a period of a dozen years, about 125,000 Scots-Irish migrated to the North American colonies,[30] as many as had migrated in the four decades from 1717 to the outbreak of the French and Indian War. This amounted to about 1 percent of the entire population of the trans-Atlantic British Empire—a significant drain from Ulster and the Scottish Lowlands—and about 10 percent of the preexisting population of the colonies. It was one of the largest immigrations in proportion to preexisting population in American history, similar in magnitude to the Irish and German immigration of 1847–56 and the Ellis Island immigration of 1900–14. The number arriving each year approximated the population of Boston, then the third-largest city in the colonies; in the first two weeks of August 1773 some 3,500 arrived in Philadelphia, which then had a population of about 30,000. Every spring and summer they streamed southwest in great numbers down the Great Wagon Road; by 1775 the previously unsettled backcountry of North Carolina just to the east of the mountains, centered on the town of Salisbury and the Yadkin River, had 60,000 settlers and the backcountry of South Carolina had 83,000, most of them Scots-Irish.[31] The Scots-Irish, a people with "a natural disposition to wandering and adventure" in the words of Sir Walter Scott,[32] took to wandering and adventure at an unprecedented pace.

They headed from the valleys and bays of Ulster and Lowland Scotland to a zone of settlement in the American backcountry, up to and just beyond the first Appalachian chains from western Pennsylvania to South Carolina. It spread across colonial boundaries and across the 1763 Proclamation line, and was already staked out by the Scots-Irish migrants of the previous half century. Most colonial historians have understandably concentrated on what was happening in the colonial capitals on or near the Atlantic coast, particularly in the rising discontent with the British authorities that led to the American Revolution. But in those years when the Stamp Act was being denounced, the Boston Massacre was taking place, and the Continental Congress was assembling, tens of thousands of Scots-Irish migrants, fierce and proud, were disembarking at Philadelphia and other nearby ports and heading determinedly inland.

AMONG this wave were a Scots-Irish couple, Andrew and Elizabeth Jackson, the parents of President Andrew Jackson, who more than any other individual stamped the Scots-Irish imprint on the North American continent. Jackson's parents were in many ways typical of the Scots-Irish migrants of the 1763–75 surge. They were not impoverished but were part of a vibrant web of commerce that extended across the Irish Sea. Andrew was the fourth son of a linen weaver and merchant in Carrickfergus, a town on Belfast Lough in Northern Ireland, and he leased a farm, raised flax, and made linen thread; Elizabeth was also from a linen-making family. Their range of relationships spanned the Atlantic. Andrew's brother Sam was a sailor; his brother Hugh was a veteran of General Braddock's army that was defeated in western Pennsylvania in 1755 and of General Wolfe's army that successfully stormed the Plains of Abraham in Quebec in 1759. Elizabeth had four sisters living in the Carolinas who wrote her letters telling of their lives there.

So they were not headed to uncharted territory when, having paid for their passage by selling their lease and livestock, they sailed out of Belfast Lough for the Delaware River in the spring of 1765. From there they headed west and southwest on an already well-trodden path, along the Great Wagon Road that led to Lancaster County, across the Susquehanna River, and then down the Shenandoah Valley on the Great Wagon Road, then over to the Piedmont of North Carolina to the Waxhaw district near the Catawba River on the boundary between North and South Carolina. This was no longer an empty frontier but a region buzzing with settlers; residents of one North Carolina town counted one thousand wagons going through that summer. Salisbury, North Carolina, and Camden, South Carolina, about 40 miles north and south of the Waxhaw district, were established market and courthouse towns; prominent Scots-Irish families such as the Polks and Alexanders were planning to build a Mecklenburg County courthouse in between, in the little settlement they called Charlotte. Slaves were brought from dockside in Charleston up through Camden and were sold, some to Elizabeth's sister and brother-in-law Jane and James Crawford. Thoroughbred horses came in over the trails as well, as did cattle in numbers sufficient for settlers to set up cow pens to fatten the animals before driving them to market in Charleston. The Jacksons bought 200 acres on Twelve Mile Creek some 10 miles from the Crawfords', built a log cabin, and plowed the red soil. Guns were plentiful, though the local Catawba Indians were friendly, and there was a Presbyterian church with a learned minister where women brought in their family Bibles for Sunday services. In this frontier at the edge of British settlement in North America the Jacksons and their fellow settlers were building communities in many ways similar to those they had left behind on the other side of the Atlantic.

But it was a rough land that exacted a toll. Andrew Jackson Sr. died suddenly in February 1767, a month before his third son, Andrew, was born in the house of one of his mother's sisters (there has been a continuing dispute as to whether the birth took place in North or South Carolina, but in any case the border then had not been finally determined). Andrew Jackson was later depicted by political opponents as being unlettered and unschooled, a description he may have regarded as politically useful. But in fact his mother saw that he attended academies run by Presbyterian ministers, unlike the common school attended by his older brothers, and she hoped he would become a minister. He did read widely, though his spelling was irregular, and though he never mastered much Latin or Greek, he found a hero in Scotland's Sir William Wallace (depicted as Braveheart in the 1995 movie) and a favorite book in Oliver Goldsmith's *The Vicar of Wakefield*. But he had a ferocious temper, would not abide being laughed at, and was always ready for a fight. "I could throw him three times out of four," one of his childhood neighbors remembered, "but he would never stay throwed." He loved wrestling, foot races, horses, cockfighting, and guns. Tall and thin, with piercing blue eyes, he was quick to take responsibility and from an early age commanded respect in a society where no man conceded that he was not the moral equal of another but where everyone respected a man who showed the superior talents of a natural leader.

British authorities were not a commanding presence in the Waxhaws, and in the late 1760s and early 1770s Scots-Irish were already heading west across the Proclamation Line into the Watauga district amid the mountain ridges of what would become east Tennessee and through the Cumberland Gap north to the Bluegrass country of what would become Kentucky—even as the settlers were receiving news of the protests in seaboard towns and colonial capitals against the Stamp Act and the tea tax and were sending crops to Boston when its harbor was closed.

But the Revolutionary War did not come to the backcountry until May 1780, when British forces captured Charleston and bands of redcoats led by Col. Banastre Tarleton and Lord Cornwallis rode inland to subdue the southern colonies. This was the most brutal fighting of the Revolutionary War, just as the battles in Ireland and Scotland fought by ancestors of the Scots-Irish were the most brutal fighting attendant to the Glorious Revolution of 1688–89. Tarleton's 300 cavalrymen killed 113 Patriot soldiers in the Waxhaws, and the Jacksons tended the 150 wounded. Andrew's oldest brother, Hugh, joined William Richardson Davie's regiment and died after a battle. Jackson, his brother Robert, and his mother moved about frequently in the summer of 1780 to avoid the redcoats and Tories, and Andrew at thirteen started drilling with the militia and rode in the Battle of Hanging Rock in August.

It was "a damned rebellious country," Lord Cornwallis declared, "a veritable nest of hornets." Cornwallis won a major victory over Horatio Gates later in August, when Andrew and Robert Jackson were captured and marched to Camden; their mother went to Charleston to tend the wounded and died there. When a British officer commanded Andrew to clean his boots, the thirteen-year-old refused, claiming prisoner-of-war status; the officer therefore swung his sword and cut Andrew's hand to the bone and slashed his head, which became scarred for the rest of his life. This outburst of war lasted less than a year, with Scots-Irish frontiersmen utterly defeating Cornwallis's troops at King's Mountain in October 1780, Cowpens in January 1781, and Guilford Court House in March 1781.[33] Cornwallis withdrew to the seemingly more defensible Yorktown on Chesapeake Bay, where his troops surrendered upon being surrounded by American troops and a French navy.

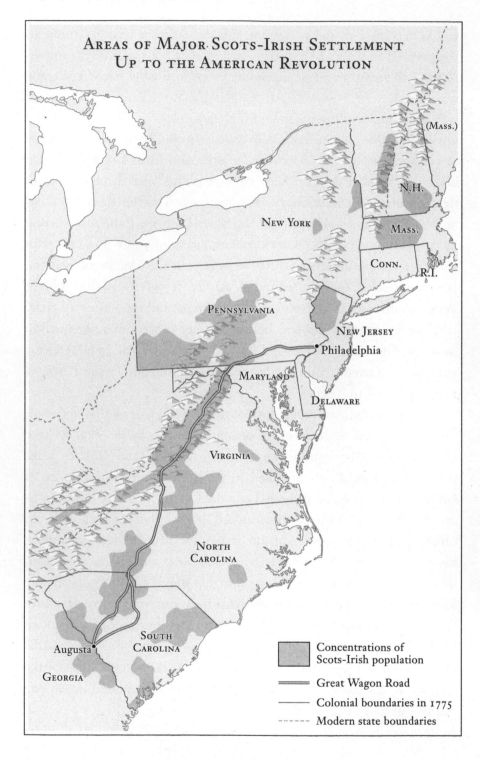

AREAS OF MAJOR SCOTS-IRISH SETTLEMENT
UP TO THE AMERICAN REVOLUTION

(MASS.)

N.H.

NEW YORK

MASS.

CONN.

R.I.

PENNSYLVANIA

NEW JERSEY

Philadelphia

MARYLAND

DELAWARE

VIRGINIA

NORTH
CAROLINA

SOUTH
CAROLINA

Augusta

GEORGIA

Concentrations of
Scots-Irish population

Great Wagon Road

Colonial boundaries in 1775

Modern state boundaries

The surge of Scots-Irish migration had thrust far in less than a generation and would thrust even farther west and southwest in the two generations to come. The Scots-Irish migration across the ocean ended abruptly with the outbreak of the American Revolution, when passage on ships became unavailable. But the dozen-year surge was just the beginning of a two-generation surge of the Scots-Irish inside America that spread out to the southwest from the Appalachian zone of initial settlement. After the war, with his parents and brother dead, Andrew Jackson did not return to the Waxhaws but, fortified with a £400 inheritance from an uncle in Ulster, gambled and drank away his money in Charleston. He read law in Charleston and then made his way westward, past the Watauga region, to the newly settled fertile lands along the Cumberland River near the frontier town of Nashborough, soon renamed the more American Nashville.

Jackson was not the first to move. In May 1769 a small group of men from the Yadkin Valley of North Carolina led by Daniel Boone hacked their way through the forest of the Cumberland Gap to what is now Kentucky; for two years they hunted buffalo, elk, and deer in the woods and wandered in the Indian country. They were followed by others who surveyed the falls of the Ohio River, the site of Louisville (named after the American ally King Louis XVI) in 1773, founded Harrodsburg in the Bluegrass country in 1774, established a settlement in Lincoln County, and built the stockade at Boonesborough in 1775. In 1775 Richard Henderson signed a peace treaty with the Cherokees, the one Indian tribe occupying lands in the mountains in what is now western North Carolina and southeast Tennessee; his Transylvania Company purchased rights to all the lands between the Kentucky and Cumberland Rivers—most of Kentucky and the part of middle Tennessee around Nashville.[34] Earlier, in 1772, North Carolinians in the valleys of the Holston and Watauga Rivers formed the Watauga Association to govern lands outside any colonial jurisdiction (the first assertedly independent American government).[35] In 1774 Lord Dunmore, the governor of Virginia, launched an expedition to Pittsburgh and then to Point Pleasant, where the Kanawha River emptied into the Ohio, and made a treaty with the Shawnees, who had blocked migration into what is now West Virginia.[36] But westward movement into this continually mountainous zone was limited. Instead Scots-Irish and other settlers headed west through the mountains toward expanses of open country where the land rolled down to the Ohio River over limestone hills. During the Revolutionary War, amid wolves and buffalo, caravans stretched a mile long on the tortuous trail from Bristol on the Holston River, over the Appalachian chains to the Clinch and Powell Rivers, to, in a narrow defile between high mountains, the Cumberland Gap; from there the wagons forded the Cumberland and Rockcastle Rivers to the Bluegrass country around Boonesborough and Harrodsburg.[37]

The Scots-Irish, loyal to the British Crown in Ulster and Scotland earlier in the century, mostly supported the Revolutionary cause. The British were allied with the Indians and tried to keep the colonists from going west, while the fast-breeding Scots-Irish were relentless in their quest for land. As one contemporary described them, "They launched into a new World breathing a Spirit of Liberty and a Desire of every individual becoming a Proprietor, where they imagine they can still obtain land for themselves, and their flocks of Cattle at a trifling Rent, or of conquering it from the Indian with the Sword,"[38] as many of their ancestors had obtained land in Ulster from the Catholic Irish. They were a hard people, inclined to play practical jokes and tell tall tales, to treat animals cruelly and to stage elaborate charivaris at weddings, to hold shooting matches as well as quilting bees and dances. They listened to day-long sermons on Sundays and thronged in great numbers to carefully organized multiday camp meetings like one at the Cane Ridge Meeting House in Bourbon County, Kentucky, that attracted ten or twenty thousand people at a time when only two thousand lived in nearby Lexington.[39] They had little contact with the seaboard colonies, but could be stirred to armed revolt as in the Regulators movements in the Carolinas in the 1760s[40] and the Whiskey Rebellion in western Pennsylvania in 1794. They administered a rough justice that could take on the character of lynch law.[41]

This was a society egalitarian in its manners but very far from egalitarian in wealth. Large landholdings were the common pattern, and deference was paid to those who accumulated wealth and demonstrated bravery and competence in battle; social distinctions were vivid but not permanent.[42] As David Hackett Fischer writes, "Inequality was greater in the backcountry and the southern highlands than in any other rural region of the United States."[43] But large landholders were expected to treat their neighbors as equals; this was not a society where men bowed or women curtsied. In the still largely deferential society of the early republic, their egalitarianism was ahead of its time, a foretaste of the democratic mores Alexis de Tocqueville would document in *Democracy in America*. Few of the Scots-Irish had a sentimental regard for or even interest in Ulster or Scotland—far less than many later immigrants would have in their countries of origin—and they proved ready to leave Presbyterian churches for Methodist and Baptist churches as well as to throng to camp meeting revivals.[44] "Long before the first Continental Congress assembled, the backwoodsmen," wrote Theodore Roosevelt, whose mother was a Scots-Irish Bulloch from Georgia, "whatever their blood, had become Americans, one in speech, thought, and character."[45] This was apparent in their near-unanimous support of the Revolutionary cause (in contrast to the ardent Tory sentiments of the Highland Scots settled in central North Carolina around present-day Fayetteville). "We are free born sons of America," Andrew Jackson proclaimed in his call for Tennessee volunteers to serve in the War of 1812, "the citizens of the only republick now existing in the world; and the only people on earth who possess rights, liberties, and property which they dare call their own."[46]

This was a society particularly suited to men like Jackson. In 1788, while the coastal states were in the process of ratifying the Constitution, Jackson, having read some law in Salisbury, made his way across the mountains to Jonesborough in the Watauga district and then to Nashville.[47] He was only twenty-one, but he quickly bought a slave, fought a duel, and established himself as a lawyer and land speculator, soon spending $20,000 on land purchases and owning at least sixteen slaves. In 1794 Governor William Blount appointed him attorney general in Nashville. In 1796, when Tennessee was admitted to the Union, he was elected its first member of the House of Representatives. A year later, at thirty, the youngest age permitted by the Constitution, he was elected by the legislature to the United States Senate.[48] Jackson did not serve there long—he was mortified when his first speech prompted ridicule—but he remained for nearly half a century one of the leading citizens of Tennessee. This interior state, like its neighbor Kentucky, which had been admitted to the Union in 1792, seemed to have great prospects. Before the Revolution the American colonists were better off economically, except for the top 2 percent, than their counterparts in Britain and probably enjoyed the highest average incomes in the world. And the southern colonies had been richer than New England or the middle colonies, with high per capita incomes even if slaves are counted. But the Revolution and the chaos of the 1780s produced a serious economic downturn, and the world war between Britain and Revolutionary and then Napoleonic France, which raged with little interruption from 1793 to 1815, severely reduced the economies of the South Atlantic states, which had depended heavily on export of agricultural commodities. Tobacco crops had exhausted the soil of much of Virginia, Maryland, and North Carolina, and crop yields were much higher in the broad fertile lands of the Cumberland Valley and the Bluegrass country. The interior lands pioneered by the Scots-Irish and like-minded others had the potential to be a land of plenty.

But there were obstacles. Overland transportation was dreadful and the cost of shipping far exceeded the value of agricultural commodities—one reason for the 1794 rebellion against the whiskey tax in western Pennsylvania, since the only cheap way to ship corn was to distill it into whiskey. The rivers of the interior drained into the Ohio and Mississippi Rivers, the outlet of which was in New Orleans, owned by Spain from 1762 to 1803—and the one place in the world, Thomas Jefferson pointed out, where the possessor of which was the natural enemy of the United States. The Spanish also had title to Florida in 1783, not only the present state but also West Florida, which included what is now the Gulf coast of Alabama and Mississippi and the Louisiana parishes west to Baton Rouge and the Mississippi River. The northern boundary of Florida was in dispute, but the lands in question, indeed most of the territory now in the states of Georgia, Alabama, and Mississippi, was inhabited by Indians—the Cherokee, who in the early nineteenth century developed an alphabet and an agricultural economy very much like that of the whites, and who were settled in southeast Tennessee, northwest Georgia, and northeast Alabama; the Creeks, who occupied most of Alabama; the Chickasaw in northern Mississippi and west Tennessee; the Choctaw in southern Mississippi; and the Seminole, who were mostly Creeks who had escaped into almost uninhabited Florida. The trans-Appalachian settlers had forged west through the mountains and were building communities on the first fertile lowlands they found, but they felt cramped and confined, cut off from commercial outlets and penned in by the claims of others.

They formed an already large constituency for further expansion in the young republic. The 1790 Census reported that one-quarter of the population of Pennsylvania lived west of the first Appalachian chain; about one-third of Virginia whites lived west of the Blue Ridge; about half of North Carolina whites lived in the Piedmont or western counties; and about two-thirds of South Carolina whites lived in the up-country area. The census counted 73,000 people in what in 1792 became Kentucky, most of them clustered in the Bluegrass country around Lexington, and 35,000 in what in 1796 became Tennessee, clustered in the mountain valleys in the extreme eastern end and on the Cumberland plateau around Nashville. Altogether about one-fifth of the population of the United States and more than one-quarter of the whites were found in the backcountry areas heavily settled largely by the Scots-Irish in the preceding seven decades.

The Louisiana Purchase of 1803 made the Mississippi an American river and New Orleans an American port, and it opened up a vast land to the north and northwest. But it left the Spanish in possession of Florida (including the Florida parishes of Louisiana and Mobile and the Mississippi Gulf coast, seized by Americans in 1810 and 1813) and of the Mexican frontier of Louisiana. The Natchez Trace, a narrow road from Nashville to what would become the richest town in Mississippi, was traversed by traders including Andrew Jackson, but there were no steamboats yet on the Mississippi, just barges heading downriver from Kentucky and Tennessee, and the country inland was wild.

Many American leaders feared that Spain would try to absorb American territory, not without basis. Gen. James Wilkinson, commander of U.S. military forces and governor of the northern Louisiana Territory, was long in the pay of the Spanish,[49] and former vice president Aaron Burr, disgraced after he killed Alexander Hamilton in a duel in 1804, journeyed southwest to meet Wilkinson. On his way he lodged in Nashville with Andrew Jackson, who had resigned from the Senate and was serving as a judge and general.[50] Burr's role in the duel with Hamilton certainly did not bother Jackson, who had killed a man named Dickinson in a duel in May 1806. "Never tell a lie, nor take what is not your own, nor sue anybody for slander or assault and battery," Jackson told friends he remembered his mother telling him. "Always settle them cases yourself."[51] In any case Burr and Jackson had cordial conversations, the substance of which has never been determined, but Burr seems to have had in mind creating some kind of new confederation in the Southwest. He journeyed to Natchez and New Orleans, then returned to Nashville to be hosted by the Jacksons, who held a ball for him. Burr may have tempted Jackson with the prospect of a military attack on the Spanish—always "the Dons" to Jackson—not only in Florida but also in Santa Fe and Mexico. But Burr also was conferring with Wilkinson, and perhaps conspiring with him to make New Orleans the center of a new southwestern empire including both American and Spanish land, and when Jackson got wind of it in November 1806, he was furious and fired off a letter to President Jefferson. Jackson was authorized to muster an army to quell the conspiracy. But Burr headed upriver with no conspiracy in sight; he was arrested at Jefferson's insistence and acquitted in a trial in Richmond presided over by Chief Justice John Marshall in 1807, while Jackson managed to avoid negative fallout from his meeting with Burr,[52] but his willingness to listen to Burr's proposals shows how eager he was to expand the zone of American control far beyond the Cumberland plateau even at a time when the United States seemed at peace. He wanted the lands to the south and west cleared of Indians, whom he regarded as a menace to civilized white men, although he and his wife raised a Creek Indian as their adopted son, and he wanted the lands beyond liberated from the Spanish and freed from any threat by the force always potentially just over the horizon, the British navy.

The outbreak of the War of 1812 gave Jackson his chance to lead men in war. He called for volunteers and prepared to lead a detachment of Tennessee militia to New Orleans and to attack Florida. But once they were in Natchez, Jackson was dismissed and told to return to Tennessee. His determination to share hardship with his men on the march home gave him the nickname "Old Hickory." Back in Nashville Jackson got involved in a duel in which Jesse Benton was shot in the buttocks and his brother Thomas Hart Benton, the future senator from Missouri, shot his former friend Jackson in the shoulder.

The frontier settlements of Nashville and Tennessee seemed to be under a pincer attack. The Shawnee chief Tecumseh, allied with the British, was campaigning not only on his home ground in Michigan, Indiana, and Ohio, but was encouraging his allies the Creeks to attack near the Florida-Alabama border; and the British navy had access to Spanish ports in Mobile and Pensacola. The Red Stick Creeks, led by their chief William Weatherford, also known as Red Eagle, and encouraged by Tecumseh, massacred 250 at Fort Mims, Alabama, in August 1813.[53] Jackson, still suffering with bullets in his arm and chest from past duels, saw his chance to defeat the Indians and strike a blow against the Spanish and British. He led his militia and regular army troops, plus a contingent of White Stick Creeks and Cherokees, south into Alabama. He was poorly supplied by Tennessee authorities and was barely able to hold his troops together, but persevering through many hardships and quelling mutinies mercilessly, he won several victories, culminating in a decisive defeat of the Red Stick Creeks at Horseshoe Bend in March 1814.[54] In his force were the twenty-one-year-old Sam Houston (great-grandson of "John Houston, Gent.," who migrated from Belfast to the Shenandoah Valley in the 1730s and who had been raised in east Tennessee and as a teenager lived for large parts of three years with the Cherokee)[55] and David Crockett, also of Scots-Irish background—both of whom would move to Texas and play leading parts in its battle for independence. They had no doubt what their families or peers expected. "My son, take this musket and never disgrace it," Houston's mother told him when he left home. "For remember, I had rather all my sons should fill one honorable grave than that one of them should turn his back to save his life. Go, and remember, too, that while the door of my cabin is open to brave men, it is eternally shut against cowards."[56]

Jackson proceeded to impose a harsh treaty on the Creeks, depriving his allies the White Sticks as well as his enemies the Red Sticks a vast swath of territory, some 20 million acres, including most of Alabama and part of Mississippi.[57] The hostile Madison administration, bereft of victories in the war's other theaters, appointed him major general over regular army troops in territory covering New Orleans. He marched to Mobile, forced the British to withdraw from Pensacola in Spanish Florida, then headed west to cut off a British attack on New Orleans. With superhuman determination he kept together a skeleton army until reinforcements arrived and rallied the disparate peoples of New Orleans and even the pirates of Barataria and won a spectacular victory over the British in January 1815.[58] This made Jackson a national hero, though Americans later learned that their negotiators had made peace with Britain in Ghent, Belgium, a month before. Of more lasting importance was his vanquishing of the Creeks, an integral step in a policy of Indian removal he followed throughout his career, and which he carried forward through far larger expanses of territory the policy followed by his Scots-Irish predecessors. As his generally admiring biographer Robert Remini puts it, "In the long history of the Indians

in North America the Creek War was the turning point in their ultimate destruction. The certain, the inevitable, the irreversible turn
toward obliterating the tribes as sovereign entities within the United
States now commenced. The Creek Nation was irreparably shattered.
All other tribes would experience the same melancholy fate."[59] Andrew
Jackson was the instrument and, in his determination to expand American territory, the personification of a Scots-Irish southwestward drive
that took the Scots-Irish from lands just east of the Appalachians, like
the Shenandoah Valley and the Waxhaw district, west into Tennessee
and then south and west to the Gulf of Mexico and ultimately to the
Rio Grande and the Pacific Ocean.

In the first three decades of the republic, most of the land of
Kentucky and Tennessee filled up and became as thickly settled as
the coastal states. Census data tell the story. Kentucky's population increased from 73,000 in 1790 to 564,000 in 1820, when only
the rugged eastern mountains and the lands at the western end of
the state—the Jackson Purchase, obtained from Indians in 1818 by
Jackson—were left unsettled. Tennessee's population increased from
35,000 in 1790 to 422,000 in 1820, with west Tennessee and a sliver
on land in the southeast, around Chattanooga, still unsettled, and the
thickest population concentration in the middle Tennessee counties
around and south of Nashville. The wider area settled wholly or par-
tially by the Scots-Irish—Virginia west of the Blue Ridge, the Carolinas and Georgia west of the fall line, Kentucky and Tennessee, the
northern parts of the Alabama and Mississippi Territories, northern
Louisiana, Arkansas—had increased in population from 800,000 in
1790 to 1.3 million in 1810 and 1.8 million in 1820. Fewer than one-
fifth of these people were slaves, compared with the slave majorities
in coastal South Carolina and central Georgia, Alabama, Mississippi,
and southern Louisiana.

The population of this territory would increase again in decades
to come, to 2.6 million in 1830 and 3.3 million in 1840, as the southwestward drive continued. Jackson was a pivotal figure throughout. In
1818 president James Monroe sent him to quell violence among the

Seminoles, as the Indians and blacks who had withdrawn to the Spanish territory of Florida were called. Jackson advanced and executed two British subjects who had been aiding the Indians, then took the Spanish capital of Pensacola. Spain and Britain protested the executions, but Secretary of State John Quincy Adams backed Jackson and cited his actions to convince the Spanish ambassador Onís that, since his country could not defend Florida, it should cede it to the United States, to which Onís agreed in February 1819.[60] Almost all of Alabama and the remaining lands of Georgia, Tennessee, and Kentucky were opened to white settlement in these years, with Jackson negotiating some of the treaties. When President Adams annulled a Creek treaty of 1825 as fraudulent, Georgia governor George Troup moved in to survey the lands and another treaty was signed.[61] The Cherokees proved especially hard to dislodge. In north Georgia and adjacent corners of Tennessee and North Carolina they built a thriving agricultural economy, with significant towns, a legal code, Christian churches, and even an eighty-six-letter alphabet devised by the remarkable Sequoyah. But the 13,500 Cherokees counted in an 1825 Georgia Census were far less than the 340,000 whites and blacks counted in Georgia in the 1820 Census, three-quarters of them north of the fall line, an area settled in large part from the Scots-Irish holdings in up-country South Carolina and the Piedmont of North Carolina. When the Cherokee found gold near Dahlonega in the hills of north Georgia in 1829, triggering America's first gold rush, the Georgia legislature moved to declare the Indian treaties protecting the Cherokee invalid and to impose state law on their territory in 1830. In 1828 Jackson defeated Adams for reelection, and in 1829 called for an Indian Removal Act and told the Five Civilized Tribes "to emigrate beyond the Mississippi or submit to the laws of [the] states." The Indian Removal Act was signed in May 1830, and the removal of the Five Civilized Tribes to the territory that became Oklahoma began soon after. The Cherokee sued in the Supreme Court, but the justices sidestepped the issue in March 1831; then two Christian missionaries, arrested by Georgia authorities, brought another case, and Chief

Justice Marshall declared the Georgia law void. This was the case of which Jackson is supposed to have said, "John Marshall has made his decision, now let him enforce it."[62] He probably did not say those words, but that was the result. The Cherokee were induced to sign a treaty relinquishing their lands and joined the other Civilized Tribes on the "Trail of Tears," which some 46,000 Indians took across the Mississippi to the Indian Territory.[63]

Through his long career Andrew Jackson consistently sought to extend American territory south and southwest, free of Indians and open to white men and their black slaves. His goal, writes historian Daniel Walker Howe, not one of his great admirers, was "the extension of white supremacy across the North American continent."[64] In the way was the Spanish and Mexican land of Texas, in the early nineteenth century "a borderland where the Spanish, French, British and American traders, soldiers and settlers rotated a kaleidoscope of alliances, trade agreements and wars with each other and the Kiowa, Comanche, Wichita, Jumano, Caddo, Apache and more."[65]

In 1819 Jackson approved John Quincy Adams's treaty with Onís relinquishing rights to Texas in return for the cession of Florida and conceding the Spanish claim to lands north of the Arkansas River and, west of the Rockies, lands north of the 42nd parallel (the northern boundary of California), but he later vehemently denied having done so. As president and even more so afterward, he sought to gain Texas for the United States.[66]

Americans were already there. In the 1820s the newly independent Mexican government encouraged Americans under Stephen Austin to settle in that region. They came primarily from Tennessee and nearby states, and paid little heed to the Mexicans' legal requirement that they become Catholic (they just refrained from building Protestant churches) and the abolition of slavery (they drew up ninety-nine-year contracts for slaves' services). By the 1830s, the Anglos outnumbered Hispanic Tejanos and the few German immigrants, and rebellion broke out in 1835 against the dictatorial Mexican president Antonio López de Santa Anna. Santa Anna's army swept into San Antonio and wiped out the defenders of the Alamo Texans, undaunted, and issued a declaration of independence. To command their troops the Texans enlisted Sam Houston, who had served under Andrew Jackson at Horseshoe Bend, had been elected to Congress and as governor in Tennessee in the 1820s, and then after his wife left him had gone to live with the Cherokee in what is now Oklahoma.[67] Houston routed Santa Anna's troops unguarded at San Jacinto in April 1836 and got Santa Anna to cede all the land north of the Rio Grande to the Republic of Texas. Jackson ordered U.S. troops to the Texas border and on his last day in office in March 1837, after Congress passed a resolution of approval, he gave diplomatic recognition to the Texas Republic.[68]

Jackson's chosen successor Martin Van Buren backed off from efforts at annexation out of concern for the antislavery opinions of northern voters, especially the New England Yankee stock who had settled most of his home turf of Upstate New York. But John Tyler, who became president after William Henry Harrison died a month after taking office in 1841, was worried lest Britain extend its influence over Texas, particularly that it might encourage abolition of slavery there, and in April 1844 his secretary of state, John C. Calhoun, signed a treaty of annexation with representatives of Texas. The news of the treaty and Calhoun's justification of it as advancing the cause of slavery was leaked by an antislavery senator, on the same day the front-runners for the Democratic and Whig presidential nominations, Van Buren and Henry Clay, both came out against annexation. Andrew Jackson, seventy-seven years old and ailing in the Hermitage outside Nashville, came out against his longtime protégé Van Buren and in favor of James K. Polk. Polk was from a prominent North Carolina Scots-Irish family and moved to Tennessee, where Jackson helped to arrange his marriage; he was little known nationally but had served as Speaker of the U.S. House and governor of Tennessee. In May 1844 the Democratic National Convention, after a deadlock between Van Buren and Lewis Cass, nominated Polk, the first "dark horse" presidential nominee in American history. Jackson then engineered the withdrawal of the incumbent, John Tyler, from his independent candidacy in August, and rejoiced when Polk was narrowly elected in November. This was and remains extraordinary: no other president in American history has ever played such a decisive part in determining a successor eight years after leaving office. Jackson proceeded, from his sickbed at the Hermitage, to lobby for a joint congressional resolution admitting Texas to the Union, and one was finally passed, to his great satisfaction, in the last days of the Tyler administration in March 1845.[69]

The dark horse Polk, in the one term to which he limited himself, proved to be one of the most effective and consequential presidents in American history. With Texas in hand, he secured an agreement with Britain that added the Oregon Territory to the United States, and he provoked a war with Mexico in 1846 that resulted in American victories under Whig generals Zachary Taylor around Monterrey in 1846 and Winfield Scott in Mexico City in 1847. The Treaty of Guadalupe Hidalgo, negotiated contrary to Polk's orders in 1848 but accepted by him, secured California and the territory between it and Texas. In line with Jackson's vision the United States now extended from sea to shining sea. But the Union was also suddenly faced with the issue that would split it apart in 1861: whether slavery would be allowed in the territories.

The Civil War can be seen as a conflict triggered by competing internal migrations—by the *drang nach* southwest of Scots-Irish led in many ways by Andrew Jackson, by the migration of southern planters and their slaves from the Atlantic seaboard to the Black Belt cotton lands farther west, and by the migration of New England Yankees across the northern tier of the nation, across Upstate New York to northern Ohio, Indiana and Illinois, southern Michigan and Wisconsin, and eastern Iowa. The southern planters pursued a vision of a nation secured for slavery and were willing to secede from the Union to preserve a zone where their almost capitalist form of plantation slavery could prosper. The New England Yankees pursued a vision of a nation open to free labor in which slavery would be confined to old ground and would in time wither away.

The Jacksonian Scots-Irish played a more ambiguous role, favoring expansion to new lands open to slavery but insisting that the Union be maintained—as Jackson had when South Carolina led by his first vice president John C. Calhoun, of Scots-Irish descent himself, took the side of the southern planters and asserted the right to nullify federal law. Jackson favored expansion of the nation and in particular of the zone in which a white yeomanry—small farmers and merchants, usually with only a few slaves—could thrive. He had nothing but scorn for abolitionists and those who wished to restrict slavery, but was also ready to employ overwhelming force to subdue slaveholders or others who challenged the authority of the Union. We can be sure that Jackson would have cheered the acquisition of territory from Mexico, that he would have favored the Kansas-Nebraska Act, and that he would have supported the Dred Scott decision with all the vehemence and force he could command. But would he have considered himself as helpless as his fellow Democratic president James Buchanan did to stop the secession of southern states after the election of Abraham Lincoln in 1860? Would he have supported Lincoln's attempt to put down the rebellion, as his fellow Democratic presidential nominee Stephen Douglas did in 1861?

No one can answer those questions for certain. As Stephen A. Douglas exclaimed to James Buchanan when the latter claimed Jackson would have supported his position, "Mr. President, General Jackson is dead." But we do know that the victory of Lincoln, whose strongest support came from the New England diaspora, and the secession of southern states starting with Calhoun's South Carolina, split the Jacksonian Scots-Irish. Sam Houston, once again the governor of Texas, opposed secession and was ousted from office; Andrew Johnson, a Democratic congressman from and twice-elected governor of Tennessee, became the Union's military governor of the state; Francis Preston Blair, a member of Jackson's "kitchen cabinet," supported Lincoln's campaign, and his son Montgomery Blair was Lincoln's postmaster general; Ulysses S. Grant, of Scots-Irish descent and born across the Ohio River from what is now West Virginia, became

Lincoln's greatest general. On the other side, a large portion of the Confederate army and many of its greatest generals—Albert Sidney Johnston, Stonewall Jackson, Jeb Stuart, Nathan Bedford Forrest— were of Scots-Irish descent.

Some parts of Scots-Irish America remained stubbornly attached to the Union: Kentucky; east Tennessee; the mountain counties of Virginia, which became the state of West Virginia in 1863; the western counties of North Carolina, which resisted secession; southwest Missouri; and Winston County in Alabama, which seceded from the state when it seceded from the Union. East Tennessee's three congressmen despite their state's secession took their seats in the U.S. House in 1861. Others were strong Confederate territory—north Georgia, Alabama, Mississippi, parts of central Missouri, almost all of Louisiana, and Texas. The ambivalence of the Scots-Irish was symbolized by the politically shrewd Sarah Childress Polk. Her marriage to James K. Polk had been encouraged by none less than Andrew Jackson himself, and she was not only a charming hostess for her charmless husband but was also his chief and only secretary, sharing his office with a desk of her own. He died shortly after leaving office in 1849, but she remained in the Nashville mansion they had built until her death in 1891. During the Civil War she declared herself neutral in the conflict and received courtesy calls from both Confederate and Union generals.

The Scots-Irish have been the least ethnically conscious of America's migrant groups. From Jackson's time to the 2010 Census, they have tended to describe themselves not as being of Scots-Irish (or Scotch or Irish) ancestry but as simply being American. In the years after the Civil War the Scots-Irish, who had surged across so much of the nation in generations after the Revolution, mostly stayed put. Only the most severe economic stress prompted significant migrations, like the flight of the Okies from parched Oklahoma to the Central Valley in the 1930s; this was vividly portrayed in John Steinbeck's 1939 novel *The Grapes of Wrath*, and chronicled in Dan Morgan's 1992 nonfiction *Rising in the West: The True Story of an "Okie" Family from the Great Depression Through the Reagan Years*. But demographically this was a very small movement during a decade in which American mobility was at its lowest ebb in history. Similarly, the migration of mountaineers from West Virginia, Kentucky, and Tennessee to work in the auto factories of Detroit and the rubber factories of Akron in the 1940s and 1950s was dwarfed in numbers by the simultaneous migration of southern blacks to the large metro areas of the industrial Midwest and Northeast.

Nowhere is the tendency of the descendants of the Scots-Irish to stay put clearer than in the political statistics. Hundreds of counties in West Virginia, Kentucky, southwest Virginia, Tennessee, northern Alabama and Mississippi, Arkansas and Oklahoma, rural Missouri and Texas, continued for a century to vote as they fought in the Civil War, and many still do so today. (In Oklahoma, the former Indian Territory, the descendants of the Indians sent westward by Andrew Jackson on the Trail of Tears, are difficult to distinguish from their Scots-Irish neighbors—and enjoy living standards considerably better than those on most Indian reservations.) The percentages cast for Democratic and Republican candidates have been far less volatile in states like Kentucky and Tennessee than in the nation as a whole; from 1880 to 2008, Kentucky cast no more than 60 percent of its votes for any presidential candidate except in the landslide years of 1964 and 1972, and Tennessee did so only in 1932, 1936, 1940, and 1972. While most of Tennessee voted Democratic, east Tennessee was stubbornly Republican; the first congressional district in the easternmost part of the state has not elected a Democratic congressman since 1860. Whether the Democratic candidate was the laissez-faire Grover Cleveland or the populist William Jennings Bryan, the conservative John W. Davis (a native of West Virginia) or the liberal Harry Truman (whose grandmother was a Confederate sympathizer) made little difference. Some developments made a difference: John L. Lewis's United Mine Workers of America moved several coal counties of southern West Virginia and eastern Kentucky toward the Democrats.

This part of America retains the warlike spirit exemplified by Andrew Jackson. It has produced more than its proportionate share

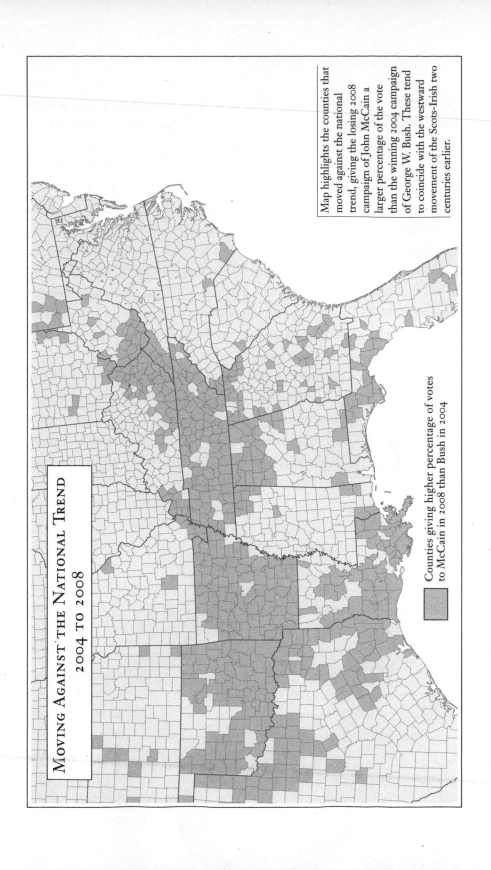

MOVING AGAINST THE NATIONAL TREND
2004 TO 2008

Map highlights the counties that moved against the national trend, giving the losing 2008 campaign of John McCain a larger percentage of the vote than the winning 2004 campaign of George W. Bush. These tend to coincide with the westward movement of the Scots-Irish two centuries earlier.

Counties giving higher percentage of votes to McCain in 2008 than Bush in 2004 of American military personnel, and it has reacted very negatively, both in Democratic primaries and general elections, against candidates perceived as more inclined to conciliate than to confront America's enemies, notably George McGovern in 1972 and Barack Obama in 2008. Fascinatingly, you may track the Scots-Irish pre–Civil War march to the Southwest in maps showing the county percentages favoring Hillary Clinton in the 2008 primaries or casting higher percentages for John McCain in 2008 than for George W. Bush in 2004, as if Andrew Jackson's Tennessee volunteers were still on the tracks of the Creeks' chief Red Eagle nearly two hundred years after Horseshoe Bend. And you can see the same pattern if you map the counties in which the most common answer to the Census Bureau's question asking for national origin is simply "American."

Having done so much to expand the United States and to put their stamp on the still readily recognizable zone into which the Scots-Irish expanded from 1763 to 1848, the Scots-Irish have largely stayed put, cultivating their own way of life independently of others and always remaining ready to answer their country's call in time of peril.

2. YANKEES AND GRANDEES

IN 1783 in the Treaty of Paris the British government recognized the independence of the United States and its title to the territory east of the Mississippi River and south of the Great Lakes except for Florida, which it ceded to Spain. But there were few white settlers west of the Appalachians except where the Scots-Irish were surging into Kentucky and Tennessee, and the infant republic was unable to exert control over this vast territory. Most of it remained Indian country and in the Northwest Territory established by Congress in 1787—the land west of Pennsylvania, north of the Ohio River, and east of the Mississippi—the British refused to yield military posts until Gen. Anthony Wayne's victory in the Battle of Fallen Timbers in 1796. In the years that followed there were two surges of migration that shaped the character of the nation and put in play the conflict over the extension of slavery that led to the Civil War. In the North the Yankee diaspora poured out of New England, settled Upstate New York, and moved rapidly westward. The South saw the expansion of plantation slavery by southern grandees from the Atlantic coast states. The Yankees and the Southerners came from different and in many ways antagonist cultures, whose distinctness was apparent in the colonial years and became even more pronounced in the process of internal migration, which was a sort of colonization of the interior United States. These two migrations changed the nation in the first half of the nineteenth century, and the conflict between them produced the bloodiest war in the nation's history.

FOR nearly two centuries, New England was almost an island, sending out traders to Britain and the Caribbean but isolated from the rest of North America. Then, starting suddenly in the decades after the American Revolution, New England Yankees surged westward across much of the northern United States, spreading their particular brand of American culture, setting up colleges, starting reform movements, inventing new machines, and establishing new businesses. The Yankee diaspora dominated Upstate New York, northern Ohio, and southern Michigan; it established Chicago on the shores of Lake Michigan and headed westward to the peaceful plains of Iowa and the violent plains of bleeding Kansas; it established Yankee enclaves in Omaha and Denver and Los Angeles. The surge started slowly, with New England Yankees founding Syracuse some 200 miles east of the Berkshires in 1805, then they plunged west to dominate much of the Midwest by the 1840s and established beachheads on the Pacific coast by the time of the Civil War. New England Yankees and their descendants founded new religions such as Mormonism and reform movements including women's rights. They provided almost the entire political base of support for abolitionism and the dominant base for the Republican Party, founded by Yankees in 1854 to stop the spread of slavery in the territories.

The continental reach of the New England diaspora, extended temporarily even into the Deep South as Yankee carpetbaggers attempted to uphold the rights of freed slaves during Reconstruction, is a vivid contrast to their geographical, cultural, and even biological insularity in colonial America. The New England Yankees of the new republic were almost entirely the descendants of 21,000 Puritans who arrived between 1629 and 1640, the years when Charles I ruled without a Parliament and archbishop William Laud was persecuting those at variance with his High Church beliefs.[1] Yankee settlers in southern New England quickly outnumbered the local Indians, who suffered from serious disease kill off even before the Pilgrims landed at Plymouth Rock, and the Indians' numbers dwindled even more after

King Philip's War in 1676 and the Deerfield Massacre in 1704. New England merchants sailed the seas, hauling slaves from Africa (only a few were settled in New England, where the cold climate proved unhealthy for Africans) to the seaboard colonies farther south and hauling molasses and rum north from the Caribbean. But the New Englanders seldom ventured beyond their colonies except in battle with the French in Nova Scotia or Upstate New York, and few moved away from their homeland. Benjamin Franklin, who left his native Boston for the freer air of Philadelphia at the age of seventeen in 1723, was very much the exception.[2]

New England Yankees were moralistic and intolerant, believers in what historian David Hackett Fischer called ordered liberty, so stern and determined in their beliefs that they early on split into offshoot colonies—New Haven and Connecticut, later united, which practiced a sterner Calvinism than Massachusetts; Rhode Island, which allowed greater liberty; and New Hampshire, which in the eighteenth century, as it does three hundred years later, lived free from the trade and tax restrictions of neighboring Massachusetts, which between 1652 and 1820 also included the current state of Maine. Few outsiders settled in the New England colonies; the Scots-Irish who headed there found a frosty reception from their fellow Calvinists and settled only a few towns, such as Londonderry, New Hampshire.

In literature and lore colonial New Englanders have been depicted as stern Puritans, insisting on a grim moral code and sexual morality. But in fact the Yankees were a lusty people, celebrating the carnal pleasures of sex within marriage, and the New England colonies had some of the highest birth rates in the world. They also had one of the lowest death rates, thanks to the chilly but bracing climate that prevented the spread of malaria and other diseases that plagued colonies to the south. As a result the white population of the New England colonies, descended largely from some 21,000 migrants in the 1630s, grew to 90,000 in 1700; 167,000 in 1720; 281,000 in 1740; and 437,000 in 1760.[3] Inevitably this expanding population filled up the towns that had been first settled, and the practice of partible inheritance—dividing property equally among heirs—left many young New Englanders with only patches of land and an incentive to move outward, from the Atlantic coast and up the navigable Connecticut River, to the north and west. Colonial legislatures and governors authorized new towns in an orderly fashion, with town meetings and established Calvinist churches. With only small Indian populations surviving settler-borne diseases and the Indian war of 1676, there was room within the New England colonies for expansion throughout the colonial period.

There were also limits. To the north and northeast were the French colonies of Quebec and Acadia, with populations also growing rapidly from a small base of initial settlers. The nineteenth-century historian Francis Parkman wrote a series of books on the colonial conflict between the French and British, which this Bostonian saw as a contest between two civilizations—Catholic versus Calvinist, dirigiste versus democratic—for control of North America. Much territory between the two realms remained unsettled until the British won the Battle of Quebec in 1759, and in the Treaty of Quebec in 1763 France formally ceded Canada to the British (though the boundary between Maine and Canada was not finally settled until the Webster-Ashburton Treaty of 1842. The presence of the French was something of a barrier to New England expansion even after the French defeat, as the British Parliament, to secure the loyalty of the French-speaking colonists, recognized as legitimate the French culture and Catholic religion in the Quebec Act of 1774; only a small number of New Englanders settled in the Eastern Townships southeast of Montreal.

The barrier to the west was the colony of New York, controlled by the Dutch until 1664 and thereafter kept more firmly under the control of the Crown than the New England colonies. This was brought home to New Englanders in 1688 when King James II's appointee Edmund Andros combined New York and the New England colonies with New Jersey into a Dominion of New England. When Bostonians in April 1689 learned of James's ouster[4] they drove Andros out of town and into exile.

The New Englanders were serious Calvinists—intolerant of other faiths (they were outraged when Andros allowed the celebration of Christmas and promoted the Anglican church) and unwelcoming to those of different folkways like the boisterous Presbyterian Scots-Irish. They were ethnically uniform, with roots mostly in eastern England and with few black slaves (less than 3 percent of the population in 1760), though New England merchants profited from the slave trade. New York in contrast was ethnically polyglot, with a large Dutch population (Theodore Roosevelt's grandfather spoke Dutch at extended family Sunday dinners in the mid–nineteenth century) and smaller French and German contingents. It was religiously tolerant, with an Anglican establishment, dissenting Protestants, Catholics, and a small number of Jews. A few New Englanders did establish the towns of Southampton and Easthampton on the east end of Long Island in the seventeenth century, but their efforts to secede from New York failed. New England farmers who were used to owning land were reluctant to settle as tenants in the Hudson Valley, where vast estates were owned by Dutch patroons and families, including the Schuylers and Livingstons. Nor did many New Englanders move to Albany, a fort more than a town, the center of the British fur trade and the primary colonial contact point with the Indians of the interior of eastern North America.

The Indians of New England had mostly died out or migrated westward. The Indians of Upstate New York were numerous and the most well organized in North America. These were the Five Nations of the Iroquois (after 1726, when the Tuscarora joined, the Six Nations),[5] who had an extensive agricultural as well as hunting economy and who traded furs with whites in return for guns, ammunition, other manufactured goods, and cloth. In the seventeenth century the Iroquois were linked in what historian Francis Jennings called the "Covenant Chain," a series of agreements with the colony of New York and with Indians in other colonies, "something close to a condominium of multiple Indian tribes and English colonies." But in 1701 they also promised the French they would be neutral in any war between the French and the British. In effect there was something resembling a deal: the Iroquois would help the British keep the French out of the Hudson Valley, while the British would see that New Englanders and others did not settle the Mohawk Valley west of Albany.[6]

The British government, to keep the Indians friendly, forbade white settlement west of the highest ridges of the Appalachians— territory that included most of what is now Upstate New York—in the Proclamation of 1763. Farther to the south, Scots-Irish migrants and colonists from Pennsylvania, Virginia, and North Carolina paid this little heed and headed west through the mountains anyway. But in New York migrations of this kind were blocked by an extraordinary figure, Sir William Johnson, a native of Ireland who had long lived in the Mohawk Valley and was appointed the British government's agent there. He had intimate relations, politically and personally, with the Iroquois (he had several children by various Iroquois women), maintained the alliance with them, and negotiated in 1768 the Treaty of Fort Stanwix, which opened up lands largely occupied by other Indians in southwestern Pennsylvania, West Virginia, and eastern Kentucky, while maintaining the Iroquois hold on western New York; Johnson encouraged the migration of a few settlers from Scotland but not from New England.[7] That arrangement continued until Johnson's death in 1774, just before the outbreak of the American Revolution. The Iroquois, guided by Johnson's nephew Guy Johnson and the Mohawk Joseph Brant, brother of Johnson's common-law wife Molly Brant, took arms on behalf of the British in the Mohawk Valley, but their efforts proved unsuccessful, and the American victory in the war sealed their cause's fate; Joseph Brant moved to Canada, where the city of Brantford, Ontario, is named for him.[8] The way west from New England was now open.

IF the New England Yankees were cabined in by Canada and the Iroquois in Upstate New York until the establishment of the republic, the great plantation owners of the South, of Virginia and South Carolina especially but also of Maryland, North Carolina, and Georgia, were cabined in by physical factors: by the character of their soil, which became infertile after years of tobacco growing; by economic factors such as the decline in demand after the Revolution for South Carolina's indigo crop; and by the geographical fact that the Appalachians were not suitable for plantation farming. And while some migrants to Kentucky and Tennessee established large plantations there, most of the land was held by small farmers more interested in subsistence and production for local markets. All these developments made it appear that plantations cultivated by large numbers of slaves would become obsolete, and that slavery would move toward extinction.

Developments elsewhere led to the same conclusion. The leaders of the first generation of the republic were living in an English-speaking world in which slavery was increasingly disfavored. In 1772 Lord Mansfield, the Lord Chief Justice, ruled in the Somersett case that a slave brought from the West Indies to England must be free, because slavery was not authorized by law in England. Slavery is, he said, "so odious, that nothing can be suffered to support it, but positive law." Four years later Jefferson in the Declaration of Independence held as a truth self-evident that "all men are created equal," and his draft included a paragraph, dropped in deference to southern delegates, denouncing the British government for encouraging the slave trade. In England during the Revolutionary War Granville Sharp, the abolitionist who backed Somersett's lawsuit, was working with Quakers and others who opposed slavery; in May 1787 they formed the Committee for the Abolition of the Slave Trade and enlisted the support of William Wilberforce, a rich young member of Parliament who had become an evangelical Christian, and Josiah Wedgwood, the owner of the famous pottery works, whose cameos of the group's seal showing a black man in chains lifting his hands to heaven with the legend "Am I not a man and brother?" became a popular ornament.

In North America slavery was abolished in Vermont's constitution in 1777, long before it became a state in 1791, and it was abolished in Massachusetts in 1781, a course followed by other states north of the Mason-Dixon Line with the last being New Jersey in 1804. In 1784 Thomas Jefferson, as a member of the Articles of Confederation Congress, sponsored a law to prohibit slavery throughout the West, including the territories that became Kentucky and Tennessee; it was defeated by a single state's vote due, Jefferson wrote, to the illness of a single delegate.[9] The Confederation Congress in 1787 did exclude slavery from all the Northwest Territory, the lands west of Pennsylvania and north of the Ohio River.[10] Most of the delegates to the Constitutional Convention of 1787 disapproved of slavery, but delegates from South Carolina and Georgia made it clear that they would oppose any measure that disfavored it. As a result the Constitution, while avoiding the word itself, did authorize Congress to pass laws to track down fugitive slaves. But the now infamous clause counting slaves as three-fifths of a person was actually a defeat for slave owners, since it reduced the representation their states would have in the House of Representatives and the Electoral College below what it would have been if each slave had been counted as a whole person. And the Constitution also provided that Congress could abolish the slave trade twenty years after its ratification. And so on March 2, 1807, just twenty-three days before Parliament abolished the slave trade in the British Empire, President Jefferson signed a bill that abolished the slave trade on January 1, 1808.

From a twenty-first-century perspective, the trend against slavery in the young United States seems like a natural course of progression. Yet at the time it was significant. The prohibition on slavery in the Northwest Ordinance prevented Virginians, who looked longingly at western lands, from transporting their slaves north of the Ohio River. The abolition of slavery in the northern states was not insignificant: the 1790 Census reported that 6 percent of the residents of New York and New Jersey were slaves. In abolishing the slave trade, Congress was acting in the wake of the states, all of which except South Carolina had already done so. And it was acting against the commercial interests of the Charleston merchants: in 1804–07 39,310 slaves were landed in South Carolina, with nearly half, 15,676, in the final year—an apparent attempt to get them in while still legal. It is true that Congress did not provide for the kind of vigorous enforcement of abolition, in contrast to Parliament, which sent the British navy on patrol to stop slave traders in all the world's waters. And Congress provided that state law governing what happened to slaves captured on illegal slave ships.[11] Still, Thomas Jefferson was not entirely indulging in wishful thinking when he wrote a friend in 1805 hoping that slavery would somehow be ended in the United States. "But interest is really going over to the side of morality, the value of the slave is every day lessening; his burthen on his master dayly increasing. Interest is therefore preparing the disposition to be just; and this will be goaded from time to time by the insurrectionary spirit of the slaves."[12]

The 1810 Census, conducted just a few years after the abolition of the slave trade, provides data to support this view. Slavery was nonexistent in New England, in New York and Pennsylvania, in the state of Ohio, and in the territories of the Northwest Ordinance. In New Jersey 4 percent of the population was still classified as slave, because of the slow workings of the state's 1804 abolition act, but there were almost as many free blacks as slaves. In Delaware, where slavery was still legal, free blacks outnumbered slaves by more than 3–1; in Maryland there were 111,502 slaves and a not inconsiderable 33,927 free blacks. Even in Virginia there were 30,570 free blacks, more than in any other state than Maryland.

In Virginia and Maryland slaves were concentrated in the tobacco-growing counties east of the Blue Ridge. Counties with ports on Chesapeake Bay typically had less than 50 percent slave population; inland counties somewhat more so, with up to 61 percent in Maryland (Charles County) and 68 percent in Virginia (Amelia County). Virginia's slave population was the largest in the country (392,518), concentrated in land producing soil-degrading tobacco. West of the Blue Ridge, only two counties had more than 20 percent slave population. Significantly, this was the fastest-growing part of the state. North Carolina had always had fewer slaves and large plantations than its neighbors to the north and south; the heaviest concentrations of slaves were in the northeast and the area east and north of Raleigh. Across most of the Piedmont and mountain counties, settled in large part by Scots-Irish, the slave percentages were lower, no more than 26 percent in any county and as low as 6 percent in the west.

South Carolina and Georgia had the highest concentrations of slaves in the nation. In the Low Country the slave percentages were almost as high as in the West Indies—81 percent to 88 percent in Beaufort, Colleton, and Georgetown Counties, South Carolina; 72 percent in Charleston County; 77 percent to 83 percent in Liberty, McIntosh, Bryan, and Glynn Counties, Georgia; and 72 percent in Chatham County (Savannah). Low Country slaves seem to have lived a life apart from the larger nation, continuing to speak in Gullah and Geechee dialects (Supreme Court justice Clarence Thomas, raised in Savannah, can remember Geechee being spoken); they cultivated labor-intensive crops including rice and indigo while their owners spent much of their time in townhouses in Charleston and Savannah. Inland there were also majority-slave concentrations around Columbia and Augusta. But in the up-country to the north in South Carolina and inland west and south toward Indian lands in Georgia, where coastal crops were not viable, county slave percentages were as low as 15 percent.

West of the Appalachian chains, Kentucky and Tennessee were settled in large part by Scots-Irish, most of whom owned no slaves. The mountain counties had low slave percentages, never above 12 percent. The biggest concentrations of slaves were in the Bluegrass country around Lexington, where Fayette County had the state's largest slave percentage (36 percent), and in middle Tennessee around Nashville, where Davidson County had the state's largest slave percentage (40 percent). These states had significant but not huge slave populations, where most whites would not be slaveholders and where blacks would never be near-majorities, as they were in South Carolina and Virginia, much less majorities of the total population.

The recently acquired Louisiana Purchase was a different matter;

under French and Spanish rule it had tolerated slavery, and the brief interlude of French sovereignty in 1803 did not last long enough to extend the revolutionary French decree abolishing it. In the first decade of the nineteenth century Indians largely populated the area; around St. Louis, from which Lewis and Clark ventured on their expedition across the continent, was a small frontier outpost. New Orleans, near the mouth of the Mississippi River, was an important port and the marketing destination for products coming down the river, including sugar produced on slave plantations just upriver. But cane sugar was not a crop that could be produced in any other part of the United States (Florida had not yet been acquired from the Spanish and remained largely unsettled for years after it was), just as the slave plantation crops of tobacco, rice, and indigo seemed unsuitable to the up-country lands on either side of the Appalachian chain and, with the exception of tobacco lands of the Bluegrass country in Kentucky, to the lands to the west. In the opening years of the nineteenth century slavery seemed to be hemmed in on all sides.

But that did not take into account the potential of cotton. Little cotton was grown in colonial America; production in 1790 was only 3,000 bales. Two years later Cary Greene, the widow of Revolutionary War general Nathanael Greene, invited a young Yale graduate to tutor her children on her Georgia plantation. The tutor, Eli Whitney, with Greene's help invented the cotton gin to remove seeds from the fiber.[13] Whitney was not the only inventor of a new device that made cotton growing economical, but the results were astonishing. Cotton was an ideal fiber for the burgeoning textile mills in the North of England and in New England, and cotton grown in the American South was more readily transported to the mills than that from other continents. Both cotton production and textile production boomed in this First Industrial Revolution. In 1800 American cotton production was 73,000 bales, with 60 percent of the world's cotton coming from Asia, mainly India. In the following decades American cotton production rose geometrically, roughly doubling each decade to 178,000 bales in 1810; 335,000 in 1820; 732,000 in 1830; 1,348,000

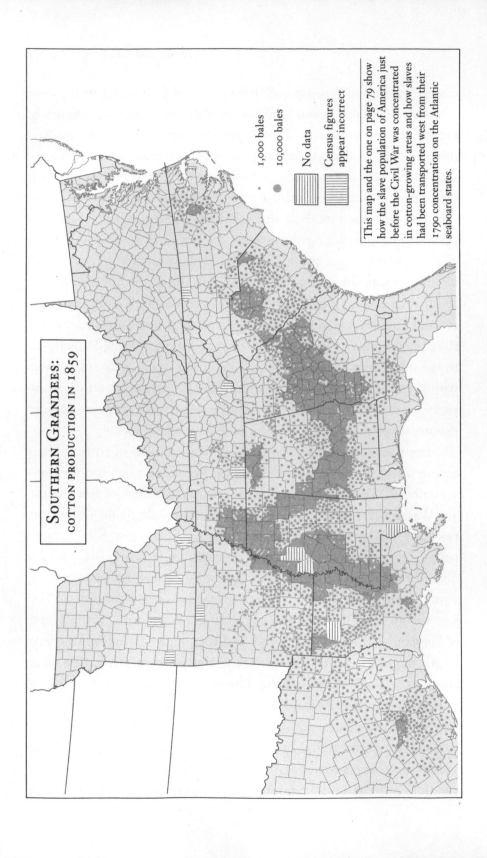

SOUTHERN GRANDEES:
COTTON PRODUCTION IN 1859

. 1,000 bales

● 10,000 bales

▨ No data

▤ Census figures
appear incorrect

This map and the one on page 79 show how the slave population of America just before the Civil War was concentrated in cotton-growing areas and how slaves had been transported west from their 1790 concentration on the Atlantic seaboard states.

in 1840; 2,136,000 in 1850; and 4,491,000 in 1861.[14] Cotton could be produced with suitable soil where there were two hundred frost-free days a year—and most of that land in America was unsettled when the slave trade was abolished in 1808. Cotton production was labor-intensive work, and slavery was legal in those lands, thanks to the failure of Jefferson's proposal in 1784. With the barriers to migration removed, the way was open for the great plantation owners, the southern grandees.[15]

BEFORE the Revolution and for some years afterward New England Yankees moved outward within New England—to Maine, then a part of Massachusetts, and to Vermont, which was contested territory, claimed by both New Hampshire and New York. Maine and Vermont grew rapidly in the early years of the republic: Vermont's population grew from 85,000 in 1790 to 217,000 in 1810 (slightly more than New Hampshire's), while Maine's increased from 96,000 to 228,000 in that period.[16] Settlers tended to move in groups, as the surplus population of younger sons and daughters from towns where the land was occupied headed out in various directions—from Connecticut northward into Vermont, from central Massachusetts and Rhode Island to Vermont, northward within New Hampshire, and from the oldest Massachusetts towns and from New Hampshire northeast to Maine. "The lines of emigration crossed and recrossed," as one historian wrote.[17]

But it was plain even before the Revolution that New England would soon run out of even marginally fertile land as its population continued to increase rapidly, and that for most Yankees settlement in British-occupied and French-speaking Canada was not an attractive alternative. The state governments of Massachusetts and Connecticut attempted to provide space for expansion by asserting title to western lands based on their colonial charters, which extended their northern and southern boundaries westward to the Mississippi River. This did not seem entirely unreasonable at a time when

Virginia and North Carolina claimed to govern the land that would become Kentucky and Tennessee. But it proved impractical. In the early republic it was considered that for representative government to be fair, county seats and state capitals should be situated in a central location, roughly equally accessible to all the people. States acted on that theory; Albany replaced New York, Harrisburg replaced Philadelphia, Richmond replaced Williamsburg, and Columbia replaced Charleston as state capitals in this period. In this context it seemed preposterous that territory near the Mississippi River could be governed from Boston or Hartford. Nor would New York willingly surrender its claims to its upstate territory. So in 1785 Massachusetts ceded to Congress its claim to southern Michigan and Wisconsin and in 1786 it relinquished its claims to sovereignty over much of Upstate New York, retaining claims to lands near Owego Creek (the Boston Ten Towns) and claims, soon sold to speculators, to the far west end of the state. Flinty Connecticut was more stubborn, but its claim to northern Pennsylvania was weakened when its settlers in the Wyoming country in northeastern Pennsylvania were massacred in 1778 and was rejected by a congressional court of commissioners in 1782. In 1786 it ceded to Congress lands it claimed comprising much of present-day northern Ohio, Indiana, and Illinois, but it held on to its claim to what it called the Western Reserve, the northeast corner of Ohio, until 1800. The Western Reserve was the one western claim of New England with consequences. Settlers from Connecticut did stake out land there, including Moses Cleaveland, who established a village that would be named after him (minus the first "a") at the mouth of the Cuyahoga River.[18] The Western Reserve was settled almost entirely by Yankees and in the years after the Civil War, when New England cities were thronged with Irish Catholic immigrants, the Western Reserve was, with Vermont, the most Yankee-dominated part of the country. Yankee domination lasted until the early twentieth century, when Ellis Islanders thronged there to work in the new steel, auto, and tire factories in Cleveland, Akron, and Youngstown.

But the first destination for the surge of the Yankee diaspora was the vast expanse of Upstate New York, directly west of New England. The Proclamation of 1763 was history; Sir William Johnson was dead, and the Iroquois had chosen the wrong side in the Revolutionary War. While their land claims would never be utterly extinguished—and their elaborate system of government and their political acuity still command deserved respect among some historians although there is no evidence they influenced the Framers of the Constitution—the Native Americans were no longer an effective barrier to settlement there by others.

As in colonial North America, land speculators entered the scene. In 1788 Massachusetts merchants Oliver Phelps and Nathaniel Gorham obtained 200,000 acres of Massachusetts-owned land along the Genesee River, south of Rochester, and settled Indian claims; in 1790 they sold much of it to Philadelphia merchant and Revolution financier Robert Morris, who bought up 500,000 acres to the west. Morris, headed toward bankruptcy, soon sold off much to a London syndicate and the Dutch-based Holland Company, which after clearing away Indian land titles hired Joseph Ellicott, the surveyor who continued and completed Pierre L'Enfant's plan for Washington, D.C., to lay out townships.[19] Revolutionary War veterans had been granted lands in Upstate New York east of Seneca Lake; in 1789 and 1790 some 1,500,000 of these state-owned acres were mostly sold to speculators. New York commissioners, assigned to name twenty-five newly created townships and noting the classical-sounding name of one Iroquois tribe, the Seneca (actually an English version of a Dutch transcription of an Indian name), applied classical names—Lysander, Hannibal, Cato, Camillus, Cicero, Manlius, Marcellus, Ovid, Homer, Hector, Ulysses, Virgil.[20] Those towns would be settled primarily by New England Yankees, and some of their names were carried by Yankee-stock migrants to townships in southern Michigan a generation later. In 1791 New York merchant Alexander Macomb purchased most of New York State north of the Adirondacks and along the St. Lawrence River and began selling off tracts to other speculators. Philadelphia privateer William Bingham bought 2 million acres in Maine (about half the size of the current state of Massachusetts) and 750,000 acres in Pennsylvania (from which he was elected to the Continental Congress and the U.S. Senate) and considerable acreage in Upstate New York.[21] Binghamton, New York (which is not a "hampton"), was named for him; he died in 1804, in Bath, England, but it is said that his estate was not settled until 1960.[22]

The New Englanders tended to migrate in groups, as extended families or bands of townsmen purchased land from speculators and planted (a New England word) new towns in Upstate New York. Thus seven pairs of brothers from seven families in Plymouth, Connecticut, headed to Oneida County, New York, where they had served during the Revolutionary War, and founded the town of Kirkland.[23] Judge Hugh White of Middletown, Connecticut, and his five sons moved to Oneida County and sent back large cornstalks, potatoes, and onions to show their old neighbors how fertile their new land was.[24] Thirty fishermen from Martha's Vineyard and Nantucket established the town of Hudson in Columbia County in 1783. A group from Durham, Connecticut, established Durham, New York, in Greene County on the other side of the river. Four sons moved from Windsor, Vermont, to Marcy in Oneida County, New York, in 1793–94.[25] Twenty heads of families came from Fairfield County, Connecticut, to Stamford in Delaware County, New York. The settlers tended to come not from the longest-settled parts of New England, the areas around Boston and the lower Connecticut River, but from the later-settled hills. They were likely to be adherents of the "New Light" Congregational-ism sparked by the rigorous preaching of Jonathan Edwards and oth-ers in the Great Awakening of the eighteenth century.[26]

As the Yankee migration continued, the population of Upstate New York (excluding the Hudson Valley south of Albany, which, like most of coastal America, grew only slowly during these years) increased lustily, from 121,000 in 1790 to 294,000 in 1800; 606,000 in 1810; 952,000 in 1820; and 1,375,000 in 1830—at which point Upstate New York had more people than any other single state. Movement was facilitated by the Erie Canal, built by the state government, begun in

1817 and completed in 1825—the first big interior transportation project of the young republic. The availability of cheap water transportation encouraged the development of manufacturing, notably textiles in Utica and flour milling in Rochester, and Upstate New York grew to be one of the most prosperous parts of the country. Yankee ingenuity and steady habits that had been directed outward to the world by merchants and whalers and inwardly to farming the rocky soil of New England were now directed to building a diversified and dynamic economy in what the Reverend Timothy Dwight, president of Yale College, called "a colony of New England," with people "with the same interests of every kind inseparably united" in a common culture.[27]

Ohio was particularly propitious country for New Englanders. The Northwest Ordinance of 1787 declared all the lands from Pennsylvania to the Mississippi and north of the Ohio River free of slavery. It provided that the land be divided into 36-square-mile townships, with thirty-five sections available for purchase at bargain rates and the thirty-sixth reserved for financing public schools. The British and their Indian allies were swept from the lands by the victory of General Wayne in the Battle of Fallen Timbers and the Treaty of Greenville in 1794. The first New England settlement was established at Marietta, on the Ohio River about halfway between Pittsburgh and Cincinnati, by 1788. But the larger movement of New Englanders was into the Western Reserve. In 1796 Moses Cleaveland, an officer of the Connecticut Land Company, journeyed from Canterbury, Connecticut, to Buffalo, where he met Iroquois chiefs including Joseph Brant, and then sailed to the mouth of the Cuyahoga River, between steep bluffs, on which his surveyors plotted a grid street plan with a town square in the center of the city that would be named after him. Many in Connecticut would be struck by "Ohio fever" and move westward in 1798 and later years, establishing towns and building schools, even as the state of Connecticut relinquished its claim to the land in 1800. The newcomers included the likes of Lorenzo Carter, who refused to turn over an escaped slave to his southern master, and Alfred Kelley, who lobbied successfully to make Cleveland the northern terminus of the Ohio and Erie Canal.[28] New England folk settled in scattered locations throughout Ohio, establishing a presence in the state's one large city, Cincinnati, and founding small towns like Granville, by settlers from Granville, Massachusetts. In the Western Reserve, one can still see New England–type greens at the town center of Hudson or covered bridges in Ashtabula County. Before the Civil War the northeast corner of Ohio was arguably the most antislavery part of the country, electing abolitionist Joshua Giddings during the 1840s and 1850s,[29] and the most heavily Republican congressional district in the post–Civil War years was in the northeast corner of Ohio, represented for eighteen years by the future president James Garfield.

Other parts of Ohio were settled by people from other regions— the Scioto River Valley north from the Ohio River, by Virginians and Marylanders; and much of the central part of the state, by Pennsylvanians. Ohio had enough people to be admitted to the Union in 1803, and settlement accelerated after the War of 1812 ended in 1815.[30] The state's population grew from 45,000 in 1800 to 230,000 in 1810; to 581,000 in 1820; and to 937,000 in 1830, at which point it was the fourth-largest state, trailing only New York, Pennsylvania, and Virginia. By 1840, it passed Virginia and, with 1,519,000 people, came close to equaling Pennsylvania. Its largest city was Cincinnati, settled from all directions—by Virginians and Kentuckians from south of the Ohio River, by Germans both Protestant and Catholic and even Jewish (Hebrew Union College, the oldest Jewish seminary in America, was founded in Cincinnati), and by New England Yankees heading westward to what was the largest city in the American interior in the decades before the Civil War. The Yankee settlers of Ohio quickly established schools and soon were busy founding colleges, as they had been in Upstate New York, including Ohio University in Athens (whose president in 1839–43 was William McGuffey, compiler of the McGuffey's Readers widely used in the rest of the century), Hiram College (the alma mater of President Garfield) in the Western Reserve, Baldwin-Wallace in Berea just southwest of Cleveland, Denison in Granville, Kenyon in Gambier (the alma mater of president

Rutherford Hayes), and Western Reserve (originally established in Hudson and moved to Cleveland after the Civil War).[31]

The westward movement of the Yankee diaspora was accelerated by improvements in transportation. Canals provided easier overland traveling than the primitive roads of the time, not only across Upstate New York but within Ohio and the rest of the Northwest Territory, and the first steamship on the Great Lakes, the *Walk-in-the-Water*, was launched in 1818. Steamship travel grew and, as Upstate New York counties and the Western Reserve filled, steamships opened up the settlement of the Michigan territory, governed from 1813 to 1831 by Lewis Cass, a native of Exeter, New Hampshire, and the famed War of 1812 general. In the early 1830s Upstate New Yorkers and Vermonters began arriving in Detroit on steamships from Buffalo and heading west into lands that turned out to be not as swampy as reputed. Michigan's settlers named many of their southern three tiers of counties after Andrew Jackson and members of his cabinet— Jackson, Calhoun, Van Buren, Livingston, Ingham, Eaton—but they tended to name their townships after towns in Upstate New York: Utica and Rochester, Bloomfield and Avon, Aurelius and Onondaga, Delhi and Oneida, Ovid and Scipio. The heritage of Vermont was recalled in Vermontville and the names of other nearby towns in Eaton County. Lumbermen from Maine moved farther north into the Saginaw River Valley, which became the leading source of white pine in North America.[32] Northwest Ohio and northern Indiana, slower to be settled than the southern portions of those states, attracted Yankee migrants as well, as did northern Illinois. Though far less numerous in Indiana than in Ohio, Vermonters and Connecticut men established northern Indiana towns such as Montpelier, Wolcottville, and Orland. Among its Vermont-born settlers was governor James Whitcomb, who set up the state's public school system, and its chief backer was New Hampshire–born Caleb Mills, first president of Wabash College.[33]

Yankee settlers moved across northern Indiana and, after the settlement of the Black Hawk War in 1832, into lands suddenly opened up in Illinois. Here several go-getters had the same insight as the French explorers of the seventeenth century: that the lowest and most accessible divide between the Great Lakes basin and the giant valley of the Mississippi River was in the land just west of Fort Dearborn, where the Chicago River emptied into Lake Michigan. Only 10 miles west over nearly level land—try to spot the divide as you drive across Chicago today—is the Des Plaines River, which empties into the Illinois River, a major tributary of the Mississippi; this is by far the easiest portage for boats between the Great Lakes and the vast Mississippi Valley. In 1818 Gurdon Saltonstall Hubbard, from Windsor, Vermont, and named for an ancestor who was a colonial governor of Connecticut, arrived at this site from the American Fur Company's outpost on Mackinac Island. He spied the Des Plaines River from the battlements of Fort Dearborn. As the Black Hawk War ended, Hubbard hired as his lawyer William B. Ogden, who had come to Illinois from Delaware County, New York, in search of fortune; they joined with New York investors Charles Butler and Arthur Bronson as well as with Grant Goodrich, who moved from Chautauqua County, New York, because he "had faith in Chicago."

These "versatile, risk-taking businessmen," as historian Donald Miller called them, were "Chicago's first urban elite . . . made up mostly of young, self-made men from New England and New York State," and they transformed a wilderness outpost into the great metropolis of Chicago. Their numbers included John Wentworth from Sandwich, New Hampshire, an early newspaperman and later Republican congressman; J. Young Scammon from Whitefield, Maine, a partner with Ogden in many enterprises; Walter L. Newberry from East Windsor, Connecticut, real estate investor and early railroad president; J. Stephen Wright from Sheffield, Massachusetts, indefatigable publicist of the wonders of the new city; Isaac N. Arnold from Hartwick, New York, who as a Republican congressman sponsored the law outlawing slavery in the territories; and Joseph Medill from New Brunswick, the English-speaking Canadian province east of Maine, the longtime editor of the *Chicago Tribune*. Ogden, elected the first mayor of Chicago in 1836, worked with others to persuade the federal government to build piers out into Lake Michigan at the mouth of the Chicago River in order to create a harbor and grant the state of Illinois land to build a canal. He recruited East Coast investors and put his own money into public improvements; he and his fellow investors built Archer's Road (now Archer Avenue, one of Chicago's few diagonal streets, another being Ogden Avenue) and the construction workers settlement at Bridgeport (the home neighborhood of the Mayors Daley) on the South Chicago River. Ogden formed a shipping line to set up regular service from Buffalo so that by 1840 one could travel from New York City to Chicago in six days. He and other pioneers established a raft of civic institutions—the Chicago Lyceum, the Chicago Historical Society, the Academy of Sciences, the Chicago Musical Union, the Orphan Society, and the Chicago Relief and Aid Society—as well as public schools and institutions of higher learning, including the first University of Chicago, Northwestern University, a female seminary, and two medical colleges.[34]

Their progress was rapid. The first balloon-frame structure—the method that enabled a few men to quickly and economically build millions of American houses—was built by New Hampshire-born George Washington Snow on the banks of the Chicago River in 1832. This provided the basis for one of Chicago's great businesses, transforming timber shipped from heavily forested Michigan into lumber for new settlers in the treeless prairies west of Chicago. Talented newcomers were attracted to this growing city that seemed likely to become a center of commerce. Cyrus McCormick, inventor of the mechanical reaper, came to Chicago in 1847 and immediately went into partnership with William B. Ogden in what became one of America's great manufacturing enterprises—and one that vastly increased agricultural productivity. Other Yankee migrants included meatpacking giants Philip Armour from Stockbridge, New York, and Gustavus Swift from West Sandwich, Massachusetts, the developer of the refrigerated rail car; William Wallace Chandler of Randolph, Vermont; and the department store magnate Marshall Field, from

Conway, Massachusetts. Also in 1847, Stephen A. Douglas, an ambitious politician from Vermont who originally settled in downstate Illinois, moved to Chicago in his first year as a U.S. senator (at age thirty-four). And in 1847 J. Stephen Wright sponsored a River and Harbor Convention that left one visitor from New York exulting, "In ten years Chicago will be as big as Albany" (it turned out to be nearly twice as large by 1860). Chicago's annus mirabilis was 1848. While European capitals were wracked by revolution, and just as the United States obtained the great Southwest from Mexico, the Illinois and Michigan Canal was completed in Chicago, the first telegraph line reached the city, the first oceangoing vessel arrived from Montreal, construction began on the city's first railroads and wooden turnpikes, the first grain elevators and stockyards were built, and the Chicago Board of Trade was established to provide a market in which wheat, corn, and meat could be traded. By 1857, only a quarter century after the Black Hawk War, Chicago was the center of the greatest railroad network in the world, with 3,000 miles of track, and by 1861 more railroads met at Chicago than anywhere else on earth. In these years Chicago's population rose from zero in 1830 to 4,000 in 1840; 30,000 in 1850; and 112,000 in 1860. The economic and institutional infrastructure was by then in place that would raise it to 1,099,000 in 1890 and make it the second-largest city in the nation.[35]

Chicago was not the endpoint of the Yankee diaspora. The four Collins brothers from the preacher Lyman Beecher's hometown of Litchfield, Connecticut, established Collinsville near St. Louis, and became advocates of temperance; they and their father helped set up Illinois College in Jacksonville and hired Beecher's son Edward as its president. Beecher helped guard the abolitionist Elijah Lovejoy's printing press the night he was murdered by a mob in Alton, and afterward, in Yankee-dominated northern Illinois, supported his brother Owen Lovejoy of Princeton in organizing antislavery meetings throughout the state. Much of northern Illinois west of Chicago was settled by Yankees, including Vermont-born John Deere, who set up his plow manufactory in Moline on the Mississippi River.[36] The

Yankee diaspora also continued west and northwest of Chicago and Illinois. Significant Yankee migration into Wisconsin started in the 1830s and accelerated in the 1840s. Although an even larger number of German immigrants began moving into the state then, "Wisconsin institutions," in the perhaps smug words of a nineteenth-century historian, "have been dominated by Americans of the Puritan seed from the beginning."[37]

The New England influence was significant also in Iowa— one of whose earliest towns, Burlington, was named after the one in Vermont—and came to overwhelm the more numerous initial migrants' from Kentucky and southern Illinois. Yankee migration to Iowa accelerated in the late 1840s, after statehood, as did the influx of German and other immigrants. One influential Yankee was Josiah Grinnell, from New Haven, Vermont, who became a follower of the American Anti-Slavery Society in Upstate New York. After preaching abolitionist sermons in Washington, D.C., and New York City, Grinnell was asked to resign and sought advice from the *New York Tribune* editor Horace Greeley. "Go west, young man," Greeley famously said, and assigned him to cover the Illinois State Fair for the *Tribune*. Grinnell followed that advice, venturing first to slaveholding Missouri (which he found "clinging to barbarism") and then to free-soil Iowa, where he met the engineer and railroad promoter Grenville Dodge, who migrated from Danvers, Massachusetts, to Council Bluffs, Iowa, across the Missouri River from the Nebraska Territory. Dodge advised Grinnell not to move as far west as Council Bluffs, but to settle on a potential railhead site in Poweshiek County, west of Davenport and east of Des Moines. There Grinnell and two associates bought 5,000 acres and established the town of Grinnell. His *Tribune* articles about the town attracted Yankee stock settlers, including graduates of Yankee-founded Oberlin College in Ohio; when Iowa College moved to the town, Grinnell became its president (it was renamed for him in 1909). Grinnell welcomed the already notorious John Brown to town just before his famous raid in 1859, was elected to Congress in 1860, and lived on until 1891.[38]

Dodge's career is a vivid example of the westward reach of the Yankee diaspora. Before the Civil War he lobbied Illinois railroad lawyer Abraham Lincoln to support his proposal for a continental railroad, during the war he became a Union general, and afterward he surveyed much of the Union Pacific route, including the low-altitude Great South Pass in the Wyoming Territory. The transcontinental railroad, famously completed in 1869 with the striking of a golden spike in Promontory Summit, Utah, was largely a Yankee enterprise; the Union Pacific was headed by Thomas Clark Durant, from Michigan, and financed by a group headed by Oakley Ames of Massachusetts. Its western partner the Central Pacific was headed by California's "Big Four," Leland Stanford, Mark Hopkins, Charles Crocker, and Collis Huntington, all originally from Upstate New York.

Alexis de Tocqueville on his famous visit to America in 1831–32, the basis of his classic *Democracy in America*, spent most of his time in New England and the lands of the Yankee diaspora, traveling through Upstate New York and by steamship to Michigan and through the Mackinac Straits; he also took a steamboat down the Ohio River to Cincinnati, where he noted the differences between free and slave territories.[39] He spent less time in New York City, Pennsylvania, and Washington, D.C., and made only a hurried trip through the Deep South. Tocqueville's acute observations in *Democracy in America* of New England–style town meeting government and the American propensity to create voluntary associations give great weight to characteristically Yankee phenomena. Perhaps disproportionate weight, demographically: in 1830 New England and the lands of the Yankee diaspora accounted for only about 30 percent of the nation's total population and less than 40 percent of its white population. But the Yankee cultural influence was arguably greater. The moralistic, reforming, didactic Yankee spirit produced movements that reshaped America in those years: the temperance movement that reduced Americans' alcohol consumption by more than half, the nonsectarian evangelical movement that stressed self-improvement and good works, the building of thousands of schools and dozens of colleges and the proliferation of a print culture that dominated at least the northern states. Yankee culture could be off-putting: the Mormons aroused fierce opposition and the Millerites, fierce derision, even as they established religious movements that have great vitality nearly two centuries later.

And some Yankee causes seemed to most Americans to be downright dangerous. The women's rights movement was widely reviled, even as women took a quiet but increasingly influential role in shaping public opinion and smoothing the rough edges of frontier truculence. The abolitionist movement was met with violent resistance in much of the North and with adamant repression in the South (where postmasters refused to deliver abolitionist tracts). But these movements also found friendly havens in Yankee communities and attracted more support as time went on. It is impossible to imagine that abolitionists would have become national forces in an America where the Yankee influence was not present; their only other major source of support came from quietist Quakers who, unlike the Yankees, made a point of not imposing their views on others. The Yankee diaspora, never embarrassed about imposing its views on others, made them great national movements that in time prevailed.

TO the south, the decades after the War of 1812 saw a vast migration of slaveholders and slaves. The Middle Passage across the Atlantic had brought 400,000 slaves to the United States between 1619 and 1807. This Second Middle Passage—or Passage to the Interior, as historian Ira Berlin has called it—took about 1 million slaves from the Atlantic coast states to the new states of America's interior (the Alabama and Mississippi Territories opened up by Andrew Jackson's Creek War; Louisiana, Arkansas, and Texas, where many Americans brought their slaves even before it gained its independence from Mexico in 1836). This forced migration accelerated over the decades. Historians Robert Fogel and Stanley Engerman, who put the total at

835,000, estimate that it increased from 17,000 in the 1790s to 31,000 in the 1800s; 101,000 in the 1810s; 121,000 in the 1820s; 223,000 in the 1830s; 149,000 in the 1840s; and 193,000 in the 1850s.[40] Some 85 percent of the migrant slaves were from Maryland, Virginia, and the Carolinas and some 75 percent of them went to Alabama, Mississippi, Louisiana, and Texas.

The Passage to the Interior was not as grim as the Middle Passage across the Atlantic; the death toll was orders of magnitude less. Nonetheless it was traumatic for the slaves who were uprooted from familiar surroundings, often removed from contact forever with friends and family and faced with the onerous tasks of breaking virgin soil and building new plantation buildings. Most of these slaves were transported across country in coffles—chains—for a period of six to eight weeks walking 25 miles a day and sleeping on the ground. Others were transported in coastal ships, with the required certificates that they were from the United States rather than Africa, which landed most often at the port of New Orleans. Fogel and Engerman argue persuasively, based on the meticulous records maintained in the New Orleans slave market from 1804 to 1862, which accounted for one-third of all U.S. slave sales in those years, that about one-quarter of these slaves were sold by their masters to others and that in only about 2 percent of cases were families broken up.[41] Nonetheless the existence of such cases and the possibility that something similar could happen if, for example, a master died or went bankrupt, must have caused great apprehension and much distress. Of all the surges of migration in American history, the Middle Passage and the Interior Passage were the only ones that were involuntary. Berlin argues persuasively that these experiences gave black Americans a "passionate attachment to place" and made them exceedingly, and to sympathetic whites surprisingly, unwilling to migrate again.[42] And indeed the surge of black migration from the rural South to the urban North that began abruptly in 1940 was initiated by government's demand for defense workers and by technological developments—particularly the invention of the mechanical cotton picker, which reduced the demand for black labor in the cotton fields as abruptly as Whitney's cotton gin had increased it five generations before.

The migration of slaves, and the movement of the geographical center of gravity of slavery, is illustrated vividly by comparing the numbers of slaves recorded in each census from 1790 to 1860 in three groups of states—the seaboard states from Delaware to South Carolina; the upper South states of Kentucky, Tennessee, and Missouri; and the lower South states from Georgia and Florida west to Arkansas and Texas. Georgia is included in the lower South category because almost all of the state was unsettled in the early years of the republic.

YEAR	SEABOARD	Region UPPER SOUTH	LOWER SOUTH	TOTAL
1790	604,427	12,430	29,264	646,121
1800	737,906	53,927	59,699	851,532
1810	873,386	125,096	105,218	1,103,700
1820	993,860	216,261	298,983	1,509,104
1830	1,137,405	331,912	514,903	1,984,220
1840	1,114,284	423,857	943,791	2,481,932
1850	1,238,988	537,862	1,423,784	3,200,634
1860	1,313,317	616,133	2,021,071	3,950,521

Thus, in 1810 79 percent of American slaves lived in the seaboard states; by 1840 that percentage was reduced to 45 percent, and in 1860 it was just 33 percent. The percentage of slaves living in the upper South states was 11 percent in 1810, rose to 17 percent in 1830, and was 16 percent in 1860. The big difference was in the lower South— the cotton kingdom where the great majority of the American cotton crop was produced. These states accounted for only 10 percent of slaves in 1810; that rose to 38 percent in 1840 and 55 percent in 1860. The lower South accounted for almost half the growth in the national slave population in the 1810s and 1820s and the great majority of it in the 1830s, 1840s, and 1850s—evidence of the magnitude of the Passage to the Interior forced by the southern grandees. Virginia in particular gained a reputation as a breeding ground for slaves; historian Frederic Bancroft estimated that about 10,000 Virginia slaves were sold each year to western states, a total of 300,000 over thirty years, a period in which the number of slaves in Virginia rose by only 21,000.[43] This made economic sense since slave owning was much more profitable in cotton-producing areas than in the exhausted soil of the Chesapeake country. In addition, slaveholders in Delaware and Maryland, with large numbers of free blacks, and in Missouri, where the large majority of whites were not slaveholders, sometimes sent slaves to markets in states farther south, for fear that slavery would be abolished in their home states.

This movement of 1 million slaves was the product of decisions made by a much smaller number of slaveholders. In the antebellum republic the majority of slaves were held by the 5 percent of slaveholders who owned twenty or more slaves,[44] almost two-thirds of whom lived in the cotton-producing states from South Carolina west to Texas.[45] These men were motivated, as the merchants and entrepreneurs of the North were, by the potential to make large profits. Cotton cloth, taken for granted today, was far superior for many articles of clothing than wool and linen, the alternatives with which people in Europe and the Americas had had to make do for centuries, and the demand for cotton from the mills rising above the fast-flowing rivers of Lancashire and New England was roughly doubling every decade.

Southern planters were acutely sensitive to trends in markets—abandoning the indigo crop quickly when it became unprofitable, responding to rises and falls in the price of tobacco, taking up cotton quickly as its potential became apparent.[46] They were, as two economic historians write, "on the whole, a highly self-conscious class of entrepreneurs who generally approached their governmental responsibility with deliberation and gravity" and "strove to become steeped in the scientific agricultural literature of the day."[47] They also had

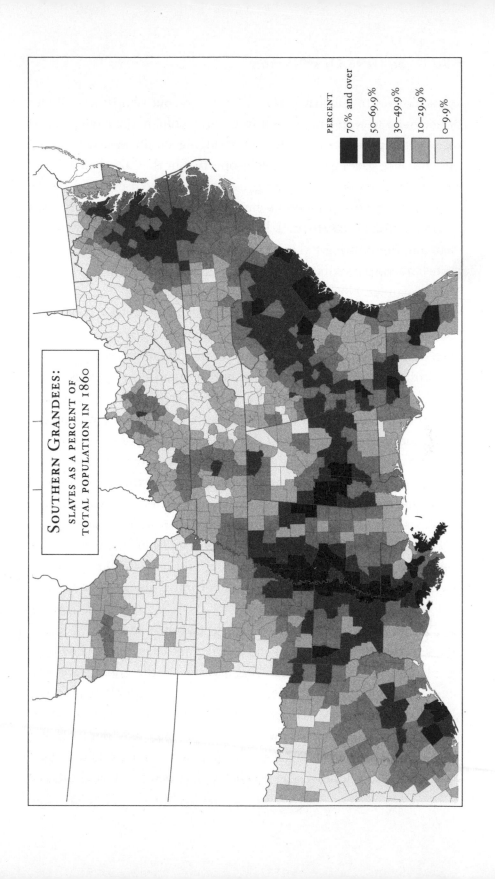

SOUTHERN GRANDEES:
SLAVES AS A PERCENT OF
TOTAL POPULATION IN 1860

PERCENT

70% and over
50–69.9%
30–49.9%
10–29.9%
0–9.9%

some motives to treat their slaves humanely and sympathetically, to direct them to work that would most fully employ their talents, and to help them maintain stable and steadying family relationships, if only because slaves were valuable property. But they also had motives to keep them in bondage. The greatest profits from cotton growing came from massive plantations employing slaves in the gang system, forcing cotton pickers to work long hours with little relief. It was efficient and unremitting toil so grueling that, as historian Robert Fogel writes, no nonslaves, black or white, could ever be persuaded to work in that manner.

So just as New England merchants such as Francis Cabot Lowell, who had made vast profits from the carrying trade during the 1792–1815 war between Britain and France, soon afterward spotted the profit potential of building cotton textile mills on the falls of the fast-flowing Merrimack, southern planters spotted the potential of raising cotton on the Black Belt soil strata that passed through central Georgia and south-central Alabama into Mississippi and on the even richer alluvial soil on the side of the great river in Mississippi, Louisiana, and Arkansas. This was not a static aristocracy but a fluid class. Statistics indicating that at any given time only a small number of whites owned more than ten or twenty slaves are misleading, since many whites who started off with no slaves accumulated many, while some large slaveholders suffered reverses and had to sell their slaves. So even if the proportion of slaveholders shrank, the absolute number ballooned to nearly 400,000 in 1860.[48]

Some major planters from South Carolina and the seaboard states invested in cotton lands in Alabama and Mississippi. The largest planters accumulated great wealth visible in the grand plantation houses of Natchez in Adams County, Mississippi, which in 1860 was the wealthiest county per capita in the nation (the nation's twelve wealthiest counties that year were all in slave states).[49] "But there was always substantial mobility into and out of the slaveholding class," writes historian James Oakes.[50] The typical planter started off as a young man in a hurry, for example, a lawyer lighting out for new territory where lawsuits were rife or a minister's son who acquired land and one or two slaves and then, if things worked out, more land and more slaves. The building of a grand mansion was usually indefinitely postponed.[51] The risks were high, but so were the rewards.[52] In both the antebellum North (except for the port cities and factory towns) and South the population of the coastal region was demographically and economically stagnant, and as lands there, and then in Kentucky and Tennessee, became filled, migration was at least as common in the South as in the North and for slaveholders was seen as a prerequisite to success.[53] But as in the booming new cities in Upstate New York and the Great Lakes states, so in the cotton lands of the South there was a continuous churning of the local elite.

Dallas and Lowndes Counties, in the heart of the Black Belt of Alabama, was settled in the 1820s by the likes of William R. King (a former congressman from North Carolina who was elected to the Senate from Alabama and who served six months, until his death in 1853 as vice president of the United States) and Dixon H. Lewis (from Hancock County, Georgia, who was elected to the U.S. House and Senate and who, at 500 pounds, was probably the heaviest member of Congress in history). By the late 1850s, King and Lewis were gone and most of the properties in the area had changed hands, some many times.[54]

The southern grandees were not like the English aristocracy, most of whose wealth came from possession of land. Their slaves were worth more than their land—this was true even of small slaveholders—so they were ready to move from one place to another as the market dictated, employing the source of their wealth, their slaves, in whatever land seemed available at the best price.[55] The rule-proving exception was the Creole planter class of Louisiana, of French and Spanish heritage; those who made up that contingent were noted for their unusual habit of holding on to their land, with their beautiful mansions, rather than seeking higher profits elsewhere.[56]

AT the center of Yankee culture was religion. Massachusetts and Connecticut were founded by Calvinist Puritans and had established Congregational churches; while they fostered considerable theological debate, they discouraged other forms of worship. New Hampshire dropped its established church in 1790, but Massachusetts and Connecticut, as permitted by the First Amendment, which barred Congress from passing any law "regarding an establishment of religion," did not abolish their established churches until 1818 and 1833. By that time, many Congregationalists in and around Boston, the hub of New England, embraced near-secular forms of belief like Unitarianism and Transcendentalism, while more exacting forms of belief found followers among New Englanders who had gone west.

But the New England Yankees heading west into Upstate New York embraced more rigorous forms of religion that encouraged the proliferation of good works. They were quick to start schools and found colleges. They produced dozens of newspapers and other periodicals, many of them religious. They brought a Yankee frame of mind and are described by historian Whitney Cross as having a "frank curiosity, pride in independent thinking, a feeling that action should be motivated by sound logic and never by whimsy, a profound skepticism of any rationalization looking to less than the supposed ultimate good of society, and, once arrived at, an overweening confidence in one's own judgment."[57] "It was the Yankees who were described as yearning to constitute a social and cultural elite that would sponsor and support higher education, literary societies and lecture courses, and follow their inclination to regulate the morals of the whole society," writes a historian of Indiana, where Yankees were in the minority. "Taxed with being busybodies and meddlers, apologists own that the instinct for meddling, as divine as that of self-revelation, runs in the Yankee blood; that the typical New Englander was entirely unable, when there were wrongs to be corrected, to mind his own business."[58] And they were determined to impose their values on the entire nation. "One of the most distinguishing features of the Yankees of the nineteenth century had been their confidence that theirs was a superior vision and that America's future depended on their ability to impose their order on the life of the nation. . . . They established thousands of public schools and private colleges, filled churches and lodge halls with committed believers and codified their version of morality in the statute books."[59]

The Yankee diaspora produced a flowering of religious enthusiasm and new religious sects as copious as any in American history. Just as the originally Presbyterian Scots-Irish in their move southward were attracted to many religious denominations, so the originally Congregationalist New England Yankees as they moved westward joined or formed Presbyterian, Methodist, and Baptist churches and even Quaker meetings. They were filling a vacuum: the New York colony, while it had an established Church of England, was home to multiple sects and none had much of a presence in the frontier country west of Albany before the Revolution. The winter of 1799–1800 saw a religious revival in Upstate New York, as it did in Kentucky, with Yankees providing leadership, especially in Oneida County in the Mohawk Valley and the Genesee country in the west. Even the seemingly irreligious were attracted. "Most of the persons usually described by Baptist and Presbyterian clergymen as irreligious, immoral or profane went to church regularly and expected at some future time to experience conversion during a revival," as one historian wrote.[60]

Millennial movements contemplating the end of the world were more common here than in any other area of the country. Upstate New York was the home of unusual sects and utopian communities— notably the Shaker settlement at New Lebanon, near the Massachusetts border, and Jemima Wilkinson's utopian colony in Yates County, both of which required sexual abstinence,[61] although thanks to converts the Shaker flock persisted until 1947[62]—and of frequent revivals in which ministers of all denominations would flock to preach.[63] Wayne County, New York, was the birthplace of the Mormon Church, founded by Joseph Smith, whose parents brought him from their native Vermont; he was not unusual in receiving messages from the Almighty or believing that the Indians were descended from the Lost Tribes of Israel.[64] When he decided to leave Upstate New York his first stop was Kirtland, Ohio, in the Yankee-dominated Western Reserve. At about the same time William Miller, born in Massachusetts and raised in Upstate New York and Vermont, began preaching that the second coming of Jesus Christ was imminent, and his Millerites, having sold all their possessions, gathered on hilltops in Upstate New York and Ohio to witness it on October 22, 1844, only to experience what they called the Great Disappointment. Many later gravitated to the Church of the Seventh Day Adventist.

One key site in New York State was the village of Western in Oneida County north of Rome, which hosted a three-day meeting with more than twenty preachers in 1802. Oneida County, covering the divide between the Mohawk River, which drained into the Hudson, and smaller rivers that drained into Lake Ontario, became the center of "the burned-over district" where one religious fervor followed another. It was there that Charles Grandison Finney began his triumphal preaching career in 1825.[65] Finney was born in Litchfield County, Connecticut, in 1792 and grew up in Oneida County, part of the first generation of Yankee Upstate migrants. As a young lawyer in Jefferson County, New York, he had a vision of Jesus in 1821 "like a wave of electricity going through and through me." He walked back to his law office and told a client, "Deacon Barney, I have a retainer from the Lord Jesus Christ to plead his cause, and I cannot plead yours." With no professional training and no theological orientation, but with a booming voice, luminescent blue eyes, and a commitment to a businesslike approach to evangelical preaching, he decided to become a traveling preacher, and in the American free market of religion, he was a gifted entrepreneur. He challenged local farmers, mechanics, lawyers, merchants, and canal workers to make a personal decision for Christ and to abandon sin, which in his view was selfishness. He kept an "anxious bench" of sinners directly before him and addressed them by name. He relied increasingly on women to speak and pray in his meetings. Men and women should be "useful in the highest degree possible" and should "make the world a fit place for the imminent return of Christ." Finney preached in the burned-over district around Oneida County and on the Erie Canal from Utica to Troy.

In 1830 and 1831 Finney conducted a months-long revival in the booming flour mill town of Rochester, then the fastest-growing city in the country. He converted 800 to 1,200 men and women, including many leading citizens, ending with a five-day protracted meeting that brought business to a close. "Here was religion," writes historian Walter McDougall, "of the sort most Americans craved, a religion of the heart promising instant improvement in every household and community, the blessings of heaven in this life, in America, perhaps even 'the complete moral renovation of the world.'"[66] Historian Sean Wilentz writes, "The converted learned that life, and receiving life everlasting, was a matter of personal moral choices. Bad choices—intemperance, slothfulness, extravagance, dishonesty, violence—blocked the sinner from redemption. Good choices, coupled with prayer, opened the way to personal salvation and hastened the moral perfection of the world that, Finney taught, would precede Christ's second coming." Finney preached against the evils of tobacco and alcohol and actively opposed slavery. In 1835 he preached to thousands in New York City and refused communion to slaveholders. His theater was burned, but with financing from the evangelical businessmen Arthur and Lewis Tappan he built the three-thousand-seat Broadway Tabernacle in New York City, the largest building in the nation's largest city, and conducted nonstop revivals. In time polyglot Manhattan proved to be alien territory to Yankee preachers. In 1837 Finney left New York City and followed the trail of thousands of New England Yankees to the Western Reserve in northeast Ohio, which with its town greens and covered bridges was almost a replica of New England.

Among them was the already famous Presbyterian minister Lyman Beecher, born in Connecticut and educated at Yale, who embodied the Yankee propensity for cultural reform. As a Presbyterian minister in East Hampton, Long Island (a Yankee town), in

1804, he denounced dueling after the death of Alexander Hamilton; as a minister in the Yankee heartland of Litchfield, Connecticut, after 1810, he organized circuit-riding ministers and lay moral reform groups in Connecticut and Upstate New York, then moved to the Park Street Church across from Boston Common in 1826. Beecher eschewed the gloomy doctrine of predestination for a belief that men and women could choose to refrain from sin. He encouraged revivals where preachers would urge listeners to make a positive choice for Christ; he started a mass-circulation religious magazine and established America's first school for the deaf and dumb. He and his allies formed the American Sunday-School Union, the American Tract Society, the American Home Missionary Society, and the American Society for the Promotion of Temperance. In 1828 he formed the General Union for Promoting the Observance of the Christian Sabbath, supported by flour merchant Josiah Bissell of Rochester and silk merchant Lewis Tappan of Manhattan. He founded the American Temperance Society in 1826, and it had considerable success: Americans' consumption of alcohol fell from 7 gallons a year per person in the mid-1820s to 1.8 gallons in the late 1840s. "Through such issue-oriented organizations," writes historian Daniel Walker Howe, "reformers transcended geographical and denominational limitations to wage nationwide campaigns. The voluntary associations became a conspicuous feature of American society from that time forward. . . . They devised new means of influencing public opinion outside of politics: education, literature, magazines, religious revivals, and organized reform. They engaged the energies of people in all walks of life, not simply a privileged elite. . . . They distributed Bibles and tracts, supported missions foreign and domestic, and addressed such varied social problems as poverty, prostitution, and the abuse of women, children, animals, convicts and the insane. Most momentous of all their activities would be their crusade against slavery."[67]

In 1831 Beecher arrived in Cincinnati to head the newly founded Lane Theological Seminary with his children, Henry Ward Beecher and Harriet Beecher Stowe. "The West is a young empire of mind, and

power, and wealth, and free institutions, rushing up to a giant man-
hood with a rapidity and a power never witnessed below the sun. And
if she carries with her the elements of her preservation, the experiment will be glorious," he wrote. "Population is rushing into the West
like the waters of the flood, demanding for its moral preservation the
immediate and universal action of those institutions which discipline
the mind, and arm the conscience and the heart."[68] Cincinnati then
had 25,000 people, more than any other American city except New
York, Philadelphia, Boston, Baltimore, New Orleans, and Charleston
and, facing Kentucky across the Ohio River, it stood on the boundary between slave and free territories. In that setting it was daring for
Beecher to agree to sponsor a debate in February 1834 on whether
slavery should be abolished immediately and whether the colonization movement, which advocated returning slaves to Africa, should
be abandoned in favor of abolitionism. Those issues were debated for
eighteen nights, including testimony from former slave James Bradley and former slaveholder James Thome and spirited speeches from
abolitionist Theodore Dwight Weld, a native of New England who
had studied with Charles Grandison Finney. The verdict among the
students was unanimous: for abolition and against colonization. This
was widely unpopular in Cincinnati and, during Beecher's absence on
a trip to New York, the Lane trustees ordered Weld dismissed and the
antislavery society abolished.[69]

Most of the Lane students embraced abolitionism and left the
seminary. They joined Weld and found housing with the help of a
young Cincinnati lawyer named Salmon P. Chase, a New Hampshire
native who had moved to the city in 1830. The "Lane rebels" decided
to move en masse to Oberlin College, which was recently founded
in the town of Oberlin in the Western Reserve. They arranged for
financing from Arthur Tappan, for Finney to move to Oberlin, and
for the school to admit blacks—the first college in the United States
to do so. Two years later Oberlin became the first school to admit
women as well. Oberlin immediately became a major center for the
transmission of reformist Yankee culture, graduating advocates of

women's rights such as Lucy Stone and of blacks' civil rights such as Erastus Cravath, founder of Fisk University. The First Church at Oberlin was for many years the largest building west of the Appalachians; Finney as well as Frederick Douglass and William Lloyd Garrison preached there, and Oberlin became a central station on the underground railway in the 1850s. Oberlin graduates spread its ideas by founding similar colleges across the Midwest—in Hillsdale, Michigan; Ripon, Wisconsin; Grinnell, Iowa; and Northfield, Minnesota (later renamed Carleton).[70] Back in Cincinnati, Lyman Beecher's son Henry Ward Beecher moved toward the abolitionism he would in time preach in Brooklyn. His daughter Harriet married Calvin Stowe, a professor at Lane Seminary and an opponent of slavery; she drew on her knowledge of slavery in nearby Kentucky when writing her novel *Uncle Tom's Cabin*, the first installment of which appeared in 1851; it was published as a book in 1852 and by 1853 an astonishing 1,200,000 copies had been sold.[71] "Is this the little lady," asked Abraham Lincoln when he met her, "who started this great war?"

SLAVEHOLDERS, like all human beings, were not just rational economic calculators. If New England Yankees heading west in search of better farmland and economic opportunity were also determined to propagate their vibrant moralistic culture across the young nation, so the southern planters, while alert to economic incentives, were also determined to spread their way of life westward. It has been said that large slaveholders had an aristocratic, pre-capitalist ethos, but in practice they were successful capitalists. And, as historian Eugene Genovese writes, "The aristocratic ethos, however offensive to many in its extreme foundations, rested squarely on a world view in which some (slaves, women) were naturally subordinate to others whose dominations they accepted in return for a protection without which they could not hope to survive. This view of the world had its strongest foundation not in the ideal of the aristocratic seigneur but in the ideal of the male head of an extensive household that included economic and social dependents as well as natural family members—the ideal captured in the common expression, 'my family, white and black.' "72 The antebellum South was an overwhelmingly rural society, with only one large city in the Deep South, New Orleans, whose French cultural heritage set it conspicuously apart from the rest of the region; other large southern cities were either isolated, like Charleston, or at the northern edge of the region, like Baltimore, Louisville, and St. Louis. And in each southern county, long established or newly settled, the large landholders, who were almost inevitably the largest slaveholders, were the most respected and honored citizens. They were proud of their martial prowess and equestrian skills, they were often learned in the classics or the law, and they were determined to proclaim their liberty and to defend their honor. That liberty included, perverse as this may seem to twenty-first-century readers, the liberty to own slaves, to derive economic benefit from their labor, and take responsibility for their well-being.

These southern planters did not see themselves as just local notables or even as national leaders; they also saw themselves as indispensable participants in an expanding and progressive world economy. Like the leaders of Great Britain, the world's leading industrial pioneer, they tended to favor free trade, and with the British textile manufacturers they were responsible for an industry that was providing cheap and comfortable clothing for an ever-increasing percentage of the people in the world. By the 1850s, cotton accounted for more than half of all American exports and was the foundation of some of America's greatest fortunes. All of this depended, the planters believed, on the continued subjugation of their slaves, which was threatened, as they could see, by northern abolitionists and opponents of expansion of slavery in the territories. It was from this perspective that South Carolina's James Henry Hammond rose in the Senate in 1858 and proclaimed that "cotton is king." Hammond argued that the North dared not destroy America's most productive commodity and threatened that the South would secede—and prosper—if slavery were threatened. Hammond was less than an ideal spokesman for the planter class—he took liberties with white female relatives and young slave women (and perhaps with males as well), exercising something like a feudal droit du seigneur on his grand plantation—but the sentiments he expressed were emblematic of a class that had moved out from coastal America and staked its claim to the Cotton Belt.[73]

Just as the New England Yankee diaspora did not confine itself to one of the two political parties that emerged in the 1830s, neither did the migrating southern planters. Yankees favored Whigs over Democrats, but by no means unanimously, while in the early years of the nineteenth century, southern voters in each state tended to rally, sometimes almost unanimously, to their local political champions. In 1832, for example, Tennessee voted 95 percent for Democrat Andrew Jackson of Nashville while Kentucky voted 54 percent for Whig Henry Clay of Lexington. But soon another pattern emerged. Counties with many large slaveholders and large numbers of slaves, anxious for internal improvements and willing to endure tariffs, tended to vote for Whigs who supported such measures from 1836 to 1848. In 1836 the heavily slave-owning and cotton-producing counties in Georgia, Alabama, Mississippi, and Louisiana all voted for the Whig Hugh White, a former Jackson ally, who managed to carry Georgia and Tennessee and came close to carrying Mississippi and Louisiana. This Whig bloc continued faithful in 1840, 1844, and 1848, when the Whig nominees were William Henry Harrison of Ohio, Henry Clay of Kentucky, and Zachary Taylor of Louisiana (all born and raised in Virginia and the latter two slaveholders). The Whigs' opposition to territorial expansion apparently pleased those who were already large landowners, while the Democrats' support for annexation of Texas, expansion in the Oregon Territory, and war with Mexico evidently appealed to those with less property. Whig support of internal improvements presumably appealed to large slaveholders more than their support of protective tariffs repelled them. But by 1852 the large slaveholder areas mostly deserted the Whigs for the doughface (pro-Southern) Democrat Franklin Pierce, and in 1856 they were split between Democrat James Buchanan and the American Party's Millard Fillmore, who as a Whig was Taylor's successor and supported the Compromise of 1850 with its fugitive slave provisions.

The southern planters of the West, tied by geography to the Mississippi Valley, seem not to have been eager for the South to secede from the Union. The large planters in South Carolina were another matter. The state's Low Country had the nation's largest concentration of really large slaveholders, with more than a hundred slaves each: the 1860 Census recorded twenty-three such slaveholders each in Beaufort, Colleton, Charleston, and Georgetown Counties, more than in any other comparable area in the country. South Carolina's great political leader John C. Calhoun, who began his career as a war hawk in the War of 1812 and as a nationalist secretary of war afterward, by 1832 was attempting to nullify federal legislation and by the late 1840s was close to encouraging secession, though he held back until his death in 1850. South Carolina politicians were not averse to taking to violence to redeem their honor; Congressman Preston Brooks, enraged by Massachusetts senator Charles Sumner's speech attacking his uncle Senator Andrew Butler, thrashed Sumner with a cane and inflicted injuries that kept him out of public life for years. In that spirit other South Carolinians plunged ahead toward disunion, and when the Yankee-backed Abraham Lincoln was elected president in November 1860, it was South Carolina that led the way to secession in December. The large slaveholders of the cotton lands to the west went along, with varying degrees of enthusiasm, with secession and supported the Confederacy.

This turned out to be disastrous. Military confrontation ended the cotton trade with the North and the Union naval blockade effectively cut off cotton exports to Britain in 1861. In 1862 Union forces captured New Orleans, the South's largest city, port, and slave market, and Abraham Lincoln's Emancipation Proclamation freed all slaves behind Confederate lines in 1863. The Union's victory was complete in 1865: all slaves were freed by the Thirteenth Amendment and blacks were given civil and voting rights at least for a moment by the Union troops stationed in the South during Reconstruction. Most of the wealth of the southern planter class was effectively destroyed or confiscated. The South became for a century distinctly less prosperous than the North, with a much lower standard of living. Incomes of southern cotton planters fell far below antebellum levels: the British found new sources of supply and, more important, the efficient gang system was no longer feasible, since free men and women simply would not accept such harsh discipline. The southern planters had intended to transfer a way of life across the South. But the way of life they ended up transferring most effectively was not the commercial aristocracy of which they were exemplars but the way of life of the African-Americans who were their slaves and after the war became in many cases their tenants, sharecroppers, and dependents. The southern planters' migration was the interior migration of black Americans, a migration that brought 1 million of them to where many of their descendants live today. For while the planter class prized mobility, migration for black Americans was wrenching and dismaying, an experience they looked back on with grief and which they were reluctant to repeat. The grueling travel overland and/or on shipboard, the reality sometimes and the threat always of families being split and separated for the rest of their lives, the daunting labor required to tame virgin soil and build new housing—these were just some of the reasons, enshrined as folk memories, that made the slaves' descendants look on the prospect of moving with something akin to horror. After some initial moving around in the years of Reconstruction, black Americans mostly remained rooted in the counties to which their ancestors' masters had carried them until the exigencies of war and other factors sparked the great northward migration of 1940–65— a story that is the focus of a later chapter in this book. Meanwhile, the internal migration of the southern planters and their black slaves can be seen on the contemporary political map, as the rural counties where they flocked show up as voting by large margins for Barack Obama in both the primaries and the general election of 2008.

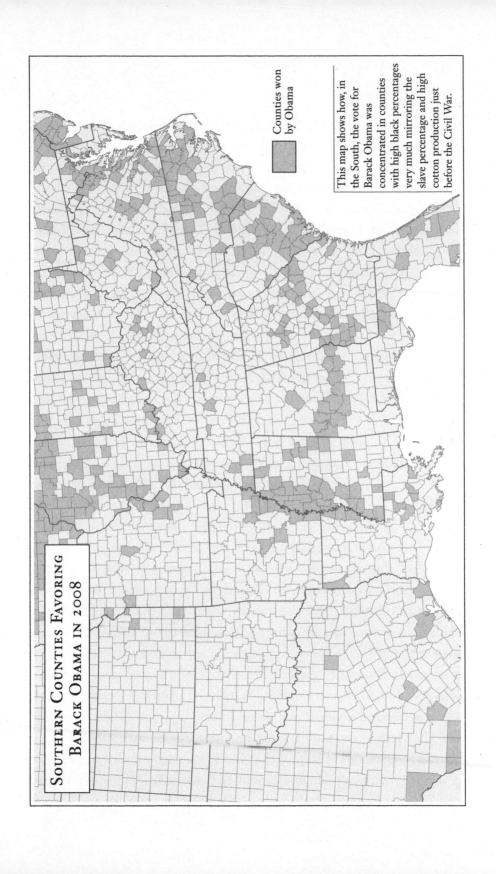

SOUTHERN COUNTIES FAVORING
BARACK OBAMA IN 2008

Counties won
by Obama

This map shows how, in
the South, the vote for
Barack Obama was
concentrated in counties
with high black percentages
very much mirroring the
slave percentage and high
cotton production just
before the Civil War.

THE Yankee success in cultural proselytization contrasts with the Yankee failure to dominate electoral politics in antebellum America. Southern slaveholders held the presidency for fifty of the sixty-one years between 1789 and 1850. Two New England presidents in this period, John Adams and John Quincy Adams, were defeated for reelection; the third, Franklin Pierce of New Hampshire, alienated Yankee voters through his support of the extension of slavery. From 1796 to 1816 New England was the base of the Federalist Party, along with the demographically stagnant coastal states of Maryland and Delaware. But the Federalists' decisive defeat in the election of 1800 brought the House of Virginia to the White House for a quarter century, leaving some Federalists disaffected enough to threaten secession from the Union in the Hartford Convention of 1814. In the party system that emerged from the politics of the 1820s, the biggest loser was New England's John Quincy Adams, defeated for reelection as president in 1828. In the decades that followed New Englanders and the Yankee diaspora tended to support Henry Clay's Whigs against Andrew Jackson's Democrats, but by no means unanimously. Those parties' chief differences were over the tariff, the Bank of the United States, and internal improvements, issues on which opinion was not closely related to Yankee cultural attitudes. Maine and New Hampshire tended to vote Democratic even as Vermont stayed staunchly Whig. Historian Lee Benson's careful examination of township returns in New York in the elections of the 1830s and 1840s shows that the Yankee vote was split, with majorities voting for the Whig Party but sizable minorities voting Democratic. The Whig Party in that state arose from the anti-Masonic movement of the late 1820s, nurtured by the farsighted politician William Seward, elected governor in 1838 and senator in 1849, and the talented political organizer Thurlow Weed.[74] But the Whigs, like the Democrats, sought to be a national party, with support in the slaveholding South as well as the North; that meant compromises on principle that many Yankees could not stomach. New England and the Yankee diaspora produced most of the votes cast for the Liberty

Party candidate in 1844 and for Free Soil Party candidates in 1852, which were fatal to the Whigs' chances in those years, and for Martin Van Buren's Free Soil candidacy, which was fatal to the Democrats in 1848. Many Yankee voters were rejecting both national political parties because both seemed unsatisfactory on slavery.

The uniting of the Yankee reforming spirit and a political party came in response to passage of the Kansas-Nebraska Act in May 1854 and the almost immediate formation of the Republican Party in July 1854. The Kansas-Nebraska Act repealed the Missouri Compromise of 1820, which prohibited slavery north of the 36°30' line west of Missouri and instead allowed voters in each new territory to determine whether or not they would allow slavery—popular sovereignty. This was seen as an attempt to spread slavery into areas where it was previously forbidden and to endorse the principle backed by Democrats from Andrew Jackson on to allow free citizens to take their slave property anywhere. The bill was opposed by most northern Whigs and by some Democrats, including those who had broken off from the party and supported Free Soil (antislavery expansion) tickets in 1848 and 1852; it was supported by a majority of southern Whigs and all southern Democrats.[75] Kansas-Nebraska was not the only non-economic issue roiling the political waters in 1854. There was also temperance, promoted largely by Yankees in Upstate New York and New England, where Maine passed the first prohibition law in 1851. And there was a movement for restrictions on immigration and immigrants, prompted by the enormous migration of Irish Catholics and Germans in the previous decade. This was embodied in the Know-Nothing movement, which spread rapidly in both North and South, in some places with sworn-to-secrecy confederates taking over local Whig or Democratic Party conventions, in some places by the forming of the American Party, whose chief aim was to limit or end immigration. (All this occurred as the old issues raised by Andrew Jackson's Democrats and Henry Clay's Whigs—the Bank of the United States, tariffs, expansion to Texas and the West Coast—were being settled. As a result, historian Michael Holt writes, "the congressional, state and local elections between August 1854 and December 1855 were the more labyrinthine, chaotic and important off-year contests in all of American political history.")[76]

In those years not a single northern state had straightforward two-party races between Democrats and Whigs, but the Democrats fared poorly against coalitions variously composed of Whigs, Free Soil Democrats, and Republicans. *New York Tribune* editor Horace Greeley, a Whig with a widespread following, urged a new coalition of Kansas-Nebraska opponents and found listeners in midwestern states where Whigs had been faring poorly. A group of Whigs, Free Soilers, and antislavery Democrats met in Ripon, Wisconsin, in February 1854 to recommend the formation of a new Republican Party; by July 1854 Republican state conventions were held in Wisconsin, Michigan, Indiana, and Ohio, and Republican tickets swept to impressive victories in all four states.[77] In Iowa the Whig candidate for governor was endorsed by Free Soilers and temperance advocates and won the general election. In Stephen Douglas's Illinois, where almost all Democrats joined him in supporting Kansas-Nebraska, congressional races were run on the issue, with Whig politicians, such as former congressman Abraham Lincoln, declining to identify as Republicans and remaining Whigs but working in alliance nonetheless.[78] In the East, Whigs co-opted the Free Soilers successfully in Vermont, while there were mixed results in Maine, where the prohibition forces were strongest. In these two states and in New Jersey, where Whigs did well, the American Party had little influence.[79] In Pennsylvania, Whigs allied with Free Soilers but were split by Know-Nothings, who endorsed candidates of the Native American Party in some races and essentially took over the Whig Party in Philadelphia. In Massachusetts, where opposition to Kansas-Nebraska was universal, Free Soilers joined the Know-Nothings, who were energized by the inrush over the previous decade of Irish Catholic immigrants into Boston, and the Know-Nothing candidates won almost all the seats in the legislature plus the governorship with 63 percent of the vote. In New York, the nation's largest state, both Democrats and Whigs were split into hostile factions; nativism and prohibition became issues more prominent than Kansas-Nebraska; Know-Nothings nominated a separate candidate for governor after a convention of Free Soilers and temperance advocates endorsed the Whig on a platform of repeal of the Fugitive Slave Act—which required escaped slaves to be forcibly returned to their owners, and called for an exclusively northern fusion party to nominate a presidential candidate in 1856. The result was a narrow Whig victory for governor and a big Whig increase in the congressional delegation, due in large part to Know-Nothing endorsements.

The results in New York were particularly momentous. Former president Millard Fillmore, the factional rival of Senator William Seward, proceeded to embrace the Know-Nothing cause as one that, with both northern and southern support, could nominate him as the American Party's candidate for president in 1856. Southern Whigs, who picked up seats in the House, were alienated from their northern copartisans by their alliances with Free Soilers and their opposition to the Fugitive Slave Act. Seward and his manager, Thurlow Weed, moved to join the nascent Republican Party, which would run a presidential ticket seeking support only in the North. In the meantime the Democratic Party saw its congressional majorities disappear and faced dismaying prospects in the North.[80]

Out of this partisan turmoil the Republican Party, dominated by and responsive to the New England Yankee diaspora, emerged as the chief rival of the Democrats. By 1856, the Whig Party disappeared, the American Party became a national anti-immigrant party (though not on the ballot in the far northern states of New Hampshire, Vermont, Michigan, and Wisconsin), and the Republican Party, dedicated to opposing the expansion of slavery in the territories, became the chief opposition to the Democratic Party in every free state except California while not appearing on the ballot in any slave state.[81] In the 1852 presidential election Democrat Franklin Pierce beat Whig Winfield Scott 51 percent to 44 percent in the popular vote, with 5 percent for Free Soil candidate John Hale. In the free states Pierce won by 49 percent to 44 percent and in the slave states he

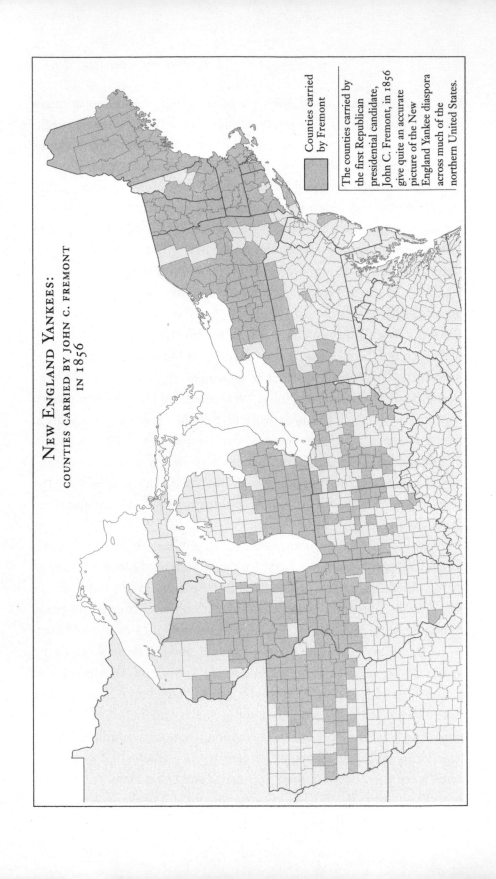

NEW ENGLAND YANKEES:
COUNTIES CARRIED BY JOHN C. FREMONT
IN 1856

Counties carried
by Fremont

The counties carried by
the first Republican
presidential candidate,
John C. Fremont, in 1856
give quite an accurate
picture of the New
England Yankee diaspora
across much of the
northern United States.

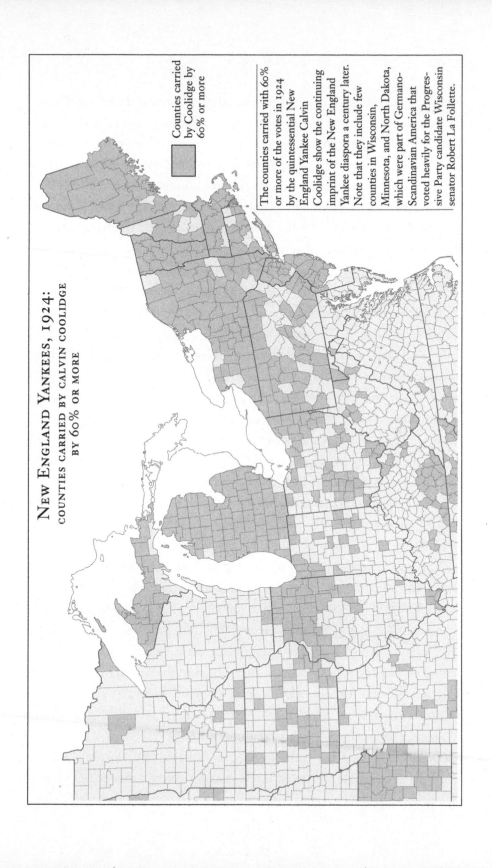

NEW ENGLAND YANKEES, 1924:
COUNTIES CARRIED BY CALVIN COOLIDGE BY 60% OR MORE

Counties carried
by Coolidge by
60% or more

The counties carried with 60%
or more of the votes in 1924
by the quintessential New
England Yankee Calvin
Coolidge show the continuing
imprint of the New England
Yankee diaspora a century later.
Note that they include few
counties in Wisconsin,
Minnesota, and North Dakota,
which were part of Germano-
Scandinavian America that
voted heavily for the Progressive Party candidate Wisconsin
senator Robert La Follette.

won 55 percent to 45 percent. In the 1856 presidential election Democrat James Buchanan won the national popular vote by a seemingly similar margin, 45 percent to 33 percent for Republican John Fremont and 22 percent for American Party candidate Millard Fillmore. In the slave states his popular vote margin was almost identical to Pierce's: 56 percent to 44 percent for Fillmore, who essentially won the former southern Whig vote. In the free states, however, Buchanan trailed Fillmore by a popular vote margin of 45 percent to 41 percent, with 13 percent for Fillmore. Fillmore held on to the votes of some Whigs who remained loyal to the vision of a national party. But Fremont rallied to the Republican side most of the former Whigs and a significant percentage of Free Soil Democrats.

This new Republican Party was clearly a creation of the Yankee diaspora, formed in Yankee-settled Michigan and Wisconsin. Unlike the Whigs and the American Party, the Republicans did not seek to become a national party, but were capable of winning a presidential election since the free states cast 176 of 296 electoral votes (and would add 7 more when Minnesota and Oregon were admitted to the Union before the 1860 election). This was apparent in the 1856 presidential election, when Fremont carried not only the popular vote in the free states but won their electoral votes by a margin of 114 to 62. He carried all six New England states; he carried New York with 46 percent of the vote, carrying most of the Upstate area; he carried Ohio and Iowa with 49 percent of the vote and won more than 50 percent in Michigan and Wisconsin. He ran second, with 40 percent of the vote, in both Indiana and Illinois. He ran much further behind in Buchanan's home state of Pennsylvania and in New Jersey. The map of the counties he carried is almost exactly a map of the Yankee diaspora. He carried all but a few counties in New England, virtually all of Upstate New York west of Albany, plus the northern tier of Pennsylvania counties; he got very high percentages in the Western Reserve and carried Yankee-settled counties west and north of Columbus; he carried the northern counties of Indiana and a cluster of counties around Richmond; and he carried almost every county in southern Michigan, northern Illinois, southern and central Wisconsin, and eastern and central Iowa. Strikingly, he carried almost no counties anywhere outside this map of the Yankee diaspora.[82] The Republicans, unlike any party since the Federalists, appealed to Yankee sensibilities. Its reformist spirit and its opposition to slavery in the territories were in harmony with Yankee reformism. Proclamations by William Seward of a "higher law" and Abraham Lincoln's declaration that the nation was "a house divided" and must either become all slave or all free struck a chord with Yankee idealism and the Yankees' desire to impose their moral standards on others.

The Kansas-Nebraska Act also set off what amounted to an armed struggle in the Kansas Territory. Former Missouri senator David Atchison, who had first proposed popular sovereignty to Illinois senator Stephen Douglas, organized a quasi-military force of five thousand men to secure the election of a territorial legislature that would allow slavery in the territory. From Massachusetts, textile magnate Amos Lawrence founded, and provided $5 million in funding for, a New England Emigrant Aid Society to settle New Englanders in Kansas and preserve it from slavery. A pro-slavery legislature was recognized by the territorial governor despite election fraud; antislavery settlers elected their own legislature.[83] Fighting broke out near the antislavery town of Lawrence in November 1855 and "actual civil war"[84] in May 1856. Congress failed to recognize either side as the rightful government. This conflict eventually split the national Democratic Party, as Senator Douglas in 1857 opposed President Buchanan's support of the pro-slavery forces.

The Republicans were united in supporting the antislavery forces in Kansas, but were embarrassed by excesses including the massacre of pro-slavery men in Osawatomie, Kansas, by the fiery abolitionist John Brown and even more by Brown's seizing of the arsenal at Harpers Ferry, Virginia, in 1859 in an attempt to foment a slave rebellion. The Democratic Party split in two in 1860, when its initial convention in Charleston, South Carolina, stormed by grandees opposed to Douglas, had to be adjourned; it reconvened in Baltimore and nominated

Douglas, while a southern Democratic convention met and nominated future vice president John Breckinridge, who supported a pro-slavery policy in Kansas.

The Republicans, meeting in the Yankee city of Chicago, nominated Abraham Lincoln, in large part because his opposition to the anti-immigrant stands of the American Party made him acceptable to many German voters in Pennsylvania, Ohio, Indiana, Illinois, Iowa, Wisconsin, and Minnesota. Lincoln, who was on the ballot in only two slave states, Delaware and Missouri, won 40 percent of the popular vote, only 7 percent more than Fremont had four years before. But he carried Pennsylvania, Indiana, Illinois, and California, which Fremont had lost, plus the newly admitted states of Minnesota and Oregon. He won every state where his name was on the ballot except for New Jersey (where he still won 4 of the 7 electoral votes), Delaware, and Missouri. A map of the counties Lincoln carried would show him carrying Yankee diaspora counties by larger margins than Fremont and show him expanding Republican territory southward, to the Pennsylvania Dutch country of Pennsylvania plus the Philadelphia area and southern New Jersey, to most of central Ohio and Indiana, to western Iowa and southern Minnesota.[85] Lincoln's rejection of anti-immigrant appeals was critical in his securing the nomination and gaining the marginal votes needed to prevail in key states. Lincoln was of Yankee stock on his father's side but, born in Kentucky and raised in southern Indiana, he seems to have developed views congenial to the Yankee diaspora on his own rather than as part of a Yankee community.

Lincoln's election and his successful conduct, over four agonizing years, of the Civil War, was a victory of the North over the South. But it was also a victory of the Yankee diaspora and a stark reversal of the freezing out of political power of Yankees during the preceding six decades. Despite their failure at the presidency, the Yankee diaspora had an enormous impact in stimulating the growth of the economy and in shaping the culture of the great mass of Americans during that time. The economic dynamism of Yankee-founded cities such as Rochester and Chicago transformed the nation from Jeffersonian agrarianism to a Hamiltonian innovative commercial and industrial dynamo. The self-improving evangelism of Charles Grandison Finney and Lyman Beecher changed national mores and opinion. Yankee moralism and bossiness finally found its political engine in the Republican Party and its charismatic leader Abraham Lincoln— although Yankee intellectuals like Ralph Waldo Emerson and Henry David Thoreau were slow to recognize this, slower than the onetime Brooklyn Democrat Walt Whitman.

The Yankee reformist impulse was given full play in the four years of Abraham Lincoln's administration. His Republican Party passed the Morrill Act (1862) encouraging land grant colleges—in line with the Yankee impulse toward higher education—and the Homestead Act, which aided plain farmers to become self-sufficient property owners. It encouraged manufacturers of arms and other products and financiers of both the public debt and the grand public works projects such as the transcontinental railroad. The two most successful Union generals were both of Yankee stock and imbibed Yankee values: Ulysses Grant abhorred the abasement of Mexicans in the 1846– 48 war, in which he served with distinction, and William Tecumseh Sherman was appalled by the mores of Louisiana slaveholders when he was stationed there in the decade before the Civil War. Not all of the Yankee reformist impulses were successful. Grant's and Sherman's efforts to enforce the rights of southern blacks during Reconstruction were cut short by voters impatient with heavy military spending and unsympathetic to the notion that whites should treat blacks as equals. But the character of the republic changed: the presidency, which was held almost without exception by slaveholders and their sympathizers during the sixty years before the Civil War, was held with only small exceptions by those who were unsympathetic with this view for almost all of the next sixty years. The Civil War can be seen as the Yankee conquest of North America, as the military and political subjugation of the conflicting American culture of slaveholders with the support of the emerging Germano-Scandinavian America and the partial but arguably decisive cooperation of a large share of Scots-Irish America.

3. THE IRISH AND GERMANS

*T*HE early years of the republic saw little immigration to the United States from foreign countries. The surge of Scots-Irish migration ended abruptly with the outbreak of the Revolutionary War and did not resume in great numbers thereafter. Britain and France were at war during almost all of the years between 1792 and 1815, and the American economy suffered a serious recession in 1819. Official records for 1820 indicate total immigration of just 8,385, with 6,024 coming from the British Isles and exactly 1 from Mexico.[1] While vast internal westward migrations were under way, immigration from abroad reached only 60,000 in 1832; 79,000 in 1837; 104,000 in 1842; and 114,000 in 1844. These were small numbers with little demographic imprint at a time when the nation's total population was increasing from just under 10 million in 1820 to 20 million in 1845.

The United States seemed very far from being a nation of immigrants. It was surely unprepared for a sudden spike of immigration to come, and from places that had produced only a small share of settlers in the colonial period. In the decade between 1846 and 1855, there began two enormous surges of immigration—1,288,000 immigrants, most of them Roman Catholics, arrived from Ireland, and 976,000 from Germany. This was one of three short periods when immigration as a percentage of preexisting population was at its highest levels in American history, the other two being the surge of Scots-Irish migration in 1763–75 and the Ellis Island immigration of 1900–14.

In all three cases lands, which had produced only a relatively small number of newcomers before, suddenly, and without forewarning, produced very large numbers of immigrants whose cultures were unfamiliar to most Americans and who were seen as threatening by many. In all three cases the immigrants clustered heavily in specific parts of the nation and created communities that took some time to be interwoven into the American fabric. And in all three cases these surges of migration occurred at a time when Americans were coping with the creative destruction produced by vibrant economic growth and would be faced with wrenching issues of war and peace.

IN July 1845, just before harvesttime, the green leaves on the potato plants in Ireland suddenly turned black. Farmers desperately tried to cut off the black leaves, but even when they did, they found that the potatoes underground had already turned putrid. This was the beginning of the great Irish potato famine. The infecting agent, *Phytophthora infestans*, apparently came from North America, an unwanted migrant on eastbound ships; to crops in much of western Europe it proved fatal, turning ripening potatoes to black rot. Ireland was especially vulnerable. Its population had increased sharply, from 5.5 million in 1801 to 6.8 million in 1821 and 8.2 million in 1841, but unlike England and Scotland, which were growing at a similar pace, Ireland had not developed industrially or economically. Peasants lived on small plots of land, surrounded by stone fences far from any feasible roads, and depended almost entirely on potatoes. The potato blight destroyed only about one-third of the crop in 1845, but it returned in 1846 and destroyed almost the entire potato harvest. It abated in 1847 but returned in full force in 1848; not until 1855 did potato production return to the levels of the early 1840s. But by then, despite the efforts of some landlords, Catholic and Protestant clergymen, Irish and British Quakers and Irish-Americans, between 1.1 and 1.5 million Irish people died from starvation and famine-related disease. Ireland's population declined to 6.6 million in 1851 and 5.8 million in 1861.[2]

The famine produced one of the greatest outmigrations proportionate to population—if not in all of history at least within the last two hundred years. About 2.5 million Irish left Ireland between 1845 and 1860 and went to the United States, Canada, and Australia, and perhaps another half million left for Britain. In the ten years of heaviest migration, from 1846 to 1855, 1,288,000 Irish arrived in the United States—a number equal to 7 percent of the U.S. population at the beginning of this period.

This surge of migration had as great an impact on mid-nineteenth-century America as the surge of Scots-Irish migration that crested in the dozen years immediately before the American Revolution. But these were very different migrations. The Scots-Irish migration was a migration almost entirely of Protestants, from Scotland and the North of England as well as from the province of Ulster in northeast Ireland. The mid-nineteenth-century migration was a migration almost entirely of Roman Catholics, largely from the west, south, and center of Ireland, the areas most heavily affected by the famine. The Scots-Irish migration to the Appalachian chain had been going on for two generations before it accelerated immediately after the British victory in the French and Indian War, which opened the way for more western settlement. There was some Irish Catholic migration to the United States before the potato blight struck—though it is not clear what percentage of the 445,000 Irish immigrants recorded in the twenty-five years from 1821 to 1845 were Catholic—but the pace and extent of the migration surged enormously when disaster struck. The Catholic percentage in the United States increased from 5 percent of total population in 1840 to 8 percent in 1850 and 12 percent in 1860[3]—huge increases in numbers considering this was a time when the total population was increasing by about 30 percent each decade. And the Irish immigrants who fled from the famine headed not to the frontiers or to farmland, but settled in overwhelming numbers in the rapidly growing cities on the eastern seaboard.

The Ireland that they left was very different from the Ulster or Scotland that the Scots-Irish had left seven decades before. The Scots-Irish Presbyterians were a people connected with Britain rather than separated from it by the Irish Sea, and they had developed an economy that traded linen products and other goods with Britain. And at the time of mass migration they were less than one generation away from a time of armed rebellion against the British Crown, the latest of a long history of violent uprisings and constant fighting. At the same time they all spoke English (if with a Scots accent) and tended to be literate, thanks to the Presbyterian doctrine that every person should interpret the Bible for himself or herself.

The Irish Catholics by the mid–nineteenth century were a people with folk memories of pitched battles more distant in the past, in the years up to 1690, when the Catholic James II was defeated by the Protestant William III at the Battle of the Boyne. But an undercurrent of potential violence was often present in the Catholics' resentment at their treatment by the outnumbered Protestant landowners and gentry. Meanwhile, ties with Catholics on the continent of Europe—with the Irish Catholic soldiers (the "wild geese") given leave by the British to flee to France or with the seminary in Douai where English-speaking Catholic priests were trained—became attenuated as they blended into their new communities and the British government authorized and subsidized Irish seminaries at Maynooth and Carlow as alternatives to Douai. The isolation of Irish Catholics was all the greater because even as their numbers vastly increased in the early nineteenth century half or more spoke only Irish (what Americans refer to as Gaelic) and knew little or no English.

In the decades just before the famine the Irish Catholics developed not an advanced industrial economy but a mass democratic politics. After the Battle of the Boyne severe laws were passed against Catholics: they were barred from voting for or serving in Parliament; they were ineligible to be lawyers or local government officials; with some exceptions they could not own land. Restrictions on landowning were relaxed in the late eighteenth century, and in 1793, 40-shilling freeholders (those owning property that rented for £2 a year) were allowed to vote. But Catholic emancipation—the right of Catholics to vote, to freely own land, to practice law—was blocked by King George III in 1801 when Parliament passed the Act of Union abolishing the separate Irish Parliament and giving Ireland representation in the British Parliament in London. This created a demand for Catholic emancipation in both Ireland and Britain and, in Ireland, a mass politics of a kind not seen before. The key organizer was Daniel O'Connell, a west Ireland landowner and a Catholic who spoke Irish as well as English and was educated in France. A lawyer elected to Parliament in 1828, he became one of the great orators in the House of Commons. In 1823 he formed the Catholic Association, which, with strong support from the Catholic Church, quickly became a mass organization capable of raising the impressive sum of £20,000 a year.

This was arguably the first European mass political party, developed around the same time Martin Van Buren was organizing the supporters of Andrew Jackson into the Democratic Party in the United States. O'Connell, writes historian William O'Connor Morris, "formed the bold design of combining the Irish millions, under the superintendence of the native priesthood, into a vast league against the existing order of things, and of wresting the concession of Catholic claims for every opposing party in the state by an agitation, continually kept up, and embracing the whole of the people, but maintained within constitutional limits, though menacing and shaking the frame of society."[4] He led what were called monster rallies, "backed up," as historian R. F. Foster writes, "by the implicit threat of mass disobedience, of unilateral withdrawal of allegiance, even of a refusal to recognize the legitimacy of the state."[5] A Catholic Association candidate was elected to Parliament in 1826; the Catholic Association had deployed priests, hired salaried agents, established travel facilities for outlying voters, and provided alternative jobs or housing to tenant voters harassed by their landlords.[6] O'Connell, elected two years later, led a bloc of thirty-six Irish members to force passage of the Catholic Emancipation Act of 1829, which removed restrictions against Catholics in politics and landholding, but at the price of dissolving the Catholic Association and raising the requirement for life tenants' voting from 40 shillings to £10.[7] Maintaining his Irish Members of Parliament as a key balancing force in the 1830s, O'Connell began to demand repeal of the 1801 Act of Union, though he was careful to remain ambiguous about an alternative. In 1843 he planned a massive rally for repeal in Clontarf, near Dublin, then canceled it under pressure from prime minister Robert Peel.[8] He was prosecuted anyway and sentenced to a year in jail, but the House of Lords quashed the conviction. O'Connell took no part in politics after the famine—he died on a pilgrimage to Rome in 1847—but he had developed a sectarian Catholics mass political party as well as what Foster calls a "lively culture of political engagement."[9] By the famine year of 1846, Catholic Ireland was economically stagnant but politically vibrant.

The migration of the Scots-Irish in the years before the American Revolution was triggered by a sense of opportunity in a new land that was nevertheless still part of the British Empire. The migration of the Irish Catholics in the famine years was triggered by disaster that befell a people poorly prepared to move to a foreign country. As historian Kerby Miller writes, "In 1845–55, an unprecedented proportion of the Irish immigrants were traditionalist peasants, often Irish-speakers, who might never have emigrated under normal circumstances and who carried to the New World pre-modern attitudes and behavior patterns diametrically opposed to those . . . characterized as typically American."[10] These immigrants were further weakened by the rigors of the Atlantic crossing in sailing ships—regularly scheduled steamship travel began in 1838 but was still the exception rather than the rule—and 9 percent of those headed westward died in what became known as "coffin ships."[11] Yet they did not include the most destitute who typically lacked the means to pay for passage across the Atlantic and, in the counties hardest hit by the blight, the deceased were buried unrecorded by the hundreds of mass graves.[12] The emigrants included those whose visions of opportunity in the market economy seemed occluded by personal circumstance as well as the horrifying destruction wreaked by the potato blight. One such seems to have been Patrick Kennedy, who in 1849 left Dunganstown in County Wexford, in the southeast corner of Ireland, the part of the island with the lowest famine fatality rate, for Liverpool and Boston. He was a third son stuck working on the family farm inherited by his older brother; he was literate in English and had enough money to afford passage on a clipper ship, the *Washington Irving*, and to bring his fiancée over a few months later. In these respects they resembled the parents of Andrew Jackson, who had embarked from Carrickfergus eighty-four years before: they left a disadvantageous position in a commercial society for the possibility of vast improvement in a more dynamic but less settled society. Such were the great-grandparents of John Fitzgerald Kennedy, elected president of the United States 111 years after their marriage. The relatively affluent Kennedys seem to have been the exception, not the rule, in a migration mostly of poor farmers; Patrick and Bridget's son P. J. was a prosperous saloonkeeper in East Boston and a member of the Massachusetts legislature for twelve years; his son Joseph P. Kennedy graduated from Harvard and made millions as a banker, speculator, movie producer, and liquor importer, enough to make him one of two $50,000 contributors to Franklin Roosevelt's 1932 campaign.

Most Irish immigrants lacked the talents and advantages of the Kennedys, but they did have one thing in common: they headed to and stayed in the big cities of the United States rather than going to the interior to make their livings on farms. This was the first surge of American migration that ended in cities rather than the countryside. This was not a natural choice at the time. In 1840 only about 5 percent of Americans lived in cities that had more than 100,000 people. Only two, New York (351,000) and Philadelphia (185,000), had reached a magnitude similar to Dublin (232,000) or Liverpool (250,000), with three more—Boston, Baltimore, and New Orleans—hovering just a bit over 100,000; all were very much smaller than London, whose population reached nearly 2 million in the Census of 1841. And yet a majority of Irish headed for those cities rather than seeking jobs on the long-settled countryside or striking out, as most German immigrants did in these years, for the prairie frontier. Why did the Irish stay in the cities, when the vast majority of them had worked as farmers before traveling to the United States?[13]

For one thing it was lonely on the prairie, and there were few if any Catholic churches outside the cities. In addition, in those years before the Homestead Act it required at least some cash to buy land—and the famine migrants came with little or no cash.[14] And given their experience, perhaps they simply didn't want to farm. They had been tenant farmers in Ireland, with few opportunities to manage, and the one crop most of them knew, potatoes, had failed them miserably. "Our forebears, landing on the eastern seaboard of the United States," writes Irish-American author Frank McCourt, "hesitated to move inland, where they could have farmed to their hearts' content. Oh, no, they weren't going to be caught again. Look at what the land had done to them in Ireland. They'd stay in the big cities, never again to become victims of the treacherous spud."[15]

There was precedent for this: Irish Catholics who migrated to England and Scotland in the years before the famine headed to fast-growing industrial cities like Manchester, Liverpool, and Glasgow with their cotton mills and shipyards, and to London. The Industrial Revolution started in Britain and the massive farm-to-factory migration started at least a generation earlier there than anywhere else, after the Scots-Irish migration of 1763–75 but before the Irish Catholic migration of 1846–55. So Irish Catholic immigrants, accustomed to industrial destinations, tended to stay put in the American ports where they landed, especially Boston, New York, and Philadelphia, while those who did go inland typically worked on railroad or canal construction or converged on mining areas, like the anthracite country of northeast Pennsylvania.[16]

The result was that Irish Catholics, a small minority in the 1830s, became a major presence in the big cities by the 1850s—more than one-quarter the population in New York, Boston, and Philadelphia and in smaller cities in between: Providence, New Haven,

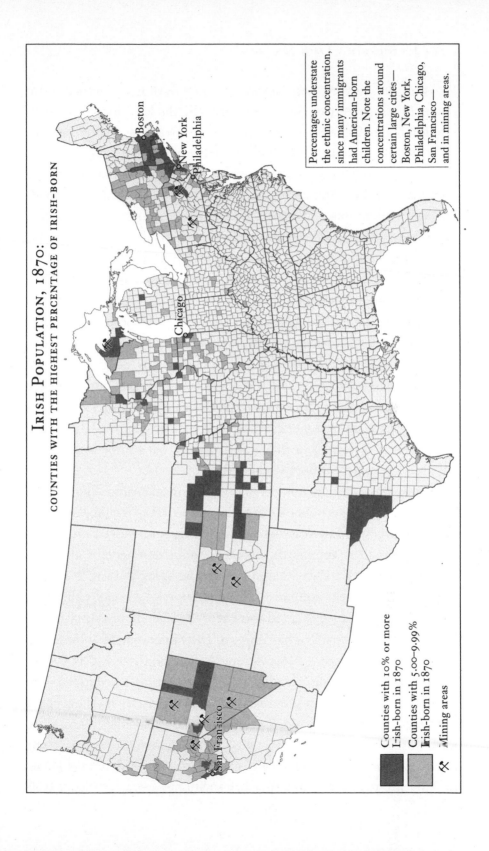

IRISH POPULATION, 1870:
COUNTIES WITH THE HIGHEST PERCENTAGE OF IRISH-BORN

Boston

New York
Philadelphia

Chicago

San Francisco

Percentages understate
the ethnic concentration,
since many immigrants
had American-born
children. Note the
concentrations around
certain large cities—
Boston, New York,
Philadelphia, Chicago,
San Francisco—
and in mining areas.

Counties with 10% or more
Irish-born in 1870

Counties with 5.00–9.99%
Irish-born in 1870

Mining areas

Hartford, Jersey City, and Newark.[17] They were not only numerous but, as historian Patrick Blessing writes, "by the late 1850s most Irish immigrants in American cities were isolated from the rest of the population,"[18] in separate predominantly Irish neighborhoods. This was profoundly unsettling both to their American neighbors and to the Irish Catholic immigrants themselves. "Had I fallen from the clouds amongst this people," historian Kerby Miller quotes one as saying, "I could not feel more isolated, more bewildered." "We are a primitive people," said another, "wandering wildly in a strange land, the nineteenth century."[19] Just as unsettling for many Americans was the sudden presence of so many Catholics in a nation that, while imposing no religious test for office and tolerating all forms of worship, was nevertheless overwhelmingly Protestant in religious preference and cultural attitude. Opposition to "Popery" was deeply ingrained in many Protestant sects, and the opposition of Pope Pius IX to the revolutions sweeping Europe in 1848 and to democratic institutions was so unpopular in America that construction of the Washington Monument was stopped in 1854 due to claims that a stone he had contributed was somehow booby-trapped with a bomb.

Moreover, Irish neighborhoods were insalubrious and crime-ridden. "The native public's reaction to the Irish included moving out of neighborhoods en masse as the immigrants moved in; stereotyping them all as drunkards, brawlers, and incompetents; and raising employment barriers exemplified in the stock phrase, 'No Irish need apply,'" writes economist Thomas Sowell. "The jobs the Irish did find were those considered too hard, too menial, too dirty or too dangerous for others. The hardships of their lives may be summed up in a nineteenth century observation, 'You seldom see a gray-haired Irishman.'"[20] There was something to these charges. Used to living in rural areas, the Irish were more casual than other city dwellers about sewage and garbage disposal, leading to cholera epidemics centered on Irish wards and high infant mortality. And although the homicide rate in Ireland was lower than in the United States, the Irish homicide rate in America was four to five times the national average.[21] Scots-Irish immigrants had also been violent and crime-prone in America,[22] but out on the frontier that attracted less attention than the Irish Catholic crime rate in the cities. "Crammed together in flats without water or sanitary facilities, they fought constantly to defend their territory and whatever scraps of dignity they still had,"[23] writes legal scholar Randolph Roth. Coming from a society in which they were in some respects second-class citizens, freed from the supervision of local landowners and priests and faced with hostile neighbors, young male Irish immigrants behaved much more violently than those around them. In the 1840s and 1850s the Irish crime rate in America was about 12 per 100,000 adults, twice that of free blacks and three times the rate of non-Irish whites.[24] In New York the homicide rate rose from 4.4 per 100,000 in 1840–45, before the potato famine immigration, to 10.8 in 1860–65.[25] The Irish were largely responsible for a national spike upward in the white homicide rate[26] and an increase in "serious violence" in "interracial riots" with blacks in the 1840s and 1850s.[27]

IN 1898, when asked what would be the most significant fact of the twentieth century, the German statesman Otto von Bismarck answered, "The fact that the North Americans speak English." Or so the story goes; it is one of those quotations the speaker should have said if he didn't, and in this case he surely would have been pleased had he said it. By this time Bismarck was retired, but he surely remained aware of demographic and economic trends as well as the latest developments in diplomacy and war. The German Empire that he had united in 1871 by a series of wars and diplomatic triumphs was now the giant of Europe, with a rapidly growing economy and 57 million people, significantly larger than its longtime enemy France (41 million) or her potential ally Britain (42 million) and, together with Germany's onetime rival but now ally, Austria-Hungary (46 million), it was a counterweight to Russia (133 million). But bring the

United States (76 million), with an economy and technology rivaling Germany's, into the picture on the side of Germany's enemies and she would be outweighed, as indeed happened two decades later. As the twentieth century was dawning, more people in Europe spoke German than any other language except perhaps Russian. But German immigrants and their descendants in America, perhaps 8 million in number, spoke English.

Most of those immigrants came over before there was a united Germany. When they began arriving, in the seventeenth century, they came from parts of the Holy Roman Empire. This was not a unified state but a collection of dozens of kingdoms, principalities, duchies, margraviates, landgraviates, counties, free cities, archbishoprics, bishoprics, and other units. The area had been devastated, with substantial population loss, in the Thirty Years' War of 1648, the complicated struggle between Protestants and Catholics, the Hapsburg Holy Roman emperors and their Bourbon rivals in France and Vasa rivals in Sweden. The Treaty of Westphalia in 1648 institutionalized the principle of *cuius regio, eius religio*, in which residents of each political unit would follow the religion of its ruler. Some of these were in effect pacifist havens, while others were military bastions, with the German states of Hesse-Kassel leasing out their young men to fight as mercenary soldiers and Prussia developing an army that would rival the emperor's.

It was from the pacifist havens that German migrants came to colonial America. In 1681 the pacifist Quaker William Penn began recruiting German pietists in the valley of the Rhine to settle in his colony of Pennsylvania, and Mennonites settled Germantown, now a neighborhood inside the city of Philadelphia. Starting in 1709 there was significant emigration from the Palatinate, at the junction of the Rhine and the Moselle, a war zone then in the War of Spanish Succession (1701–13), including many sectarian pietists like Mennonites, Baptist Dunkers, Schwenkenfelders, and Moravian Brethren as well as members of the Lutheran and Reformed Churches. Their numbers swelled until one-third of colonial Pennsylvanians were German—the ancestors of the Pennsylvania Dutch. Benjamin Franklin, a political opponent of the Quaker pacifists and the colony's Penn family proprietors, both of whom won German support in the politics of the colonial assembly, deplored large-scale German immigration. "Few of their children in the country learn English. The signs in our streets have inscriptions in both languages," he noted in 1753. "Why should the Palatine Boors be suffered to swarm into our settlements, and by herding together establish their language and morals to the exclusion of ours?"

Immigration from German lands was minimal during the American Revolution, the years of economic depression in the 1780s, and the two decades of world war between Britain and revolutionary and Napoleonic France between 1792 and 1815. Immigration was also very limited in the years after the sharp economic downturn of 1819. Two developments changed that, however, and prompted a surge of immigration from Germany at the same time as the surge of Catholic immigration from Ireland. One was the development of regularly scheduled steamship traffic across the Atlantic, starting with the race between the *Great Western* and the *Sirius* across the ocean in 1838. Steamships could hold many more migrants than the sailing ships of the eighteenth century, the journey was much shorter, and the risk of danger or death was very much reduced. The second development was the potato blight. The same year it struck Ireland, 1845, it also struck Germany. Peasants there did not depend as heavily on the potato for sustenance as the farmers of southern and western Ireland, but the blight caused considerable distress, exacerbated by an economic crisis and crop failures due to adverse weather in 1846 and 1847. The population of the German states, declining or relatively stagnant in the seventeenth and eighteenth centuries, started rising sharply after the Napoleonic wars, even as the birth rate in France (until Napoleon's time the demographic giant of Europe) was slowing down. Population pressure and the scarcity of land surely played some part in prompting many Germans to leave for North America, as it did many in the neighboring Low Countries and Switzerland, whose rates of emigration to the United States were higher in the 1846–55 decade than at any other time in history.

Napoleon had abolished the Holy Roman Empire after more than a thousand years of existence and drastically reduced the number of German states. The Congress of Vienna, which settled affairs after Napoleon's defeat, accepted most of these changes and encouraged an alliance of royal powers to maintain something like the ancient regimes of the period before the French Revolution. Leading this enterprise was Prince Klemens von Metternich, the dominant minister for four decades of the Hapsburg rulers of Austria and Hungary, who created a German confederation including the western Hapsburg lands, most of the kingdom of Prussia (but not East Prussia), and a dozen or so German principalities and free cities in between. These German states seemed as classically serene and disciplined as the Biedermeier furniture that was the favorite of the affluent at the time. But underneath the placid surface some currents were stirring. The German economy, no longer held back by war, was growing, but few large factories had yet been built. There was no culturally and politically dominant capital city like London or Paris. But the German states did have universities and scientific institutes that were surpassing those of any other nation in many disciplines, and if they did not equal Britain in literature or France in visual arts, they outshone both in music and produced at least one polymath genius in Goethe. The universities were centers not only of cutting-edge scholarship but also of philosophical discontent with the status quo. Professors and professionals demanded representative government, inspired perhaps by revolutionary France but even more by the neighboring Swiss Confederation and by the limited monarchy of Great Britain. Feudal ties to the land had been largely severed and the barriers against emigration and movement from one state to the other had been reduced. It was this not-yet-united Germany that produced a surge of migration that amounted to some 5 million immigrants to the United States in the half century from 1846 to 1895 and almost one-third of all immigrants during all but the last decade of this period.

AS tenant farmers the Irish had little experience operating in the market economy, but they did have experience with activist politics and with active religion. There was remarkably little upward economic mobility among the Irish[28]—the Kennedys were an exception, not the rule—but they did much to shape two fundamental American institutions, the urban political machine (usually but not always Democratic) and the American Roman Catholic Church. In both cases they built on preexisting institutions, but they made them immensely larger and more powerful.

In Ireland the Catholic Church was almost an underground institution, disfavored by the state, which was deeply involved in Daniel O'Connell's mass political movement and enjoying the allegiance of the large majority of the people. Even today Ireland's Roman Catholic cathedrals are located on obscure side streets, while prominent spots on town squares and broad avenues are occupied by cathedrals of the Anglican Church of Ireland. In the United States before the famine migration the Catholic Church was entirely legal, generally tolerated, with members carrying no unique ethnic identification and uninvolved in politics (interestingly, the one Catholic signer of the Declaration of Independence, Charles Carroll of Maryland, was also the longest-lived, dying in 1832, two years before the appointment of another Maryland Catholic, Roger Taney, as chief justice of the Supreme Court). The huge waves of famine immigrants changed that. In a few years the number of American Catholics quadrupled, forming 12 percent of the nation's population in 1860,[29] and the American Catholic Church took on a kelly green hue.

The most consequential leader of the American Irish Catholic Church was John Hughes, born in Ireland in 1797, bishop and archbishop of New York from 1838 until his death in 1864. He was a man of enormous energy, organizational ability, and fearlessness—nicknamed "Dagger John." He encouraged an ethnically exclusive, militantly Catholic church under conservative clerical leadership and hostility to Protestants, public schools, and mixed marriages.[30] And he was not a man to counsel passivity in the face of threats. "In 1844," writes Daniel Patrick Moynihan, "when the good folk of Philadelphia took to burning Catholic churches, Hughes issued a statement that 'if a single Catholic church were burned in New York, the city would become a second Moscow.' None was burned."[31] Hughes called in the Irish-based Sisters of Mercy and the St. Vincent de Paul Society to serve poor Irish Catholics, established doctrinal unity, paid off debts, tripled the number of churches, and created charitable organizations. Remembering how Catholic cathedrals in Ireland were isolated on side streets, Archbishop Hughes secured an entire block on Fifth Avenue, where the mercantile aristocrats were building their palaces, and laid the cornerstone there for St. Patrick's Cathedral, which has been seen from his day to ours as the capitol building of Irish Catholic America.[32]

Hughes was also a pioneer in education. Noting that public schools featured Protestant Bible study, he sought state support for separate Catholic schools and gained the support of William Seward, elected governor in 1838, who wanted his Whig Party to get a share of Irish Catholic votes. But the state legislature, elected most from Upstate New York, the heartland of the Yankee diaspora, refused to go along. In response, Hughes and his successors in New York and Catholic bishops elsewhere built a system of Catholic schools that expanded as rapidly as the public schools while managing to remain affordable for low-income parents.[33] For more than a century, the American Catholic hierarchy, priesthood, and religious orders remained overwhelmingly Irish—the first Italian-American bishop was not appointed until 1954—replenished by fresh recruits from Ireland.[34] This amounted to the creation of an Irish Catholic culture largely separate from the Protestant-dominated national culture, confident in its rectitude, severe in its disapprobation of dissent, determined to keep its constituents from entirely mixing into Protestant society. "The dominant American culture was more than happy to let Irish Catholics build their own society within a society,"[35] writes Terry Golway, and the Irish Catholic clergy seemed content with this insularity. Daniel Patrick Moynihan, who unusually for an Irish Catholic was not educated in Catholic schools or universities, toted up the cost in the early 1960s. "The Catholic Church does not measure its success by the standards of society. In secular terms, it has cost [the Irish] dearly in men and money. A good part of the surplus that might have gone into family property has gone into building the Church. This has almost certainly inhibited the development of the solid middle-class dynamics that produce so many of the important people in America. . . . The celibacy of the Catholic clergy has also deprived the Irish of the class of ministers' sons which has contributed so notably to the prosperity and distinction of the Protestant world."[36]

Where the Irish Catholics did dominate an institution that had a major and continuing impact on the larger society was in politics, and specifically, though with a few exceptions, through the Democratic Party.[37] It is the oldest political party in the world, already well established before the famine immigrants arrived. The first Democratic National Convention assembled in 1832 to nominate Andrew Jackson for a second term as president and to nominate for vice president the gifted political operator Martin Van Buren of New York. One asset Van Buren had was a close acquaintance with the turbulent politics of New York City, which had been growing lustily since the completion of the Erie Canal, connecting it to the Great Lakes, in 1825.

New York City, then confined to the lower end of Manhattan, had 123,000 people in 1820; 202,000 in 1830; and 312,000 in 1840. By the end of that period, it, together with Brooklyn across the East River, was almost twice as large as its chief rival, Philadelphia. Even before the famine immigrants arrived, New York City was developing a robust and sometimes violent politics that the Catholic migrants arriving from Daniel O'Connell's island would find not only familiar but also congenial. The Whig Party, formed to oppose Andrew Jackson's Democrats, attracted support from the merchant class and from those sharing New England Yankee provenance and values, including sympathy for causes like temperance and abolitionism. These values and causes were, to say the least, unappealing to Irish Catholics. They much preferred the Democracy developed amid much working-class agitation by the sachems of Tammany Hall, as described by historian Sean Wilentz: "Without abandoning economic issues like the tariff, Tammany campaigns blended lower-class racism and anti-abolitionism, class and ethnic resentments, and nationalist jingo to establish the Democracy as the anti-nativist, red-blooded party of the patriotic workingmen, the eternal foe of aristocratic, Tory, 'Federal Whig Coon Party.' "[38] The Irish were not at all put off by what Wilentz describes as "the roughhouse standards of the 1840s."[39] Irish immigrants arriving at the docks were recruited and sent to the polls by Democratic Party operatives, aware that their votes were pivotal: New York State voted just 52 percent to 48 percent for Andrew Jackson in 1832, 55 percent to 45 percent for Van Buren in 1836, but 51 percent to 48 percent against him in 1840, then 49 percent to 48 percent for James K. Polk in 1844; Polk would have lost if he had not carried New York by 5,106 votes. Bishop Hughes did his part to highlight the importance of Catholic votes when, amid his attempt to get state funding for church schools, he formed a Catholic political party for the 1842 elections and demonstrated that its endorsement could be the difference between victory and defeat for the Democrats.

But that was only a brief experiment, like Seward's attempt to win Catholic votes by supporting aid to their schools. The template that was set for the next century and more was for Irish Catholics to support and make their way upward in the Democratic Party, and for the Democracy, as it was called in the nineteenth century, in many large cities to take on a character that at times was almost as suffused with Irishness as the American Catholic Church. Like the Church, the Democratic Party offered Irish Catholics an institutional framework in which their identity could be asserted, their tendency to violence and antisocial behavior sublimated, with the reward being a slow ascent up an established hierarchy and the security of knowing they would be taken care of—three square meals and a bed, as the saying went—no matter what. The federal or state government, like the British government in Ireland, might be seen as distant and illegitimate;

the party organization, like Daniel O'Connell's, was close at hand and seen as beneficent and friendly and fair.[40]

Its hierarchical character made it all the more so. "The Irish village was a place of stable, predictable social relations in which almost everyone had a role to play, under the surveillance of a stern oligarchy of elders," writes Daniel Patrick Moynihan, "and in which, on the whole, a person's position was likely to improve with time. Transferred to Manhattan, these were the essentials of Tammany Hall. . . . It is possible to point to any number of further parallels between the political machine and rural Irish society. The incredible capacity of the rural Irish to remain celibate, awaiting their turn to inherit the farm, was matched by generations of assistant corporation counsel awaiting that opening on the City Court bench."[41] The downsides of machine politics were that the organization, like the Church, offered little outlet for independent thinking, few rewards for entrepreneurial originality, and a continuing confinement to a community insulated from the larger society. The Kennedys, like some other highly visible Irish Catholics, took care to make their way upward outside the confines of the local political machine, as Joseph P. Kennedy, with his Harvard degree and his wife who was the daughter of the mayor of Boston, accumulated a fortune that made Church officials and machine politicians his servants rather than his superiors. Frustrated in his own political ambitions—he was mentioned as a candidate for president in 1940, when he was ambassador to the Court of St. James and fifty-two years old—he pushed his sons into early political ascent: John Kennedy was elected congressman at twenty-nine, senator at thirty-five, and president at forty-three. Quite a contrast with, say, his fellow Bostonian John W. McCormack, who became Speaker of the House at age seventy in his thirty-fifth year as a member of Congress, in the same year in which his nephew, the attorney general of Massachusetts, was defeated for senator by the thirty-year-old Edward Kennedy.

For several decades after the famine immigration, Irish Catholics were the cogs rather than the leaders of urban political machines. They provided many of the votes and much of the organization that elected Tammany Protestant politicos like Fernando Wood mayor of New York and made William Marcy Tweed commissioner of public works before "Honest John" Kelly, Richard Croker, and Charles F. Murphy began their reigns as the heads of Tammany Hall. What did they accomplish? From the standpoint of a twentieth-century Democratic politician, not very much; the Irish, writes Daniel Patrick Moynihan, "never thought of politics as an instrument of social change—their kind of politics involved the processes of a society that was not changing. . . . In all those 60 or 70 years in which they could have done almost anything they wanted in politics, they did very little."[42] This made a certain sense, for the nineteenth-century Democracy to which they were attracted was not a party that sought social change. Its voters and its politicians shared the Irish prejudice— hostility, really—toward blacks and abolitionists,[43] to established Protestant churches that remained such in New England until the 1830s and to the reform-minded Protestant churches that preached temperance and abolitionism in the decades afterward. (Never mind that Daniel O'Connell was a vigorous opponent of slavery who got sixty thousand Irishmen to sign his petition urging abolition.) On economic issues the Democratic Party was America's laissez-faire party in the nineteenth century, opposing government aid to builders of canals and railroads, opposing protective tariffs and backing free trade, opposing a central bank and paper money. The Irish like other Democrats opposed efforts to limit slavery in the territories and, even more than many Democrats, they opposed Abraham Lincoln's efforts to force the seceding southern states back into the Union. They formed the lion's share of those who rioted against the military draft—said to target Irish Catholics and exempting blacks—and pillaged New York City for four days in July 1863, the same month as the Yankee victories at Vicksburg and Gettysburg, which resulted in their killing blacks, including in an orphanage, and setting fire to public buildings. Archbishop Hughes, though ill enough that he could not speak standing up, summoned Catholics to hear him and urged them forcefully and successfully to go home.[44]

GERMANY'S internal migration, from farm to factory, from backward-looking principalities to growing cities, led to migration across the ocean as steamships started embarking from the ports of Hamburg, Bremen, and Rotterdam. In 1846, the year after the potato blight first appeared, German immigration to the United States increased steeply, to 57,000, slightly more than immigration from Ireland that year. Irish immigration then doubled, tripled, and quadrupled; German immigration, though rising rapidly, did not quite keep up with the Irish until 1854, when it reached 215,000. Total German immigration for the 1846–55 decade was 976,000, and in each of the next four decades German immigration totaled about 1 million, except for the ten years including the Civil War, when it was a still-impressive 576,000. German immigrants were drawn from a very much larger population than Irish immigrants, and from a population that in many ways was more advanced and less distressed than the Irish Catholics fleeing the famine of the 1840s. It was also a population that came from different spiritual and political environments. Irish Catholics saw themselves as second-class citizens, barred by hostile Protestants for generations from the professions and politics, but mobilized in mass political action under Daniel O'Connell. With relatively low agricultural, artisanal, and mechanical skills, they flocked to the big cities rather than the countryside and sought advancement through the ballot box as much as in the marketplace. The Germans were generally better farmers, with higher mechanical and artisanal skills and a tradition of craftsmanship as strong as any in Europe. Some were Protestant and some were Catholic, but few saw themselves as rebels against a hostile religious establishment.

Of politics, the Germans had relatively little experience. The regimes encouraged by Prince Metternich and mostly prevailing for more than three decades after the defeat of Napoleon were run by royal or noble rulers, with little in the way of ancient councils or parliamentary bodies, no bills of rights, and plenty of censorship. But dissenting ideas were in the air, communicated by heirs of the

Enlightenment and bards of the Romantic movement, enduring in Napoleonic decrees that were not repealed abolishing feudal obligations and granting citizenship to Jews. These ideas appear to have been strongest in southwest Germany, from the Palatinate south along the Rhine to the Swiss Confederation, a republic that stood conspicuously aside from Metternich's system of alliances and common policies. "German liberals of every shade agreed on demands for some guarantees against the absolutist exercise of governmental authority. Some form of constitutionalism was generally considered necessary along with an extension of local self-government," writes historian Hajo Holborn.[45] All this gained sudden force in 1848, after the ouster of the French government of King Louis Philippe in February. Holborn goes on: "It was astonishing how in the spring of 1848 the political agitation which so far had been carried on in relatively small groups seemed to gain the elemental support of the masses. Almost overnight the liberals became the spokesmen for the whole nation, whereas a while before they had been representatives of special social and regional segments of German society."[46] Liberal governments with representative assemblies and freedoms of assembly and speech were quickly formed in Baden, Württemberg, Hesse-Darmstadt, Hesse-Kassel, Hanover, and Saxony. Metternich was forced to flee from Vienna, and Prussia lifted censorship, convoked a legislature, and called for constitutions in all the German states. These changes did not prove enduring. The revolutions were unsuccessful, the reforms were quashed, and the Metternich system continued more or less in force for some years to come.

The initial surge of German immigration seems to have been set in motion by the potato blight, which struck the German states as well as Ireland. An ongoing surge, increasingly great in its magnitude, seems to have been sustained by some combination of the pressure of rising population, which stimulated continued immigration to the United States from Britain and the Low Countries, and something like the feelings that sparked the unsuccessful revolutions of 1848. Many German immigrants called themselves Forty Eighters and said that they were seeking in democratic America what they had been unable to find in the autocratic German states. On the new steamship lines they headed primarily to New York, and in smaller numbers to Philadelphia and Baltimore, almost entirely bypassing Boston and the southern ports. Nearly half settled in the larger cities, with 37 percent of German-born residents in 1860 in cities of more than 25,000. In that year 15 percent of New York City residents were German-born. A little more than half settled on farms and in small towns. But except for New York, Germans tended not to stay in the seaports, but to head for inland cities. With their Rhineland heritage, they seemed particularly drawn to the attractive landscapes along the Ohio and Mississippi Rivers. The two largest cities in the interior of America in 1860 had very substantial German-born populations: Cincinnati had 27 percent and St. Louis had 27 percent. There was a large German immigrant population in rapidly growing Chicago (20 percent) and in Louisville (20 percent), Cleveland (21 percent), and Detroit (16 percent). Milwaukee, the largest city in Wisconsin, had the largest German-born population (35 percent). German immigrants also established communities and became a major presence in rural counties in Ohio, Indiana, Michigan, and Illinois. Religious leaders guided congregations to build German communities in central Missouri, south of the Missouri River. The onset of German immigration coincided with the admission of Iowa and Wisconsin to the Union in 1846 and 1848 and to a rush of settlement there. The boundary between those two states is the Mississippi River, bounded by rolling hills—a landscape especially reminiscent of the Rhine—which were settled in very large part by German immigrants; in 1852 the state of Wisconsin set up a bureau to encourage immigration from Germany.

Here in what was then referred to as the Northwest came a confluence of two streams of migration, the Yankee diaspora and the German migration. They can be thought of not as merging exactly, but as heading in different directions from a point roundabout Chicago: German immigrants heading north and northwest as well as directly west from that rapidly growing metropolis, Yankee offspring mostly

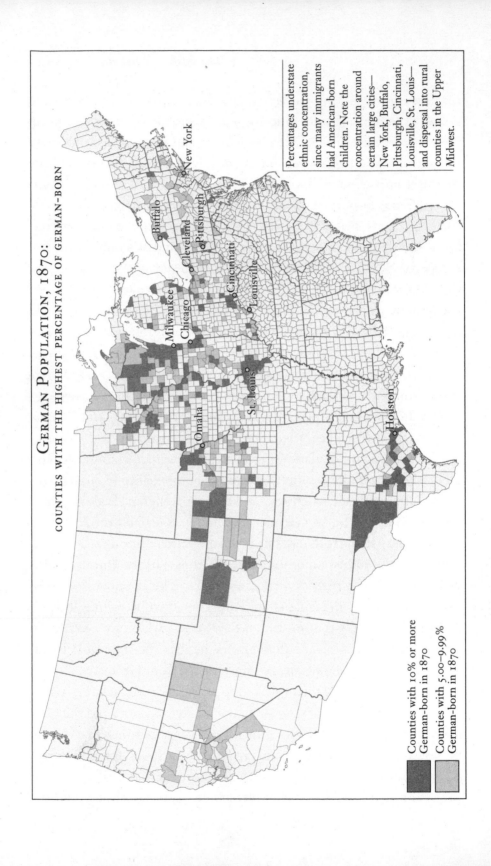

GERMAN POPULATION, 1870:
COUNTIES WITH THE HIGHEST PERCENTAGE OF GERMAN-BORN

Percentages understate ethnic concentration, since many immigrants had American-born children. Note the concentration around certain large cities—New York, Buffalo, Pittsburgh, Cincinnati, Louisville, St. Louis—and dispersal into rural counties in the Upper Midwest.

New York
Buffalo
Cleveland
Pittsburgh
Cincinnati
Louisville
Milwaukee
Chicago
St. Louis
Omaha
Houston

■ Counties with 10% or more
   German-born in 1870

▨ Counties with 5.00–9.99%
   German-born in 1870

heading various distances west, with some headed northwest. The large number of German and, starting in large numbers in the 1870s, Scandinavian immigrants in time made this Old Northwest—Wisconsin, Iowa, Minnesota, and the Dakotas—a Germano-Scandinavian province of America.

To their rural communities and city neighborhoods dotting the Midwest and growing thicker as one went west and north, the Germans brought their native culture. As soon as they could they built solid stone houses and commercial buildings. They built German Catholic, Lutheran, and Reformed churches, and they maintained German-language instruction in private and public schools for decades. They formed fire and militia companies, coffee circles, and especially singing societies, staging seasonal Sangerfeste (singing festivals). They staged pre-Lenten carnivals, outdoor Volkfeste, and annual German Day celebrations. They formed mutual-benefit fire insurance firms and building societies and set up German-speaking lodges of American associations. Turnverein (athletic clubs) were established in almost all German communities and national gymnastic competitions became common. German-language newspapers sprang up— newspaper baron Joseph Pulitzer, a German-speaking Hungarian Jew, got his start in one in St. Louis—and German theaters opened in New York, Philadelphia, Cincinnati, Chicago, and Milwaukee. Some German customs came to seem quintessentially American—the Christmas tree, kindergarten, pinochle. Unlike the Irish Catholics, the Germans had strong family ties and low rates of crime.

The German presence on the major river cities on the border between slave and free states—Cincinnati, Louisville, St. Louis—had significant political repercussions. These cities were almost German islands in a southern-settled sea, profoundly out of sympathy with the mores and opinions of their near neighbors. The German immigrants with their Forty Eighter sympathies tended to be hostile to slavery. This was true even of the small Texas German community pioneered in the 1830s in the hill country around San Antonio and west of Austin, which declined to support the Confederacy in the Civil War.

This had political significance. Immigrants in the late 1840s and early 1850s tended to adhere to the Democratic Party, which was generally more sympathetic to immigrants than its Whig rivals. They were especially repelled by the American Party, widely known as the Know-Nothings, which arose from the ruins of the Whigs in 1854 and swept elections in Massachusetts and other states with an anti-immigrant platform. The abrupt decline of German immigration in 1855 was at least in part a response to the prominence of the Know-Nothing movement.[47]

The Germans' antislavery views tended to make them sympathetic to the new Republican Party, which emerged in 1854 as a movement opposing the Kansas-Nebraska Act, which opened up the territories to slavery. The Republicans, who sought votes only in the North, quickly won wider support among the Yankee diaspora than the Whigs ever did, and eclipsed the Know-Nothings in the North by 1856. But Americans of Yankee stock and many Republicans also tended to support the temperance movement, which the beer-drinking Germans considered deranged. As a result German voters were a key target group in the turbulent politics of the 1850s. It was in large part to appeal to German voters that the Republicans at their 1860 national convention in Chicago nominated an Illinois lawyer named Abraham Lincoln. Lincoln's opposition to the Know-Nothing movement and skepticism about temperance measures (despite his own abstention from alcohol) helped win key German votes in Pennsylvania, Indiana, and Illinois, without whose electoral votes he would not have been elected president.

A major role in this was played by the most famous of the American Forty Eighters, Carl Schurz. The son of a Rhineland schoolteacher, he was a nineteen-year-old student at the University of Bonn when the 1848 revolutions broke out in Germany. He quickly founded a newspaper calling for democratic reforms and with other schoolmates took up arms in support of a constitution adopted by a rump parliament in Frankfurt. He led an artillery company in the Palatinate and Baden in 1849 and when the last forces surrendered in 1850, he escaped to

Switzerland, rescued a comrade from prison in Berlin, then moved to Paris and London. In 1852 he moved to Philadelphia and then in 1855 to Watertown, Wisconsin, halfway between Milwaukee and the state capital of Madison. Far removed from the cockpit of European politics, Schurz found himself in the midst of vast churning movements in American politics, only 50 miles from the town of Ripon, one of the birthplaces of the Republican Party just the year before. While his wife embarked on promoting kindergarten education in America, Schurz joined the Republican Party and in 1857, at twenty-eight, was the Republican candidate for lieutenant governor, losing while the party's governor candidate won by just 454 votes; evidently some decisive portion of Wisconsin's Yankee voters were not quite ready for a German candidate. Schurz persevered, even though his attempt to push the governor aside in 1859 failed, and he emerged as a national figure at age thirty, delivering at Faneuil Hall in Boston a speech on "true Americanism" that absolved the Republican Party of anti-immigrant feeling and serving as spokesman for the Wisconsin delegation at the 1860 Republican National Convention in Chicago. During the 1860 campaign Schurz served as a "hired gun" for the Republican ticket among German voters and seems to have played an important role in swinging Germans, especially Protestants, in the critical states of Illinois, Indiana, and Pennsylvania, which John Fremont had lost in 1856 and Abraham Lincoln carried in 1860.[48] Without them Lincoln would not have had an Electoral College majority.

Schurz was well known enough to have been appointed by Abraham Lincoln as ambassador to Spain in 1861 and then, at his request, as a brigadier general in the army in 1862. He served in Missouri and Virginia, at Gettysburg and Chattanooga, and was with General Sherman's army in North Carolina when the war ended. In the aftermath of the war Schurz moved around geographically and politically. He edited German-language newspapers in Detroit and St. Louis and was elected to the U.S. Senate from Missouri in 1869. He was one of the intellectual Republicans who opposed Ulysses S. Grant's Reconstruction policies seeking equal treatment for blacks in the South and he presided over the Liberal Republican convention that nominated Horace Greeley to oppose Grant in 1872. He supported Republican Rutherford B. Hayes in 1876 and was appointed secretary of the Interior in 1877, in which office he spurned political patronage appointments and tried to install nonpartisan civil service. He moved to New York in 1881, editing the *New York Post* briefly and joining the Mugwump movement that supported Democrat Grover Cleveland over Republican James G. Blaine in 1884. He represented the Hamburg American Steamship Company, served as president of the National Civil Service Reform League, and edited *Harper's Weekly*. He supported William McKinley on sound money principles in 1896 and William Jennings Bryan on anti-imperialist principles in 1900.

Over Schurz's long and varied career in American politics, he took stands that were generally supported by German-American voters and that generally prevailed in Germano-Scandinavian America: stands against slavery and for the Civil War but against serious Reconstruction and black rights, for civil service reform and organization of government on apolitical bureaucratic lines, opposed to a bellicose and assertive American foreign policy and military ventures abroad.

IRISH immigration continued in large numbers through most of the nineteenth century. After the initial surge of 1,288,000 immigrants in the famine years 1846 to 1855, Irish immigration in each of the four succeeding decades, to 1895, was approximately half a million every ten years; it then fell off to a little more than half that level in the two decades before World War I began in 1914. Thus during the three decades following the Civil War, Irish immigrants were outnumbered by about 2-to-1 by German immigrants, and during the Ellis Island period starting in 1892 the Irish made up only 4 percent of total immigrants—a huge decrease from the 42 percent proportion they accounted for in 1846–55. Even so, immigration as a percentage of Irish population was substantial, and the population of Ireland continued to decline until the 1960s; in 2010 the island's total population of 6.4 million was more than 20 percent lower than in 1841. The Irish continued to migrate primarily to big cities, especially on the East Coast but also in the Midwest, and in smaller numbers to mining communities. The later immigrants were better prepared for life in American cities; by the time of the Civil War, almost all Irish immigrants spoke English. There was also considerable upward mobility. "Second- and third-generation Irish entered skilled or middle-class occupations in droves, and by the 1880s and 1890s fewer than a tenth of all Irish [American] men were unskilled laborers—a dramatic advance since the 1850s," writes legal historian Randolph Roth. "As they entered the mainstream, their absolute homicide rates and their rates relative to those of other whites fell in cities and in northern New England and the rural Midwest."[49] New York's murder rate, which had risen from 4.4 per 100,000 in 1840–45 to 10.8 in 1860–65, largely because of the Irish, then fell back to 4.4 in 1880–85.[50]

Some of the political energies of Irish-Americans were directed back at the mother country. Unlike the Scots-Irish, who quickly took to calling themselves unhyphenated Americans and appear never to have looked back, the Irish Catholics cherished their ethnic identity, most visibly on St. Patrick's Day, and took an active interest in the Emerald Isle. Ties to the homeland were maintained to a greater extent than many today realize. Steamship travel made return trips feasible and affordable, and journals published in New York and other cities kept Irish-Americans in touch with political and cultural developments at home. There remained from the famine years a strong sense that the Protestants who ruled Britain had allowed mass starvation among Irish Catholics, and hence evolved the Fenian movement to liberate Ireland from the British yoke. It grew as vigorously in North America as in Ireland, or more so: Fenians tried to launch an invasion of Canada from Upstate New York in 1866, and in 1869 a Fenian exile and a Tammany judge formed a secret society to support violent action against Britain in Ireland.[51] Enthusiasm for Fenianism—revolutionary overthrow of the British government—tended to be greater in America than in Ireland for most of the late nineteenth and early twentieth centuries, and a sort of sentimental Fenianism, combined with a willingness to subscribe funds to buy arms for the various branches of the Irish Republican Army, persisted in some Irish-American quarters into the late twentieth century.

Irish voters had strong views on some issues—they strongly opposed prohibition, for example—but of even greater importance to most Irish-American voters then was the drive to put friends and neighbors on the public payroll. The Irish, having distrusted the state in Ireland, used Daniel O'Connell's weapon, mass politics, to take over large parts of government in New York and Boston and Philadelphia and dozens of smaller cities in the East, in the coal country, and in the industrial Midwest. The machine provided public-sector employment, and in some cases the public sector produced public goods as sturdy as the Tweed courthouse or the bridges over New York's East River built in the first decade of the twentieth century. Urban politics took different forms in different cities: with a dominant Democratic machine (Tammany Hall) in New York and a dominant Republican machine in Philadelphia, rival political factions headed by charismatic Democrats in Boston (such as John F. Fitzgerald and James Michael Curley, whose career was the inspiration for Edwin O'Connor's 1950s bestseller *The Last Hurrah*) and two-party contests between rival Democratic and Republican machines in Chicago.[52]

Only later, under Charles F. Murphy, head of Tammany Hall from 1902 until his death in 1924, did the Irish-dominated Democratic Party come to recognize and advance social reformers. In 1913 Murphy chose as speaker of the Assembly and majority leader of the state senate two relatively young and non-senior legislators, Al Smith (of Irish, German, and Italian descent) and Robert Wagner (a German Protestant immigrant), both supporters of welfare state legislation. In taking these steps Murphy shrewdly recognized the rising importance of the Ellis Island immigrants—especially the vast numbers of Jews and Italians who settled in New York City—and calculated that worker protection and welfare state policies would be needed to produce the kind of party loyalty produced in the Irish by laissez-faire policies and patronage jobs. Murphy proved prescient: Smith went on to be elected governor in 1918, 1922, 1924, and 1926 and was the Democratic nominee for president in 1928; Wagner was elected U.S. senator in 1926, 1932, 1938, and 1944 and was the chief sponsor of legislation establishing Social Security and empowering labor unions. Previous Tammany Hall chieftains had been ignored and shunned by national Democratic presidential nominees; Murphy was proud to be asked to acquiesce in the vice presidential nomination in 1920 of an aristocratic New York politician who had attacked his allies in the past, Franklin Roosevelt, and did so; and he received recompense when the 1924 Democratic National Convention was scheduled to convene in New York's Madison Square Garden. Murphy himself died earlier that year and did not live to see the convention take 103 ballots—a record number in American politics—to decide on a presidential nominee, after having divided almost precisely evenly on a resolution denouncing the anti- (among other things) Catholic Ku Klux Klan. But the approach and the policies he sponsored found full flower in Franklin Roosevelt's New Deal in the 1930s.

In the meantime Irish-Americans made other contributions to American life. While the high culture of urban elites remained Protestant with traditional regional accents—Yankee in Boston, polyglot in New York, Quaker in Philadelphia—popular culture in the great cities was increasingly Irish. In theater and in sports the Irish increasingly set the tone and won the championships.[53] Daniel Patrick Moynihan tells this story: "Let it be said that the Irish gave style to life in the slums: 'Boys and girls together, me and Mamie Rourke,/ Tripped the light fantastic on the sidewalks of New York.' They became the playboys of this new Western World. 'None can love like an Irishman' was a favorite song of Lincoln's day. By the turn of the century, it had become equally clear that none could run like them, nor fight like them, nor drink as much, nor sing as well. When it came to diving off the Brooklyn Bridge or winning pennants for the Giants, it took an Irishman. And who could write such bittersweet songs as Victor Herbert? Or enjoy life like 'Diamond Jim' Brady? All was 'bliss and blarney.' "⁵⁴

The great triumph of Irish America was the election of the first Irish Catholic president, John Kennedy, in 1960. He won the votes of 78 percent of Catholics and his Scots-Irish–descended opponent Richard Nixon won the votes of 63 percent of white Protestants. Kennedy came from anything but a typical Irish background, with a father who was one of the richest Catholics in the world and had the manner and appearance more of an English lord (one of his sisters married the Marquis of Hartington) than an Irish pol. Moynihan once again summed up the moment in a passage in the Irish chapter in *Beyond the Melting Pot*, mourning Kennedy's assassination. "It was the Last Hurrah. He the youngest and newest, served in a final moment of ascendancy. On the day he died, the President of the United States, the Speaker of the House of Representatives, the Majority Leader of the United States Senate, the Chairman of the National Committee, were all Irish, all Catholic, all Democrat. It will not come again."⁵⁵

AS time went on following the Civil War, the approximately 1 million German immigrants per decade until the mid-1890s came increasingly less from southwest Germany and the Rhineland and more from northern Germany and ultimately the eastern expanses toward East Prussia. German immigration was still made up more of family groups than of single men, but over time, as Germany became industrialized, the German immigration became more downscale, with fewer artisans and skilled workers and more agricultural laborers. In the United States, aside from the sizable number who remained in New York, German immigrants tended to head to Chicago and beyond to Wisconsin, Iowa, and Minnesota and, starting in the 1880s, to the Dakotas. North Dakota in particular was the destination of Volga Germans, farmers whose ancestors had left Germany for Russian wheatlands along the Volga River and who now flocked to familiar soil and a familiar climate in a free land. Large and cohesive German settlements were built by immigrants on virgin land. In contrast to German immigrants before the Civil War, they tended to bypass the river cities of Cincinnati, Louisville, and St. Louis, whose percentages of German-born residents dropped sharply. Milwaukee emerged as America's most heavily German large city, with a German-born population of 32 percent in 1870 and 24 percent in 1900. After the decade ending in 1895, as Imperial Germany grew more prosperous and its expanding industries produced an increased demand for labor, the number of German immigrants fell by almost three-quarters. Scandinavian immigration fell as well, but less sharply, from peak levels of 475,000 in 1876–85 and 598,000 in 1886–95, as Denmark, Sweden, and (a separate nation only in 1905) Norway developed economically. But by the later 1890s the shape of Germano-Scandinavian America was set.

In post–Civil War America German immigrants and their offspring tended to be middling folk, well educated though not often college educated, skilled workers but not heavily represented in the professions, solid citizens unconcerned with causes such as temperance and women's suffrage. There were some conspicuously successful German businessmen, like John Jacob Astor, the fur trader and accumulator of Manhattan real estate who became the richest American in the early republic, and the financier Henry Villard, one of the premier capitalists of the late nineteenth century. Some German-American fortunes were built on artisanal skill and craftsmanship: John A. Roebling and his son advanced the technology of forging steel cables and became America's great bridge builders in the second half of the nineteenth century, and Henry Steinway parlayed his skill in fashioning musical instruments into the premier piano-making firm in America, complete with a neighborhood in then bucolic Queens for its workers. Breweries were a major German business in just about every major city; those of Milwaukee were perhaps the most famous, but were rivaled by St. Louis's Anheuser-Busch and by the Yorkville brewery of Col. Jacob Ruppert, owner of the New York Yankees.

German Jews were part of this immigration, and many became peddlers, especially in the South, and then shifted to dry goods stores and cotton trading. The scions of such families in the late nineteenth and early twentieth centuries made their way to New York, where they founded Wall Street firms like Kuhn Loeb and Goldman Sachs and established institutions like the *New York Times*.

The genteel neighborhoods of the German Jewish aristocracy, like the area around Madison Avenue and 81st Street where the eminent journalist Walter Lippmann was born in 1889, or the mansions of the Milwaukee beer barons lining the streets just off Lake Michigan, were starkly different in tone from the ethnic German neighborhoods, such as Manhattan's Yorktown centered on Third Avenue and 86th Street or Milwaukee's west and north sides. German restaurants and beer gardens shared streets with solid stone German churches and delicatessens, with competitive German-language newspapers vying for readers at newsstands and German wurst peddled on the street. There was also a lively ethnic German politics. German voters never gravitated entirely to either of America's two major parties. Their aversion to temperance made them suspicious of Republicans, as did Republican opposition, signaled by an 1882 Wisconsin law, to German-language instruction in public schools. But they were wary as well of the increasingly Irish-dominated patronage politics of the Democrats and attendant corruption, and were sympathetic to Carl Schurz's great cause of civil service reform. The concept of a rationalized, disinterested, apolitical government bureaucracy, operating under the tutelage of credentialed experts rather than at the direction of crass politicians, had a considerable appeal to German-American voters. Government ownership of utilities, railroads, and major industries was not antithetical to this, and socialism after all was the product largely of German thinkers. These ideas were in tandem with developments in the German Empire unified and declared by Otto von Bismarck in 1871 after victory in the Franco-Prussian War. Socialism was gaining great ground among German voters in the late nineteenth century, and to forestall it Bismarck put through a pioneer program of old-age pensions at a time when such measures were inconceivable in other advanced industrial nations.

The bulk of German immigrants in these years were from rural and heavily Protestant northern Germany;[56] the bulk of the Scandinavians, who started coming over in large numbers in 1881, were from isolated rural Norway. Some of these Germano-Scandinavian immigrants in the 1880s stayed in New York City, but larger numbers headed to the farm country and the growing cities of the Old Northwest, to what was a rapidly growing Germano-Scandinavian America. The 1880s saw the populations of New York State and Pennsylvania rise by nearly 1 million, wide-open Texas by 644,000, and industrial Ohio by 474,000. But all the other states with population increases of about 400,000 or more were in the Germano-Scandinavian zone: Michigan, Wisconsin, Minnesota, Missouri, Kansas, Nebraska, and the Dakota Territory (split into two states when granted statehood in 1889). These new settlers occupied homestead and railroad-owned land up to the 100th meridian. Many warned them that the rainfall was too low that far west to achieve crop yields comparable to those farther east, but many settlers believed the theory that "the rain follows the plough"—settlement would produce man-made climate change. That theory seemed to be substantiated in the 1880s, but in the 1890s rainfall plunged, many new farmers were ruined, and population growth virtually halted in Kansas, Nebraska, and South Dakota. This news, like all changes in the economic or cultural environment, was quickly communicated to the old country, where in any case changes were occurring that would reduce emigration. The German birth rate started to decline in 1875, thus reducing the number of young potential emigrants by the mid-1890s, and by then the German economy had grown strong enough that there were plenty of opportunities at home. Germans might prefer working as farm owners in America to working as farm laborers in Germany, but working in a German factory was even more attractive at a time when America seemed to be running out of available farmland.[57] Similar changes were not as advanced in Scandinavia, and immigration from those nations rebounded to near 1881–91 levels in 1902–14, with the new-comers heading most often to the northern extensions of Germano-Scandinavian America—Minnesota, North Dakota, Montana, and Washington State.

The political heritage of these German and Scandinavian immigrants had reverberations in Germano-Scandinavian America, as evidenced by the fact that the capital of North Dakota, admitted to the Union in 1889, was named after Bismarck. The decades that followed saw the emergence of the Progressive movement in Wisconsin, the Farmer-Labor Party in Minnesota, and the Non-Partisan League in North Dakota—all attempts to transcend the two traditional American political parties and to use a rationalized government to provide security and freedom from exploitation by giant corporations for ordinary people. Governor Robert La Follette, a previously conventional Republican politician elected governor of Wisconsin in 1900, pioneered such measures as a legislative bureau staffed by University of Wisconsin experts, recall elections to keep public officials accountable, and workmen's compensation to provide speedy redress for injured workers. In 1905 La Follette moved on to the U.S. Senate, where he was a national figure and received 16 percent of the popular vote as the nominee of the Progressive Party in the 1924 presidential election. His political allies and his sons Robert Jr. and Philip served as governors and senators for most of the next three decades. In the meantime Milwaukee elected a Socialist congressman, Victor Berger, in 1910 and again in 1918 as well as from 1922 to 1928, and it had Socialist mayors from 1910 to 1912, 1916 to 1943, and 1948 to 1960. Minnesota's Farmer-Labor Party attracted support primarily from German- and Scandinavian-American voters who favored activist government at home and, like La Follette's Progressives, opposed American involvement in European wars; their great tribune Floyd Olson served six years as governor in the 1930s and was a model for Franklin Roosevelt's New Deal. The Farmer-Labor Party was merged into Minnesota's Democratic Party in 1944 under the guidance of a young college professor running for mayor of Minneapolis named Hubert Humphrey, and it remains the Democratic-Farmer-Labor Party today. Formed in 1918 to oppose railroads and the giant privately held grain companies, the Non-Partisan League was a latecomer in these efforts ; it elected North Dakota governors, established state grain elevators and a state bank, still operating; and its endorsees held the state's senate seats for most of three decades, until it effectively merged with the state Democratic Party in the late 1950s.

These third-party movements arising in Germano-Scandinavian America had a major effect on American public policy in the twentieth century, inspiring New Deal programs and providing critical votes from what had once been a predominantly Republican part of the nation for Franklin Roosevelt's Democratic coalition. But the ethnic basis of this Germano-Scandinavian influence has largely been invisible, because of foreign policy. Seventeenth- and eighteenth-century German immigrants to North America had been largely pacifist, drawn from the German states that eschewed the war-making practices of some of their mercenary neighbors, or from rebels against such states. Nineteenth-century German immigrants, too, seem to have been inclined to oppose American participation in wars; it may very well be that emigration to America drained off a disproportionate number of Germans disposed to be wary of military involvement, leaving Germany a more warlike nation in the first half of the twentieth century than it otherwise would have been. Many Germans like Carl Schurz fought on the Union side in America's Civil War, but overall these people who came from lands that had been the scene of much of Europe's most horrendous fighting and slaughter and destruction over the previous several centuries seemed to want to leave behind that part of their heritage. They observed the rise of the German Empire with pride and approval, and during the nineteenth century and in the early years of the twentieth century did not see it as in any way hostile to the United States. On the contrary, Germany seemed to be a progressive leader in many ways. Its innovative chemical and electrical industries were enabling it to seize industrial leadership over Britain with its aging textile mills. Its universities, not slumbering Oxford or Cambridge, were the models for American research universities and their PhD programs and they were producing more scientific advances than their British, French, or American rivals. The German pension program and rationalized German bureaucracy was a model for progressives in the United States.

Then came World War I. Most German- and Scandinavian-Americans strongly supported American neutrality in the war and many had more sympathy for Germany and its ally Austria-Hungary than for the alliance of Britain, France, and tsarist Russia. When President Woodrow Wilson reversed himself and sought a declaration of war against Germany in April 1917, six senators and fifty members of the House of Representatives voted against the declaration. Four of the senators and nearly half of the House members who voted no came from states or districts with large German- or Scandinavian-American voters.[58] Senator Robert La Follette of Wisconsin, in speaking out against the war, noted that a poll of voters in heavily German Sheboygan County participating in a local election the week that Congress voted had voted 4,082 to 17 against declaring war.[59] Even before the war, President Woodrow Wilson had spoken out against citizens "born under other flags but welcomed under our generous naturalization laws to the full freedom and opportunity of America, who have poured the poison of disloyalty into the very arteries of national life. Such creatures of passion, disloyalty and anarchism," he said, "must be crushed out."[60] The Democratic Congress promptly set about passing the Espionage Act of 1917, which authorized press censorship and banned treasonable material from the mails. Wilson appointed journalist George Creel as head of the Committee on Public Information to churn out material favorable to the war effort, and Creel assigned a network of bilingual investigators to monitor the foreign-language press for "material which may fall under the Espionage Act."[61]

The main targets of these efforts were German-Americans and socialists who opposed entry into the war. They included those who fell into both categories like Victor Berger, who was elected to Congress from a Milwaukee district as a Socialist in 1912 and 1914.

Defeated in 1916, he did not cast a vote on the declaration of war, but after he was reelected in 1918 he was denied his seat in the House and prosecuted and sentenced to twenty years in jail (the sentence was later overturned). The anti-German movement was "a brainless fury that knew few restraints," according to historian David Kennedy, and "an ultimately almost hysterical animosity to Germany and all things German," according to novelist and Wilson biographer Louis Auchincloss.[62] Some of the reaction seems almost humorous nearly a century later: hamburgers were renamed *liberty sandwiches*, sauerkraut became *liberty cabbage*, the card game pinochle was renamed *liberty*.[63] The Swiss conductor of the Boston Symphony Orchestra was dismissed and opera singer Madame Schumann-Heink was pressured to remove German songs from her repertoire; there was opposition to the playing of the music of Bach, Beethoven, Mozart, and Brahms. The Bismarck School in Chicago and the Deutsches Haus in Indianapolis were renamed, and Kaiser Street became Marne Way, named for the battles at which the Germans were repulsed in 1914 and 1918. The governor of Iowa called for banning the speaking of German in public, on streetcars, and over the telephone. More seriously, German-language instruction was banned in schools in half the states and turnverein and other German organizations were closed permanently. The number of German publications in the nation, which declined marginally from 613 in 1900 to 554 in 1910, fell to 234 in 1920. The Missouri Synod Lutheran Church switched heavily from German to English services. The National German-American Alliance was dissolved in April 1918. Out of half a million German citizens in the country, only about 1,200 were imprisoned in 1917, but at least one German was lynched in Collinsville, Illinois, outside St. Louis, with the perpetrators acquitted by a jury after only twenty-five minutes of deliberations. Vandalism, tarring and feathering, and arrests for unpatriotic utterances were common. In addition, another German cultural institution, the beer garden, was threatened with extinction by the advance of the prohibition movement during the war. In December 1917 Congress passed a constitutional amendment prohibiting the production and sale of alcoholic beverages, and in January 1919 this Eighteenth Amendment was ratified by the requisite three-quarters of the state legislatures.

Thus during just two years Americans effectively suppressed many of the outward expressions of German-American culture. German clubs and singing groups, German newspapers, and German beer gardens—all disappeared or became much less common and less noticed. The Germans became, as historian Kathleen Neils Conzen writes, "the least visible of American ethnic groups."[64] But the German-American influence could still be discerned not so much in the political dialogue—the Kaiser did not have any articulate support after World War I and Adolf Hitler had almost none in the years before World War II—but in the election returns. Politically, Germano-Scandinavian America tended to be the heartland of isolationism, whose staunchest tribune was Charles Lindbergh, the aviator son of a Farmer-Labor congressman from Minnesota who as a Senate candidate had opposed American entry into World War I. Germano-Scandinavian America swung heavily against Woodrow Wilson's Democrats in 1920, as did most of the nation, but in the 1922 off-year elections, in response to a sharp though brief economic recession, it moved away from Warren Harding's Republicans. In 1924 the sixty-nine-year-old senator Robert La Follette, famed for his progressive record in Wisconsin two decades before and his outspoken opposition to entry into World War I and the Versailles Treaty more recently, ran as the Progressive candidate against Republican incumbent Calvin Coolidge and the nominee Democrats picked on the 103rd ballot of their tumultuous national convention, John W. Davis. La Follette, running on a platform calling for big government programs, won 17 percent of the popular vote, the largest share for a third-party candidate between 1912 and 1992. He carried Wisconsin, nearly carried North Dakota, and was competitive in Minnesota, the heart of Germano-Scandinavian America. A map of the midwestern counties where he won 25 percent or more would look very much like a map showing German- and Scandinavian-American concentrations; a map of states where he had that level of support would run west from Wisconsin to include Iowa, South Dakota, Wyoming, Montana, Idaho, and Washington, plus California.

Four years later Democrat Al Smith, who had German and Italian as well as Irish Catholic ancestors, while losing nationally ran far better than previous Democrats in Catholic immigrant areas in the Northeast and Great Lakes, and he carried counties with large German Catholic populations—Brown County, Wisconsin; Dubuque County, Iowa; Stearns County, Minnesota; Ellis County, Kansas. Franklin Roosevelt's winning coalitions in 1932 and 1936 can be described with fair though not complete accuracy as a combination of traditional Democratic strength in the big cities and the South with the La Follette progressive constituency centered in Germano-Scandinavian America. But that constituency was strongly isolationist in the late 1930s and early 1940s, opposed to any effort that might embroil the United States in a war with Germany. In 1940 Roosevelt, running for a third term, moved to provide aid to Britain and to institute a military draft; he won reelection, but ran more than 10 percent behind his 1936 showings in most of the same states that had disproportionately backed La Follette in 1924. As the journalist and psephologist Samuel Lubell reported, isolationism arose not so much as a result of living far from the Atlantic seaboard as it did from a reluctance to fight one's ancestral homeland—and a feeling in some quarters, articulated more after the war than during it, that we ought to have been fighting the Communist Soviet Union rather than Nazi Germany. This, in Lubell's view, explains senator Joseph McCarthy, who beat Robert La Follette Jr. in the 1946 Republican primary in the most heavily German-American state, Wisconsin, and then in the early 1950s conducted his ill-fated crusade against Communists in government after almost all had already been ousted.

Germano-Scandinavian America has had a distinctive profile in our politics over the years as the most pacifist or isolationist or dovish geographic part of the country. The five states that are more or less coterminous with this region—Wisconsin, Iowa, Minnesota, and the

Dakotas—switched from voting more Democratic than the national average in the New Deal years of 1932 and 1936 to distinctly more Republican than average in the war years of 1940 and 1944. In the Cold War years of 1952, 1956, and 1960, when Republicans seemed the more war-averse and lower-defense-spending party, Germano-Scandinavian America was more Republican than average. During the Cold War years from 1972 to 1988, when the Democrats were seen as significantly more dovish, they ran ahead of their national average in these states, and that was the case as well in 2004 and 2008, years in which the war in Iraq was an important issue in the presidential contests. The path of the German and Scandinavian surges of migration more than a century ago, like the path of the Scots-Irish surge of migration more than two centuries ago, can be seen in our most recent election returns.

4. INCOMPLETE CONQUEST

THE end of the Civil War in 1865 came seventy-six years after the inauguration of George Washington as the first president and seventy-six years before the declaration of war following the attack on Pearl Harbor. This book has depicted the Civil War as a clash between surges of migration, an irrepressible or at least not repressed conflict between the surging Yankee diaspora and the southern grandees, with the Scots-Irish, after their southwestward surge was spent, split between the two sides, with the surging Germans taking the side of the Yankees and the surging Irish more ambivalent—perspectives at variance with usual depictions of the war.

The result was what might be called the Yankee conquest of North America, but a conquest that was less than total. Reconstruction, the efforts to defend the rights of blacks in the South, failed when the prospect of perpetual military deployment there was rejected by the voters. The surge of westward Yankee migration from New England was largely spent after two generations. Expansion into the increasingly arid farmlands of the Great Plains was limited, as was expansion to the still very lightly settled Pacific coast. But in their postsurge period, Yankees took undisputed leadership of American culture, in the growing universities and in literature, where Mark Twain, raised in a southern-origin part of Missouri, embodied the Yankee outlook as much as the editors of high-culture publications in Boston and New York did. Very successful Yankees exploited a network of elite secondary schools and colleges that served as a preparatory ground for public leadership. Abraham Lincoln sent his son Robert to Phillips Exeter Academy and Harvard in the midst of the Civil War; Franklin Roosevelt went to Groton, headed by the Reverend Endicott Peabody, and Harvard; Samuel Bush, a steel manufacturer in Columbus, Ohio, chose Phillips Andover Academy and Yale for his son Prescott Bush, father and grandfather of presidents. Yankees rose to the top in investment banks and in law firms: making up the WASP (white Anglo-Saxon Protestant) elite, as it came to be called in the 1970s, just as its dominance of the upper ranks of society was waning.

The Union victory in the Civil War ended not only the southern grandees' surge of expansion; the abolition of slavery cost them most of their wealth, and their land was worth less than before since they couldn't use gang-system cultivation to maximize the production of cotton. And the efforts of Republicans in the Reconstruction Congresses and Ulysses S. Grant's administration to enforce equal rights, including voting rights for blacks in the South, by military force threatened their political dominance. Southern whites fought Reconstruction with violence and succeeded in ending military occupation. Over three decades they set fully in place a system of legal segregation and an informal but even more effective regime of violent intimidation. This "New South," as publicists hailed it, fell farther and farther behind the North economically and remained largely apart from it culturally. It is as if it walled itself off from the nation it fought to leave. Politically, the South was a region apart. Once blacks were denied the vote, it heavily favored the Democratic Party, but the North was strongly Republican, and the South's favorite party won the northern states' electoral votes only once between the Civil War and the Depression of the 1930s, in 1912 when the Republican Party split.

The Irish and German surges of migration slowed somewhat during the Civil War, but resumed sharply afterward and remained strong for thirty years. They halted only in the middle 1890s, when the American economy was in recession and when wage and living standards in Ireland and Germany had become competitive with those in the United States. The Irish continued to migrate almost entirely to big cities; the Germans, increasingly to Germano-Scandinavian America north and west of Chicago. Large numbers of immigrants from Scandinavia started coming in 1881 and headed primarily to Wisconsin, Minnesota, and the Dakotas. Significantly, almost all of these migrants, and those from other nations as well, landed and settled in the North. The foreign-born percentage in the South, never high, declined in the decades after the Civil War, even as it was rising rapidly in the North.

Abraham Lincoln conducted the Civil War to prevent the United States from being divided into two nations. Yet paradoxically for the three-quarters of a century after Appomattox the North and the South in important ways behaved like two separate nations. Lincoln noted in his Second Inaugural Address that the great bulk of the black population was in the South. There it remained for the next seventy-five years, despite a system of racial segregation and intimidation that was almost enslaving in its effects. The economies of the two regions took diametrically opposite courses, with the South remaining predominantly rural and agricultural—cotton production actually spread out over larger portions of the South after the Civil War—while the North was industrializing and growing rapidly in population and prosperity. Wage levels for low-skill workers were approximately twice as high in the North as in the South during this entire three-quarters of a century. Yet what looks like a powerful incentive for the Southerners to migrate north did not operate in this way. During these seventy-five years about 30 million immigrants left Europe and came to the United States, almost all of them to the northern states. During the same time only about 1 million southern whites and 1 million southern blacks moved from the South to the North.

The story of migration in this middle third of the history of the republic is the story of surges of migration that happened and a potential surge of migration that did not happen. When the Irish and German surges of migration flagged in the middle 1890s, they were replaced by a surge of migration from eastern and southern Europe. These peoples had provided less than 10 percent of immigrants to America in the two decades after the Civil War. These Ellis Islanders—for the onset of their surge of migration began just after the Ellis Island immigrant processing center opened in 1892—provided 71 percent of all immigrants in the two decades between the middle 1890s and the outbreak of World War I in 1914. In effect first the Germans and the Irish provided the manpower for northern agricultural, commercial, and industrial pursuits that southern Americans were unwilling to provide (or in the case of blacks, that they were barred from doing), and then the Ellis Islanders did so. In the process they provided a cultural variety in the North almost entirely absent in the South and thus exacerbated the tensions between the two regions years after the Civil War was over.

"*THE* main causes of migration," wrote a classical economist in the 1930s, are "differences in net economic advantages, chiefly differences in wages."[1] Yet economic differentials cannot explain all migrations. Nor can it explain how economic differentials sometimes do not produce migrations. All American surges of migration involved people who could reasonably hope to become better off economically, at least in the long run, by moving. But not everyone who could have reasonably hoped to be better off chose to move. The United States has never received a large number of French immigrants; the French, it seems, prefer to stay in France or in the reasonable facsimiles thereof they have constructed in the French Community nations where you can walk into an *épicerie* and find exactly the same kinds of bread, cheese, wine, and aperitifs you can find in any part of France. Nor did the United States receive a significant number of immigrants from Spain or Portugal; the Spanish and Portuguese, it seems, preferred Spanish- and Portuguese-speaking destinations, notably Argentina and Brazil. The United States did not receive appreciable numbers of Irish Catholics or Germans before the 1840s, or of Italians, Poles, or Eastern European Jews before the 1890s, even though many of those peoples could have reasonably believed they would be better off here. It seems that few if any experts predicted these surges of migration before they began—or predicted when they would taper off, as the Irish Catholic and German migrations did in the 1890s. Experts tend to extrapolate existing trends into the indefinite future. History provides them with many surprises.

Experts looking at the United States in the months and years immediately following the Civil War might well have predicted that many Southerners would be prompted to move north. The South was physically devastated and a major portion of its wealth vanished when slavery was abolished. Migrants to the North could communicate rapidly and cheaply, through the U.S. Post Office, with those left behind and could make return visits to their former homes on railroads or steamboats. They would not have to learn a new language. Yet by and large they did not come. And in fact this had been happening in antebellum America. The Ohio River in those years was not a barrier but a highway to the west, with migrants crossing it regularly. The 1850 Census, the first to record states of birth, showed that many residents of the states north of the Ohio came from the other side of the river—16 percent of the native-born population in Indiana; 15 percent in Illinois; 27 percent in the slave state of Missouri; and 10 percent in the state of Iowa. Only 6 percent did so in Ohio, but that state had been settled earlier and the percentage undoubtedly would have been higher in earlier censuses had the question been asked then. In addition, there was appreciable migration across north-south lines into states in what was then the Southwest. In Louisiana 17 percent of the native-born population were born in the North, and in Texas 16 percent were. Similarly, in the new state of California, 18 percent of the native-born population was born in the South.

In contrast the 1890 Census showed much lower percentages of native-born population born outside the region. In only one northern state, the former slave state of Missouri, were as many as 10 percent of the native-born population born in the South; in Indiana, Illinois, Iowa, and California the percentages were 5 percent, 4 percent,

2 percent, and 4 percent. In the Census Bureau's Eastern North Central region (Ohio, Indiana, Illinois, Michigan, Wisconsin) the percentage of southern-born residents fell from 12 percent in 1860 to 3 percent in 1890 and hovered there for two decades. In the South, despite legends of northern carpetbaggers moving in during Reconstruction, the percentages of northern-born native population exceeded 10 percent only in West Virginia (11 percent), which had been spun off from Virginia and remained with the Union during the Civil War; the border state of Arkansas (12 percent); Texas (14 percent); and lightly populated Florida (12 percent). In other southern states except for Louisiana (6 percent) the percentages ranged between 1 percent and 4 percent.

Forty years later, in 1930, despite some cross-regional migration during the 1910–20 wartime decade and the prosperous 1920s, the regional isolation was still profound. In the South the northern-born percentage of native-born population was higher than 10 percent only in Florida (14 percent), Texas (12 percent), and Oklahoma (22 percent), many of whose first white settlers came over the line from Kansas. In northern states the southern-born percentage of native-born population was relatively high, 22 percent, in lightly populated New Mexico and Arizona directly west of Texas, and otherwise exceeded 10 percent only in Ohio (11 percent), whose factories were attracting West Virginians and Kentuckians, and California (10 percent). The percentage of southern-born residents in the Great Lakes states barely rose, from 3 percent in 1910 to 4 percent in 1920 and 5 percent in 1930 and 1940. Despite the highly visible migration of what were actually relatively small numbers of blacks to Chicago and New York, the southern-born percentages in Illinois and New York were just 7 percent and 4 percent in those years.

During the entire three-quarters of a century between the Civil War and World War II the South grew much less rapidly than the North, where almost all foreign immigrants settled. New Orleans, by far the largest city in the South during this period, did attract some immigrants from Ireland and Italy, but the flow of Italians stopped abruptly after a mob lynched eleven Italian prisoners accused of

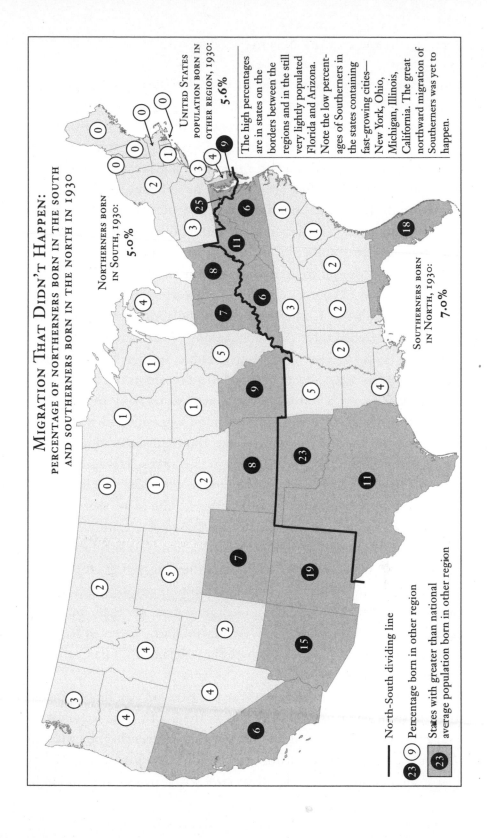

Migration That Didn't Happen:
PERCENTAGE OF NORTHERNERS BORN IN THE SOUTH
AND SOUTHERNERS BORN IN THE NORTH IN 1930

UNITED STATES
POPULATION BORN IN
OTHER REGION, 1930:
5.6%

NORTHERNERS BORN
IN SOUTH, 1930:
5.0%

SOUTHERNERS BORN
IN NORTH, 1930:
7.0%

The high percentages are in states on the borders between the regions and in the still very lightly populated Florida and Arizona. Note the low percentages of Southerners in the states containing fast-growing cities—New York, Ohio, Michigan, Illinois, California. The great northward migration of Southerners was yet to happen.

——— North-South dividing line

(9) Percentage born in other region

23 States with greater than national average population born in other region

murdering the city's police chief in 1891. The foreign-born percentage of population in the South peaked at 3.5 percent in 1860 and fell to 2.6 percent in 1890 and 2.2 percent in 1930. The corresponding figures in the North were 18 percent in 1850, 20 percent in 1890, and 15 percent in 1930, and of course these did not include immigrants' children and grandchildren born in the United States.

Behind these cold numbers are vivid human realities. Some 600,000 Americans in a nation of 38 million died in the Civil War—the proportionate number in an America of 310 million, a nation that mourns 4,000 deaths in Iraq and 2,000 in Afghanistan, would be 5,000,000 today. Many rural areas in the eastern part of the country, both Union and Confederate, lost population in the 1860s and never again reached their 1860 populations. The wounds of the Civil War were deep and lasted for many decades. Speaker Sam Rayburn, born in 1882 in Texas, lived on to see the election of the first Catholic president in 1960 and was often moved to tears by the plight of Confederate veterans—who, unlike Union veterans, did not receive pensions from the federal government; those pensions were a major share of the federal budget up through the 1890s. Harry Truman's grandmother would become visibly angry when she recalled being mistreated by Union soldiers in Missouri. The state that cast the second-highest percentage (after Rhode Island) for Catholic Democrat John F. Kennedy in 1960 was not his native Massachusetts but Georgia; Sherman had marched through the state, living off the land, destroying property, and freeing slaves, only ninety-six years before, and that still mattered to many Georgia voters. In 1944 my father asked his grandfather, born in West Virginia, why he voted Republican for president in 1944. His grandfather explained, "The Confederates burned our barn."

In the years after the Civil War the party of Abraham Lincoln tried to secure equal rights for blacks in the South. The Republican-controlled Congress passed the Thirteenth, Fourteenth, and Fifteenth Amendments and came within one vote of removing Andrew Johnson from office for frustrating their efforts to protect southern blacks from violence and ensure their participation in elections. Republican president Ulysses S. Grant, elected in 1868 and 1872, did more to ensure the rights of black Americans than any other president between Lincoln and Harry Truman, and insisted on stationing federal troops in the South to enforce black rights. But this interference with the customs of the white majority aroused opposition not only from southern grandees but from the Scots-Irish who wanted to handle local affairs and the local black minority their own way; Andrew Johnson had been a Jackson Democrat himself before supporting Lincoln and the Union, as Jackson's protégé Sam Houston, then governor of Texas, did in the crisis of 1860–61. And of course whites in states where they were a minority—the cotton-growing belt from South Carolina to Louisiana—were even more obdurate in their opposition to civil rights for blacks. In time the majority of northern voters wearied of the turmoil and expense of supporting federal military occupation of southern states to protect the rights of blacks for whom they had little sympathy, and they were scarcely ready to admit to the full array of rights in their own communities. In the off-year election of 1874 Democrats won major victories, winning majorities in both houses of Congress, majorities strong enough that they lost control of the House of Representatives only twice in the ten elections from 1874 to 1892. In 1876 the Democratic presidential nominee, Samuel J. Tilden, won a majority of the popular vote and was denied the presidency only after a commission awarded southern electoral votes in question to the Republican, Rutherford B. Hayes, in return for a promise that military occupation of the South would end. Historians sympathetic to Democrats have depicted these Democratic victories as a response to the economic downturn following the Panic of 1873 or to scandals implicating some, though not the president, in the Grant administration and in the Republican congressional leadership. But this analysis is an attempt to view attitudes in the decade before Franklin Roosevelt's birth as identical to those in the years of his presidency and to magnify supposedly scandalous behavior that in fact had been routine for decades. The actual message of American voters in the elections of 1874 and 1876, amplified by Supreme Court decisions of the time that eviscerated the legislation of the Reconstruction Congresses, was that the federal government should get out of the business of using military force and legal prosecution to ensure the rights of black Americans in the southern states and should let southern whites rule there as they pleased.

The result was that the North essentially withdrew from the South and let white southerners govern it their way. Southern historians in the generations after the Civil War depicted the Republicans' Reconstruction policies as oppression of virtuous white men and women, and so in many cases did northern historians as well. The effort to ensure equal rights for black Americans was an embarrassing enterprise, mostly forgotten, and Americans from the two regions went their own ways. It was as if an invisible wall was put in place along the Potomac and Ohio Rivers and extending westward, across which Northerners and Southerners seldom ventured and across which they averted their gaze. It took more than two decades for white southern Democrats to put in place the system of legally enforced racial segregation to buttress the existing unwritten laws of customary behavior, which certified blacks as an inferior caste in the American South. This process required also the threat of and more than occasional acts of illegal violence to punish blacks who treated whites as in any way their equal. Lynchings began under the noses of federal troops in the late 1860s and early 1870s and continued for decades, with 104 in 1891–1900, 75 in 1901–10, 55 in 1911–20, 25 in 1921–30, and 10 in 1931–40.[2] So strong was white Southerners' defense of this indefensible institution that in the 1930s Franklin Roosevelt refused to support, and Democratic Congresses declined to pass, a federal antilynching statute. Republican politicians occasionally asserted the rights of black Americans. Theodore Roosevelt, whose father paid $300 to avoid military service in the Civil War because his Georgia-born wife's family were Confederates (her brother James Dunwoody Bulloch was a leader of the Confederate navy), made an attempt at regional and racial reconciliation when, early in his years as president, he invited the black leader Booker T. Washington, who accepted white political supremacy in the South, to lunch at the White House. But the roar of rage from white Southerners was so loud and vigorous that even as brave a leader as Roosevelt was, he never invited a black to the White House again. Roosevelt, however, was liberal in comparison to Democratic president Woodrow Wilson—born in Virginia, raised in Augusta, Georgia, and a nine-year-old boy in Columbia, South Carolina, when Sherman came marching through in 1865—who imposed rigorous racial segregation in the federal government.

In many ways the United States in the three-quarters of a century between its two most deadly wars was two countries, in which the ordinary people and even the elites of North and South paid no heed to what was happening in the other region. Southern elites sent their sons to southern universities, or perhaps as far north as Princeton and Johns Hopkins, where Woodrow Wilson earned his degrees. Even in the summer heat they did not venture to cool northern vacation spots. Northern elites seldom proceeded southward, even on vacation; it was considered noteworthy that John D. Rockefeller in the early twentieth century took to spending winters in Florida, and that his business partner Henry Flagler built a railroad to Palm Beach, Miami, and Key West. Nor did northern business elites invest in any substantial way in the South. "I am not interested in any business proposition in any place where it does not snow," declared James J. Hill, the builder of the Great Northern Railway, headquartered in snowy St. Paul, Minnesota.

While the great cities of the North boomed and ballooned, the South remained a primarily rural region. Only 10 percent of Southerners lived in urban areas in 1860, just before the Civil War, and by 1900 that percentage had risen to only 18 percent. In contrast, the North's population was already 25 percent urban before the Civil War, and more than 50 percent urban in 1900—a level of urbanization that the South reached only in 1950. Much has been made by historians of the South regarding the Atlanta journalist Henry Grady's 1886 proclamation of a "New South," industrialized and progressive, "thrilling with the consciousness of growing power and prosperity." But his hometown of Atlanta had a population of 37,000 in 1880, making it the forty-ninth-largest city in the United States, and the only southern cities that were larger were New Orleans (216,000), Louisville (123,000), Richmond (63,000), Charleston (49,000), and Nashville (43,000). One might also add the much larger Baltimore (332,000), which was southern by some definitions, although with its immigrant population it increasingly resembled northern cities far more than those to the south. From 1850 to 1930 the South accounted for no more than 21 percent of the nation's urban population and as little as 14 percent, in 1880; in 1940, after a decade of depression, that rose to 24 percent.[3] The South accounted for only fifteen of the nation's hundred largest cities in 1890, with only 8 percent of their total population. By 1940, it still accounted for only twenty-four of the top one hundred, with only 12 percent of their total population. Manufacturing was concentrated overwhelmingly in the North; the South had far less railroad mileage than the North and dreadful roads; a large percentage of its population was subsistence farmers or sharecroppers. Wage levels were typically less than half those in the North, and nutrition and public health standards were far lower. "In the post–Civil War era," writes economic historian Gavin Wright, "the South constituted a separate regional labor market, outside the scope of national and international labor markets that were active and effective during that era. . . . The South was a low-wage region in a high-wage country."[4]

Yet few Southerners, white or black, left the South. The conclusion one must draw is that they thought they would not be welcome— and they were surely right. White men born in the 1830s and 1840s had been shooting and killing one another in large numbers, with many suffering disabling injuries; those who survived lived on for decades, many well into the twentieth century. Confederate veterans, whose only pensions came from state governments, had an economic as well as cultural disincentive not to move to the land of their recent foes. Union veterans, conscious that the troops and officials enforcing

Reconstruction until 1877 had been attacked as corrupt carpetbaggers and had been shunned by southern elites, had no desire to reenter what had been a scene of conflict after the troops were withdrawn. In 1898 officials in the War Department in Washington, dispatching troops to Tampa for embarkation to Cuba in the Spanish-American War, stationed sentries along the rail lines to prevent southern attacks, while one southern army officer in his delight at seeing the Spanish forces retreat in Cuba, yelled, "We've got the damn Yankees on the run."

Southern blacks had even more reason than the southern whites to shun the North, despite all the Yankees' professed devotion to the cause of equal rights. Throughout American history blacks have been the group most reluctant to move, with the lowest degree of mobility in response to economic incentives.[5] This reluctance is likely rooted in historical experiences, kept alive for generations in folk memories, of the miseries of the Middle Passage from Africa across the Atlantic in the seventeenth and eighteenth centuries and the internal passage from the Atlantic coast states to the Southwest in the years between the abolition of the slave trade in 1808 and the outbreak of the Civil War in 1861. Moving meant leaving behind forever family members, ancestral churches, familiar terrain—and facing uncertainty, new and possibly brutal masters, illness, and death. Southern blacks may not have been aware that some northern states, even those that supported the party of the Union like Abraham Lincoln's Illinois, also sought to bar the immigration of blacks, but they were certainly aware that they would have a hard time finding housing in northern cities (and certainly could not afford to buy or rent most working northern farms). "Whites did not want blacks next door," write historians Stephan Thernstrom and Abigail Thernstrom. "Even before the Great Migration, when the African-American population was too small to seem truly threatening, a color line had to be drawn."[6] That practice continued for many years. In Detroit in the 1950s, in a state that had never had legally enforced racial segregation, newspaper classified ads had separate headings for "Apartments—white" and "Apartments—colored."

That left the large majority of blacks—90 percent or more until 1900, 89 percent in 1910, 85 percent in 1920, 79 percent in 1930, and 77 percent in 1940—in the segregated South. There they were, with only a few exceptions, not allowed to vote or to serve on juries. They could not attend white schools, could not ride on public transportation in the same seats as whites. They were never addressed as *Mr.* or *Mrs.*, they were required to address white children as *Master* or *Miss*, and they were required to come only to the back not the front door of whites' houses. Interracial dating and marriage were strictly forbidden— all practices redolent of slavery and some enforced by law, although it took several decades after the Civil War before southern states fully adumbrated their racial codes. All were enforced, unofficially but usually effectively, by the threat of violent punishment, even death.

From this system of legally and violently enforced racial segregation northern whites seem to have averted their gaze. In the 1930s the University of Chicago sociologist John Dollard did fieldwork in Indianola, Mississippi, living with local residents and studying local mores and behavior much as contemporary anthropologists studied the local mores and behavior in Samoa or New Guinea. In 1937 he published *Caste and Class in a Southern Town* in which, without identifying Indianola or specific individuals, he described the system. It was received in academia, appropriately, as a serious work of scholarship and, oddly, as a revelation—despite the fact that almost everything in it was common knowledge to any ten-year-old, black or white, in Indianola. That it could come as a revelation to so many in the North is vivid evidence of how wide the gulf—or how high the wall—between the North and South had been for seven decades after the Civil War.[7]

ON January 1, 1892, fifteen-year-old Annie Moore from County Cork, Ireland, arrived at the newly opened federal immigration station at Ellis Island in New York Harbor, the first immigrant to be processed there. She was one of 104 steerage passengers on the

Nevada who were disembarked in New York and put on a barge; the 20 passengers who traveled in cabins were allowed to go onshore unimpeded. Altogether 700 steerage passengers went through the inspection that day.[8] The opening of Ellis Island coincided with two important turning points in American immigration policy: One was the assumption by the federal government from the states of the process of screening immigrants to keep out those who were diseased or, in the language of the day, likely to become a public charge. The other was a shift in the origin of most immigrants from northwestern Europe and Germany to southern and eastern Europe. The first turning point resulted from decisions made by elected officeholders and official bureaucrats. The second resulted from the cumulative decisions of hundreds of thousands of people in dozens of different nations and provinces. In the years of the Ellis Island migration, from 1892 until 1924, when restrictive immigration laws went into effect, almost precisely 20 million immigrants arrived in the United States, and 12 million of them were processed at Ellis Island.

The shift in countries of origin was stark. The years from 1881 to 1891 were high immigration years, with the annual flow averaging 519,000. The largest sources of immigration were Germany (142,000 annual average), Britain (79,000), Scandinavia (65,000), and Ireland (64,000). The economic turmoil of the early 1890s and the economic uncertainty of the later years of the decade resulted in much lower total immigration, with the annual total averaging 361,000 for the years from 1892 to 1901. But in those years the largest contributors were Italy (71,000), Austria-Hungary (63,000), and Russia (54,000), all well ahead of Germany (41,000), Ireland (36,000), Scandinavia (35,000), and Britain (22,000). Annual outmigration from 1881–91 to 1892–1901 from Britain fell 72 percent, from Ireland 44 percent, from Scandinavia 54 percent, and from Germany 71 percent. In contrast, it rose 64 percent in Austria-Hungary, 102 percent in Italy, and 129 percent in Russia. The British, German, and Scandinavian economies had developed and were providing jobs for an increasing number of natives, while Ireland's reservoir of potential immigrants simply dried up, with its population falling to half the prefamine level of 1841. It is a pattern in international migration identified by economists Timothy Hatton and Jeffrey Williamson: "Emigration rates rose steeply at first from very low levels; the rise then began to slow down, emigration rates reached a peak and subsequently they fell off."[9]

This shift persisted as immigration spiked upward starting in 1902. In the thirteen years from 1902 to 1914, immigration to the United States averaged 956,000 annually—a figure roughly the same as the average annual immigration to the more than three times as populous United States in the years from 1990 to 2007. Immigration levels from Britain and Scandinavia, though not from Ireland or Germany, rebounded somewhat upward from the 1892–1901 level, but the biggest increases were among the nations contributing about 200,000 immigrants annually—Austria-Hungary (224,000), Italy (216,000), and Russia (183,000). These were the peak years of the Ellis Island migration, when the island center would process more than 1,000 immigrants many days. The level of immigration as a percentage of preexisting population was the highest in American history, roughly tied with the 1763–75 period when the Scots-Irish arrived in record numbers and with the 1846–56 period when unprecedented numbers of Irish and German immigrants arrived. The Ellis Island surge of immigration occurred during years of great industrial expansion and productivity increases, made possible by advances in electricity and gasoline. In effect the Ellis Islanders provided the workforce for garment factories in New York and steel and auto factories of Pittsburgh, Cleveland, Detroit, and Chicago at a time when emigration from northwestern Europe was declining and when southern Americans, black and white, were still unwilling or reluctant to move north.

One reason emigration from southern Europe (primarily Italy) and eastern Europe (primarily the empires of Austria-Hungary and Russia) rose so rapidly was that it suddenly became feasible. Those who formerly could not afford a journey across the ocean suddenly could because in some cases their incomes had risen but more often because the price of transportation had lowered, just as railroads increasingly connected the far reaches of Europe with ports on the North Sea and the Adriatic, and as technological advance and market competition made steamship travel cheaper. So as the American economy boomed and the demand for workers rose, and as the flow of unskilled workers from northern and western Europe declined, unskilled workers from eastern and southern Europe—not Americans from the South—in effect took their place and provided the supply of labor for which there was increasing demand.

But the Ellis Island immigration was not just a response to economic incentives. Another factor was at work. "Explosive colonization was driven as much by dreams as by reason," writes the Australian historian James Belich, speaking about migration to Canada and Australia as well as the United States.[10] Immigrants sought a place in America that seemed unavailable in the lands of their birth. When we look at the Ellis Island immigrants, what we see are people who were second-class or second-caste citizens of large multiethnic empires. We see that the vast majority of Italian immigrants were from southern Italy, from the former Kingdom of Naples and Two Sicilies, which had become part of the northern-ruled Kingdom of Italy as a result of the military expedition of the self-starting adventurer and revolutionary Giuseppe Garibaldi. Few northern Italians came to the United States (or to those other favorites of Italian emigrants, Argentina and Brazil).[11] We see that the vast majority of immigrants from the Hapsburg Empire of Austria-Hungary were Czechs, Poles, Slovaks, Slovenes, Serbs, and Jews. Relatively few Hungarians emigrated, and fewer Austrians.[12]

Similarly, we see that the vast majority of immigrants from the tsarist empire of Russia were Poles and Jews, with smaller numbers of Ukrainians and Lithuanians. Relatively few ethnic Russians left Russia. Looking backward before the early 1890s, we can see that the Irish Catholic immigrants were of a different religion (and were considered by many to be of a different race) from their British rulers, and that as the century went on larger proportions of British immigrants were Scots or Welsh rather than English. And a significant percentage of German immigrants were either Jews, Poles, or Germans out of sympathy with the militaristic ethos of increasingly dominant Prussia or the German Empire that it created in 1871. Emma Lazarus's poem tells of nations giving America their poor, their tired, their hungry. There was something to that. But what was also happening was that the empires of pre–World War I Europe were giving the United States their second-class citizens, their subject peoples, their disfavored ethnic groups. This can even be said of Norway, the largest source of Scandinavian immigrants, for Norway was a part of the kingdom of Sweden before it gained independence and its own king in 1905.

In an age of surging nationalist feeling—when not only intellectuals but also ordinary people were coming to feel that assertion of their own ethnic and linguistic identity was an essential component of personal liberty—this feeling was articulated most strongly by those who regarded themselves, often plausibly, as the natural leaders of a newly liberated ethnically based nation, but it gained strength and momentum among ordinary people as well. The marshaling into military service of millions of young men who spoke a variety of languages under the leadership of officers who spoke German or Hungarian or Russian created tensions felt by not only these soldiers but also by their families and their communities. The language barrier in the United States must have seemed not much higher than the language barrier in Italy, Austria-Hungary, or Russia for those not fluent in the governing language or dialect. The possibility of becoming full-status citizens, in a democratic republic, was an option that did not seem open to them in their native lands.

Between 1892 and 1914 3.5 million immigrants from Italy came to the United States, more than from any other nation. An additional 125,000 arrived in 1915–19 and 460,000 in 1920–24. Italian immigration rose from an average annual rate of 35,000 in 1881–91 to 71,000 in 1892–1901 and 216,000 in 1902–14. It fell to 25,000 in the wartime years and 92,000 in the early 1920s. They came from a Kingdom of Italy that had been proclaimed only in 1861. Italian unification—the

Risorgimento—was a project championed for years by the intellectual Giuseppe Mazzini and fought for by the charismatic Garibaldi. But as a practical matter it was largely the work of the leaders of the Kingdom of Sardinia, which, despite its name, was headquartered in the Piedmont city of Turin, in the far northwest corner of Italy. The king, Victor Emmanuel, was a member of the House of Savoy, a territory just south of Lake Geneva relinquished to France (along with Nice) to repay the French emperor Napoleon III for his support of Italian reunification; the king's chief minister Camillo Cavour spoke French rather than Italian as his native language. Their intention was to expand their kingdom in northern Italy, which they did by acquiring Lombardy in a war with Austria-Hungary in 1859 and the small states of Modena, Parma, and Tuscany and the provinces of the Papal States north of the city of Rome in March 1860. It was not part of their plans to absorb the Two Sicilies, but Garibaldi launched an invasion of Sicily in May 1861 and swept through the island, then the mainland of the ancient kingdom, within four months—and presented it to Victor Emmanuel and Cavour. They had no choice but to accept.

The two halves of Italy were a poor fit. Their differences, as sociologist Robert Putnam has written, go back to the Middle Ages, when the northern city-states enjoyed independence and pioneered modern finance, while the southern kingdoms of Naples and Sicily were ruled by despotic and often absentee monarchs.[13] Moreover, most residents of the new kingdom did not speak standard Italian, based on the Tuscan dialect in which Dante wrote his *Divine Comedy* in the fourteenth century. Southern dialects, particularly Sicilian, but also Calabrian and Neapolitan, were distinctive and difficult if not impossible to understand for Northerners (especially for Cavour). In 1860 the north was on the brink of industrialization; the south was not, with large masses living in poverty in cities, including Naples and Palermo, and most of the population scratching out a living as tenant farmers. Italian immigration to the United States was minimal during the first three decades of the kingdom, reaching the 50,000 annual figure only in 1888, but then it skyrocketed despite the strained economic circumstances of the United States in much of the 1890s. Some 97 percent of Italian immigrants landed in New York: this was indeed an Ellis Island immigration. And it was a southern Italian immigration: 84 percent of those arriving between 1890 and 1910 were from southern Italy. Northern Italian migration was visible, with Northerners heading to San Francisco and the California wine country, where they prospered in what must have been a familiar climate and terrain. But the large majority of Ellis Islander Italians did not venture far from where they landed. In 1910 New York City had 340,000 Italian-born residents, more than Florence, Venice, and Genoa combined, and more than twice as many as Boston, Philadelphia, Baltimore, Chicago, New Orleans, and San Francisco combined.[14]

The large majority of Italian immigrants were males, mostly young men, and about half of them returned to Italy at some point, with some making the voyage back to New York again. They clustered at first in lower Manhattan, which may have been the most densely populated place in the world at that time: the 1910 Census showed the island with 2.3 million people, some 750,000 more than live there today, with half of them living south of Fourteenth Street. They lived in heavily but not entirely Italian neighborhoods, with concentrations of Sicilians, Calabrians, and Neapolitans, and even when they spread out into the boroughs of Brooklyn and the Bronx as subway lines were completed starting in 1906, they continued to shop and meet in the old Little Italy. Italian immigrant men worked mostly as unskilled workers, sometimes taking construction jobs around the country; significant numbers were skilled stonemasons, shoemakers, and tailors. Italian women worked in large numbers in New York City's rapidly growing garment industry. The Italians were nominally Catholic, but southern Italian men tended to shun church, and many Italians found Irish domination of the church in America uncongenial. They tended to be more entrepreneurial than the Irish and less likely to seek government jobs. Coming from a southern Italy where most people trusted few beyond their family, they had strong family ties. But that also meant that they discouraged school learning, which they feared

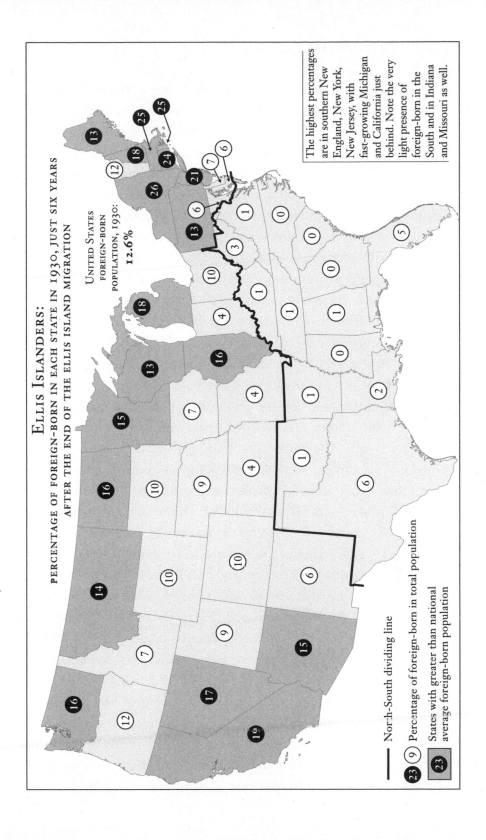

Ellis Islanders:

PERCENTAGE OF FOREIGN-BORN IN EACH STATE IN 1930, JUST SIX YEARS AFTER THE END OF THE ELLIS ISLAND MIGRATION

UNITED STATES
FOREIGN-BORN
POPULATION, 1930:
12.6%

The highest percentages are in southern New England, New York, New Jersey, with fast-growing Michigan and California just behind. Note the very light presence of foreign-born in the South and in Indiana and Missouri as well.

— North-South dividing line

23 9 Percentage of foreign-born in total population

23 States with greater than national average foreign-born population

would estrange their children from them. Coming from the nation with the highest crime rates in Europe, the Italians had a high crime rate, higher than at home, and accounted for a significant portion of the national rise in crime during the Ellis Island years; homicides were five to ten times more frequent among them than among other whites in America.[15] But crime rates were much lower than in Irish neighborhoods in the first few decades of Irish immigration. "Violence in American cities in the early decades of the twentieth century bore no resemblance to the violence in those unhappy places in the decades just past," writes criminal law scholar William Stuntz. "By today's standards, immigrant-dominated American cities were safe places."[16] But members of traditional Italian criminal organizations like the Mafia of Sicily did make their way to the United States, especially after World War I, just as Prohibition produced opportunities for enormous profits in the illegal liquor trade.

Italian immigrants, like the Irish, almost all made their way in large cities and factory and railroad towns, even though most had come from farms. The Italian communities in other large cities—especially Philadelphia, Boston, and Chicago—and in smaller cities such as Providence, Rhode Island, and New Haven, Connecticut, were in many ways similar to the Italian community in New York. But politically there were differences. Italians in New York tended to vote Democratic—though there were some staunch Republicans, and the most accomplished Italian (and half-Jewish) New York politician, Fiorello La Guardia, won elections as a Republican, a Socialist, and a nominee of the American Labor Party. Italians in Philadelphia and New Haven tended to vote Republican, while those in Providence and Cleveland tended to vote Democratic: they seem to have been responding more to local political divisions than to national political issues. But the Italians, for all their movement back and forth across the Atlantic, once in the United States tended to stay close to New York City. In 1970 two-thirds of Italian-Americans lived in the Northeast, a proportion that did not decline markedly for the next forty years, and over half lived within 100 miles of Ellis Island.

Most immigrants from Slavic ethnic groups, except for Poles, came from the Austro-Hungarian Empire ruled by the Hapsburg emperor-king Franz Josef. There are no reliable precise numbers of those from each group, since most entered the United States before World War I and were classified as coming from Austria, Hungary, or the dual monarchy. Generally speaking, after passing through Ellis Island they were much less likely than the Italians to remain in New York and much more likely to set out for the industrial cities of the American interior—places more reminiscent in location and climate to landlocked central Europe. The Czechs, geographically the westernmost group and economically the most advanced, were the first to arrive in significant numbers and the only Slavic group that settled on farms in large numbers. Czech farmers arrived in significant numbers in the years just after the Civil War and settled in Wisconsin, Minnesota, Iowa, Nebraska, and Kansas; their struggles were depicted beautifully in the novels of their Nebraska neighbor Willa Cather. But by the 1890s most Czechs were headed to cities, especially Chicago, where they were known as Bohemians and lived in a quadrant spreading southwest from the Loop. Prominent Chicago Czechs included Congressman Adolph Sabath (1907–52), Mayor Anton Cermak (1931–33), and his son-in-law, federal judge Otto Kerner, whose son Otto Kerner Jr. was governor of Illinois in the 1960s. There were also large Czech communities in Cleveland and New York.[17] The Czechs came from the Austrian half of Austria-Hungary; the Slovaks came from the Hungarian half, where most were tenant farmers on the large landholdings of Hungarian aristocrats. Agents for American railroads and coal mines journeyed to the Slovak provinces to recruit laborers in the years after the Civil War, and most Slovak immigrants were men, often in groups from the same village. Most became low-skill laborers in the factory and mining towns of Pennsylvania, Ohio, Illinois, and New Jersey.[18]

The Slovenians, most from the Austrian province that became the northernmost part of post–World War I Yugoslavia, had relatively high levels of literacy and a strong Catholic faith. Early Slovenian

immigrants were pioneers in Michigan's Upper Peninsula and north-
ern Minnesota's mining country; later Slovenes tended to settle in
Cleveland and the southern Chicago suburbs around Joliet, Illinois.
The Slovenian community produced an impressive number of suc-
cessful politicians—Ohio governor (1945–47, 1949–57) and senator
(1957–69) Frank Lausche and five U.S. House members, Minnesota
Democrats John Blatnik (1947–77) and James Oberstar (1977–2011),
Kansas Republican Joe Skubitz (1963–79), Michigan Republican Philip
Ruppe (1967–79), and Colorado Democrat Ray Kogovsek (1979–85).[19]

Croatian immigration, first from the Dalmatian coast and then
from the inland peasant farmlands, was mostly male, with many
returning home later. There were Croats in gold rush California and
in various parts of the West before 1880. Afterward Croatians tended
to come to the steel country in and around Pittsburgh and Chicago.
The most renowned immigrant from Croatia was the prolific inventor Nikola Tesla.[20]

Serbian immigrants tended to head for industrial and mining
country around Pittsburgh, Youngstown, Cleveland, Chicago, and in
northern Minnesota. Politicians of Serbian descent include the col-
orful governors Rudy Perpich of Minnesota (1977–79, 1983–89) and
Rod Blagojevich of Illinois (2003–09).[21]

The most numerous Slavic immigrants were the Poles, coming before 1890 mostly from the German Empire and afterward
mostly from the Hapsburg and tsarist empires. Their numbers cannot be stated with precision, but they made up a large share of eastern and central European immigrants. They came in mostly via New
York City but headed most often to Chicago. As with other ethnic
groups, the first to arrive often recruited and encouraged others,
family or friends or neighbors, to come: this was chain migration. A
fine example was Anton Schermann, from Posen (now Poznan) in the
German Empire. He settled in Chicago in 1851, just as its Yankee
founders were laying the foundations for its stunning growth; in his
early thirties, he worked as a laborer and opened a grocery store that
was also the home of the St. Stanislaus Kostka Benevolent Society.

This resulted in the building of a Polish Catholic church in 1869 on a site just west of the North Chicago River in an industrial area. Schermann is credited with "bringing over" 100,000 Poles to Chicago. With other Polish businessmen, newspaper editors and writers, priests and nuns, he would write to Poles back home, talking up the prospects in Chicago and arranging for steamship travel fares to be paid (by 1890, three large steamship companies had 6,500 agents in the United States for European immigrants).[22] Whether Schermann inspired a full 100,000 Poles to come, Chicago did attract more Poles than any other American city. The church still stands, highly visible since the John F. Kennedy Expressway curves around it; across the street were the homes of Joe and Dan Rostenkowksi. Joe held the post of Democratic 32nd Ward committeeman from 1935 to 1995; Dan, elevated at age thirty to Congress because his father had supported mayor Richard J. Daley against a Polish primary opponent, was chairman of the House Ways and Means Committee from 1981 to 1995. Other similar Polish communities grew up in New York City, in the industrial cities of Pittsburgh, Buffalo, Milwaukee, Detroit, and Cleveland, and in factory and mining cities such as Wilkes-Barre and Scranton, Pennsylvania; Toledo, Ohio; South Bend, Indiana; St. Paul, St. Louis, and Omaha. A multitude of Polish institutions grew: Polish churches (some 512 in 1910), cooperative building-and-loan societies, the Polish National Alliance and Polish Falcon Alliance, Polish medical and dental and lawyers' associations. But the large majority of Polish immigrants were blue-collar workers, laboring at low-skill jobs, living in close quarters in predominantly Polish city neighborhoods, with meticulous yards and lavish decorations at Christmastime. Crime rates among Poles and other Slavic groups were about the same as among whites generally, not higher as was the case with initial generations of Irish and Italians.[23]

There were relatively few southern Italians, Poles, or other Slavs in the United States before the Ellis Island era, but Jews had been immigrating to America since the colonial period. The small number of Jews in the colonies had mostly Sephardic backgrounds and worked as merchants in Charleston, Newport, and New York who traded with the West Indies and Britain. While Jews in Europe lived under harsh restrictions, those in England and its colonies could live where they pleased, and the Framers of the Constitution specifically provided that there be no religious test for federal office—a few years before revolutionaries in France removed restrictions on Jews. George Washington in his 1791 tour of New England made a point of stopping at the Touro Synagogue in Newport, and in a letter to the congregation he wrote that "Citizens of the United States . . . [a]ll possess alike liberty of conscience and immunities of citizenship. It is now no more that toleration is spoken of, as if it was by the indulgence of one class of people, that another enjoyed the exercise of their inherent national gifts. For happily the Government of the United States, which gives to bigotry no sanction, to persecution no assistance, requires only that they who live under its protection, should demean themselves as good citizens, in giving it on all occasions their effectual support."

The young republic received Jewish immigrants mainly from German-speaking lands. While a few Jews amassed considerable wealth, many if not most Jewish immigrants in the early republic became peddlers, a trade that required minimal capital, excellent calculating skills, a nexus of trusting suppliers (often relatives or townsmen from the old country), and a sensitive understanding of the rapidly changing tastes and fashions of people with entirely different backgrounds. Jews spread across the continent, with concentrations in great internal trading cities, including Cincinnati, St. Louis, and Milwaukee, which also were major centers of antebellum German immigration. Cincinnati had a particularly prominent German Jewish community and became the center of Reform Judaism, with Hebrew Union College, founded there in 1875, the chief training school for Reform rabbis.

They also were numerous in San Francisco during the gold rush years, when Levi Strauss invented the pants that still bear his name. Jewish peddlers spread across the South and ventured into the dry goods business, with some becoming commission merchants and cotton brokers.

The first American Jewish cabinet member was Judah P. Benjamin, a New Orleans lawyer and former senator from Louisiana, who became secretary of war and secretary of state in the Confederate States of America. The first American Jewish national party chairman was August Belmont, born Schoenberg, who started off as office boy for the Rothschilds in Frankfurt and became their American agent and who served as Democratic National Chairman from 1860 to 1872—longer than anyone else has headed the world's oldest political party. After the Civil War, some prominent southern Jews moved to New York—the Lehman brothers, cotton factors who set up their eponymous investment bank in New York; Lazarus and Isidor Straus, who moved from Talbotton, Georgia, to New York City, where they made R. H. Macy and Company the nation's largest department store; the eight Seligman brothers, who set up offices in San Francisco and New York in the 1850s and who underwrote U.S. bonds and clothed U.S. troops in the Civil War; and Adolph S. Ochs, owner of the *Chattanooga Times*, who moved to New York in 1896 when he bought the flailing *New York Times*.

By 1890, German Jews occupied prominent positions in American life while Jews in eastern Europe were facing increased persecution. After the assassination of Tsar Alexander II in 1881, by terrorists whose group had many Jewish members, the Russian interior ministry began strictly enforcing restrictive laws against Jews. Young Jewish men were subject to up to twenty-five years of military service and Jews were prohibited from living outside the Pale—essentially the old kingdom of Poland—including St. Petersburg and Moscow. The tsarist authorities believed that Jews were disproportionately involved in socialist, anarchist, and terrorist movements; and many Jews were in fact attracted to a system of thought that identified them not as a hated minority but as part of the great mass of oppressed people. But the Russian secret police were not bound by fact; the organization wrote the notorious *Protocols of the Elders of Zion* in the 1890s.

Jewish immigration from the Russian Empire accelerated in the 1890s and then quadrupled after 1900; Russian immigration to the United States averaged 54,000 annually in 1892–1901 and 183,000 in 1902–14. This was in part a response to pogroms in Kishinev in 1903; Odessa, Minsk, and Lodz in 1905; and Bialystok of Gomel in 1906. Persecution was not nearly as menacing in the Hapsburg Empire, but anti-Semitism seemed to be rising, as indicated by the election of the Jew-baiting Karl Lueger as mayor of Vienna in 1897 over the objections of the Emperor Franz Josef, and Jewish immigration accelerated in the same years as from the Russian Empire.

In the mid–nineteenth century most Eastern European Jews lived in shtetlach, small rural villages where they were isolated from their gentile neighbors. During the next half century about half moved to cities, where they worked as traders, craftsmen, and workers in the new clothing factories: the migration to America was thus part of this rural-to-urban movement. Unlike Italians, Jews tended to migrate in family groups and, again unlike Italians, almost none chose to return to the countries of origin. In the Russian Empire they made their way to the town of Brody, on the older Polish border, which became a great funnel point of immigration.[24] There they usually crossed the border illegally and headed to the ports of Hamburg, Bremen, Amsterdam, Rotterdam, and Antwerp for passage to the new world. Some Jews from the Hapsburg Empire also traveled to these ports, but most left through the Hapsburg port of Trieste on the Adriatic. The native language of most was Yiddish, developed in the Middle Ages from Middle High German dialects with admixtures of Hebrew, Polish, and Russian and usually written in Hebrew letters. It was, as the greatest Yiddish writer, Isaac Bashevis Singer (who wrote in New York and Surfside, Florida), said, the only language never spoken by men in power.[25]

The difference between American Jews of German origin and the new, mostly Yiddish-speaking Jewish immigrants from eastern Europe was widely appreciated. Eastern European Jews were aided in their migrations by charitable and welfare agencies set up by wealthy German Jews in America. But the German Jews were also aware that there were profound differences between them and the newcomers, and they dreaded that their acceptance in America would be imperiled by an influx of the much more numerous and much less sophisticated and polished immigrants from eastern Europe. Jewish organizations met immigrants fresh off Ellis Island and gave advice on finding housing and jobs, and settlement houses gave them lessons in public health, English, and the requirements for American citizenship.

About 70 percent of the Ellis Island Jews stayed in New York, clustering at first on a few blocks in the Lower East Side, then spreading to cover almost all the area east of the Bowery and Chatham Square and south of Houston Street, just to the east of the various Little Italys. By 1910, there were some 540,000 Jews living in 1.5 square miles of the Lower East Side—730 per acre, quite possibly the highest population density in the world at the time. They lived in five- and six-story tenement houses, sleeping three or more to a room, with most rooms opening only to an airshaft. The streets were filled with pushcarts and some 2,500 peddler stalls, horse-drawn carts, and workers carrying piles of cloth and clothing. Synagogues, ritual baths, and Yiddish theaters opened; *landsmanshaft* organizations offered life insurance, sickness and death benefits, and burial plots. No other immigrant groups produced as many voluntary organizations as the Jews. The Lower East Side was not a permanent home for most Eastern European Jewish immigrants, however. As the subways were built—the first line opened in 1906—they moved in huge numbers to Brooklyn and the Bronx, with Brownsville and Flatbush in Brooklyn and the Grand Concourse in the Bronx becoming predominantly Jewish neighborhoods. By 1920, New York City had 1.6 million Jews, by far the largest Jewish population of any city in the world.[26] Similar patterns were seen in other cities: on Chicago's West Side and in South Philadelphia, in Boston, Cleveland, Baltimore, Pittsburgh, St. Louis, and Detroit. There as in New York the Eastern European Jews tended to settle in neighborhoods far removed from German-origin Jews, and relatively few headed to the old German destinations of Cincinnati, Milwaukee, and San Francisco.

Immigrant Jews tended to find work in the garment factories, most of them small firms owned by German Jews. The workday was long, the work was painstaking, and the wages tended to be low. Immigrant Jews, drawing on their experience in the Bund, the Jewish labor movement in Russia, formed labor unions and staged strikes; in 1910 Jewish manufacturers and labor leaders reached a "protocol of peace" thanks to the mediation of Boston lawyer and later Supreme Court justice Louis Brandeis. The two major garment workers unions, the ILGWU and the Amalgamated, which formed in 1900 and 1914, plus the heavily Jewish hat and fur worker unions had 217,000 members by 1917.

The German Jews' fears that the influx of Eastern European immigrants would spur discrimination against all Jews proved justified. During the first half of the twentieth century and into the second half, Jews were largely excluded from the management ranks of manufacturing companies, from large insurance companies and major banks, from prestigious "white shoe" law firms, from the faculties of Ivy League universities, from prestigious men's clubs in the city and prestigious golf clubs in the suburbs. But this did not prevent the Eastern European Jews from rising higher and faster in other businesses and in the professions than any other identifiable ethnic group in any country in all of history. They tended to have high verbal and math aptitudes and rose to the top ranks in the public schools and city colleges of New York and other large cities. They rose to the top in the garment industry, in retail, in advertising, and in entertainment and show business, the quintessential trade in which pleasing fickle consumers delivered great rewards. Jews were amazingly successful, quickly coming to dominate the Broadway theater, Tin Pan Alley, and Hollywood.

A common element in their success stories is an exquisite sensitivity to the changing tastes and desires of people of entirely different backgrounds—a sensitivity undoubtedly honed from their experience of persecution when the ability to gauge the attitudes of goyim could literally mean the difference between not only profit and loss but also life and death. Retailers like Julius Rosenwald of Sears and advertising men like Albert Lasker of Lord & Thomas amassed great fortunes and became major philanthropists; Jews built the first transcontinental trucking company and the United Fruit Company, which pioneered the banana business. Barred from old Wall Street outfits and law firms, German-origin and Eastern European Jews established their own investment banks and law firms; barred from manufacturing corporations, they dominated the scrap metal business. Among the first generation of Jewish immigrants were astonishingly creative artists such as George Gershwin and Irving Berlin and the studio bosses who, speaking in heavily accented and tortured English, nonetheless created the movies of the 1930s and 1940s that personified the basic American character in a way that still speaks to us today.

There was an underside to this dazzling achievement. Jews were also successful in organized crime, in prostitution, in dodgy investment swindles. In politics the Jews remained a people somewhat apart from the rest of America. Many were attracted to socialist and radical movements, as their forebears had been in the tsarist and Hapsburg empires. They valued and appreciated the freedom and tolerance they received in America, but many were hostile to the capitalist system even as many were achieving extraordinary success within it. In New York, where they were most numerous, they were suspicious of the Democratic Party, with its Irish-Catholic–dominated machines, and found little in common with the Republican Party, dominated in the city by the high-prestige WASPs who systematically discriminated against them and by Yankee-stock Upstaters who seemed far removed from their world. A Lower East Side district elected the Socialist congressman Meyer London in 1914, 1916, and 1920 (he was defeated in 1918 after voting against the declaration of war in 1917 and the Sedition and Espionage Acts); and much later, in a 1947 special election, Bronx voters elected Leo Isacson, a supporter of Henry Wallace's Communist-sympathizing Progressive Party. But their favorite politicians were Franklin Roosevelt, who received the support of as much as 80 percent of Jewish voters, and Fiorello La Guardia, whose mother was Jewish and who was elected to Congress in 1920 on the Republican and Socialist tickets; he was also elected mayor in 1933 as an opponent of the machine Democrats and reelected in 1937 and 1941 as a Fusion candidate of the Republican and American Labor parties.

The Ellis Island immigrants—Italians, Poles, and other Slavs, Eastern European Jews—came from quite different backgrounds and had quite different experiences in America. But they stood out together as a new and different kind of immigrant who, in the view of many Americans, posed a threat to the basic American character of the nation. They came, after all, not only with little money but with little experience in republican traditions or democratic politics, and to most Americans they seemed to be a different race, or races, from the dominant British-origin majority or even the German- and Scandinavian-origin minorities. They spoke languages—Italian dialects, Slavic languages, Yiddish—with which ordinary Americans had no acquaintance and which seemed, though this was unfair, to have little cultural heritage worthy of respect; and a great many of them were illiterate in any language. They clustered in the nation's big cities, most especially in New York, where the influx of Italians and Jews was responsible for the enormous growth that enabled it to remain America's largest city at a time when it appeared that Chicago might overtake it. The neighborhoods where the immigrants originally clustered were tightly packed and seemed a threat to public health— advances in which were one of the great achievements of the late nineteenth and early twentieth centuries. The novelist Henry James, returning to New York in 1904 after long years in Britain and Europe, was appalled at the slums of the Lower East Side and wrote witheringly of the Italian and especially the Jewish immigrants he saw there. President Theodore Roosevelt, from an even more patrician background but with practical experience in New York politics and law enforcement, decried those who would be "hyphenated Americans" and insisted on the importance of Americanizing Ellis Island immigrants, even while recognizing their particular interests as he adopted policies and made appointments aimed at gaining their votes.

The vast tide of Ellis Islanders in the years from 1902 to 1914 sparked demands for restricting immigration. The impression that this was an enormous addition to the population was not inaccurate: those years saw the heaviest immigration as a percentage of preexisting population in American history, roughly tied with the influx of Scots-Irish in the years just before the Revolution and the huge Irish and German immigrations of the decade starting in 1846. Those tides of immigration had been halted or sharply reduced by the outbreak of wars, the Revolutionary War and the Civil War, which few had anticipated. Similarly, in the first decade of the twentieth century almost no one anticipated that the Ellis Island immigration would be halted, as it was, by the outbreak of World War I in 1914 (it was still high in that calendar year, since most immigration tended to occur in the spring and summer, when shipping conditions were most favorable, and the war started only in August). The Ellis Island immigration was contributing to economic growth, by supplying unskilled labor for the factories and garment sweatshops, but to many Americans it seemed to be changing the character of the nation, and for the worse.

Americans in the South and in the great farmlands and small towns in the Northeast and Midwest, as separate and distinct as they remained decades after the Civil War, still together feared that they would be outnumbered by alien newcomers and would be outvoted by the huddled masses in the great cities. The upper-class WASP presidents of the first two decades of the twentieth century (when graduates of Harvard, Yale, and Princeton followed each other in office, with all three running in the tumultuous election of 1912) did not favor limits on immigration: Theodore Roosevelt preached Americanization and William Howard Taft and Woodrow Wilson both vetoed bills restricting immigration. But the demand for such legislation increased after World War I, even as the expansion of government powers in wartime made such control suddenly seem feasible. After the war immigration spiked upward, from an annual rate of 234,000 in 1915–19 to 550,000 in 1920–24—well below the 956,000 of 1902–14 but still higher than in any previous period. The 1920 Census, which for the first time showed a majority of Americans living in urban areas (defined as those with populations more than 2,500), stimulated fears of change. For the only time in history Congress refused to reapportion the number of House of Representative members among the states, despite the Constitution's requirement that it do so, on the grounds that urban areas should not have such political power. And in 1921 and 1924 Congress passed restrictive immigration laws that were signed by Presidents Warren Harding and Calvin Coolidge—whose hometowns of Marion, Ohio, and Northampton, Massachusetts, were just the kind of places where residents felt threatened by the influx of Ellis Islanders. The 1924 law explicitly limited immigration from foreign countries to the percentage of the population they accounted for in 1890, thus essentially closing the doors of Ellis Island to immigrants from southern and eastern Europe. There could have been no more explicit repudiation of the Ellis Island immigration and no clearer statement that America wanted no more of it.

It has been asserted that the 1921 and 1924 laws provided America with a "time out" in which it could assimilate the newcomers. But assimilation had been going on before those laws were passed and continued in the 1920s at roughly the same pace. And even if these laws had not been passed, immigration would surely have been reduced to minimal numbers by another event almost no one anticipated, the Depression of the 1930s. In that decade immigration (and internal migration within the United States) was minimal, the lowest in our history, and some former immigrants returned to their original countries. The only immigrants who would probably have arrived then if the 1920s legislation had not been passed would have been Jews and others seeking refuge from Hitler's Germany; it is hard to argue that the United States would have been worse off opening the door to them.

THE pace and volume of northward migration from the American South in the first four decades of the twentieth century was not much greater than in the last three decades of the nineteenth, with the exception of the churning sparked by the relatively brief mobilization effort in World War I. Much has been written about the "great migration" of southern blacks to northern cities starting in World War I and continuing through the 1920s. But it was of much smaller magnitude than the truly great migration that began in 1940 and continued through 1965. The percentage of blacks living in the North (almost entirely in cities) increased from 11 percent in 1910 to 23 percent in 1940. But it increased from 23 percent in 1940 to 47 percent in 1970. Or consider the number of blacks living in the North. That number increased from 1.1 million in 1910 to 3.0 million in 1940. But that increase was dwarfed by the increase from 3.0 million in 1940 to 10.5 million in 1970. In 1940 blacks were still a relatively small minority, outnumbered heavily in most cases by those of immigrant stock, in northern cities. Only three of the ten largest cities had black percentages over 10 percent—Baltimore (19 percent), St. Louis (13 percent), and Philadelphia (13 percent)—and two of the three were in states that allowed slavery until the Civil War. By 1970, eight of the largest twenty cities had black percentages over 30 percent, led by Washington (72 percent), where the black community was established by freed slaves before the Civil War and which grew rapidly from the 1930s on; the others were Baltimore (46 percent), New Orleans (45 percent), Detroit (44 percent), St. Louis (41 percent), Cleveland (38 percent), Philadelphia (34 percent), and Chicago (33 percent). Only three, Seattle and San Diego on the West Coast and San Antonio in south Texas, had black percentages under 10 percent.

Overall, what is remarkable about the period from the Civil War to World War II is not how many southern blacks and whites moved to the North, but how few did. This is as clear a refutation as the real world affords of the theory that American migration was primarily an economic phenomenon. Southern Americans were subject to economic incentives similar to those of European immigrants—wages were much higher in the North than where they were living—and they were faced with much less formidable barriers to movement. Yet very few moved. The wounds of the Civil War stayed fresh and raw for three-quarters of a century, and the American majority in the North, after abandoning Reconstruction, was willing to let the white majority in the South run their society without interference. The migration that didn't happen shaped the nation as surely as any of the great migrations that did occur.

5. PROMISED LANDS

GREAT wars change nations. The Revolutionary War transformed the seaboard colonies into one culturally diverse nation heading westward across a continent but vexed by the increasingly irresolvable issue of slavery. The Civil War resolved that issue but split the nation, with the South largely walling itself off from the rest of the nation for three generations and the North content to leave the wall mostly unbreached. World War II, as unforeseen and undesired as the Civil War, did something like the opposite, welding together a nation flying apart from the centrifugal vectors of successive surges of migration and of the great migration that did not happen. Three-quarters of blacks lived in the segregated South. Ethnically identifiable neighborhoods were the rule rather than the exception in the great cities of the North, while the vast tide of Ellis Island immigration barely touched the vast American countryside.

Some factors were bringing Americans together. The nation's entry into World War I resulted in the muster of a large draft army drawn from across the nation and the mobilization of many workers in war industries. But the war for the United States lasted only nineteen months from the declaration of war in April 1917 to the Armistice in November 1918. And the Wilson administration's actions during that war—not just challenging the patriotism of millions of Americans, but persecuting and prosecuting opponents of the war and eradicating in large part the culture of German-Americans—tended to split some large numbers of Americans rather than unite them. In the prosperous years of the 1920s, as automobile ownership became commonplace, states began building the networks of paved roads that would enable Americans to travel about their country more easily than they could on passenger trains, which were patronized largely by the affluent. Technology made possible the development of a popular culture with near-universal appeal, silent movies starting in the 1910s, radio starting in the 1920s, talkies—movies with sound—starting in 1927 and wiping out the silents by 1930. The innovators in these universal media were not concentrated on the East Coast. Radio formats were pioneered more often in Chicago and even Detroit than in New York, while moviemakers quickly abandoned New York for the sunny skies of Southern California and Los Angeles's recently annexed suburb of Hollywood.

The movies of the 1930s and 1940s, the strongest popular culture since Dickens, presented a vision of what was typically American that continues to resonate three-quarters of a century later. Yet most of the studio bosses were Jewish immigrants or sons of immigrants who spoke in broken English or with heavy New York accents. The genius and habits of mind that enabled their ancestors to survive in the shtetlach of eastern Europe enabled them to make millions in their adopted land. They made movie stars who had Ellis Island backgrounds change their names and downplayed their immigrant roots. The nation's ethnic variety was more evident in sports, as broadcast over the radio and replayed in newsreels. Blacks were excluded from major league baseball, but Jesse Owens was a national hero when he won four gold medals at the 1936 Olympics in Berlin—Hitler skipped the medal ceremony—and in 1937 Joe Louis became an icon as heavyweight boxing champion. Baseball stars included Georgia-born Ty Cobb and many Southerners but also Jews such as Hank Greenberg and Italians like Joe DiMaggio; Babe Ruth and Lou Gehrig used to speak German with each other.

Nevertheless the Depression of the 1930s in many ways kept Americans apart. Population growth and mobility in the decade from 1930 to 1940 was the lowest in American history. The migration of the Okies in ramshackle cars over U.S. 66 to the Central Valley of California, after dust storms turned the sky black and blew the topsoil off large swaths of the Great Plains, caught the public's imagination, thanks in large part to John Steinbeck's novel *The Grapes of Wrath* and the 1939 movie based on it.[1] But even though Oklahoma's population declined during the decade, this was not a migration of the demographic heft of the others in this book; it involves tens of thousands of people, not hundreds of thousands or millions.

Of an entirely different scale were the movements and migration set in motion by World War II. Mobilization of industry started in May 1940, when William Knudsen, then president of General Motors, was appointed by Franklin Roosevelt to build up America's capacity for wartime production, which Knudsen did by persuasion rather than command over the next eighteen months.[2] Mobilization of personnel began when Congress at Roosevelt's urging approved a military draft in August 1940; the first draft numbers were plucked from a fishbowl by Secretary of War Henry Stimson in October 1940. During the five years until Germany's surrender in May 1945 and Japan's surrender in September 1945 some 16 million Americans out of a population of 131 million served in the military; a proportionate number in 2010 would be 38 million. A similar number of civilians had their lives transformed as well. Hundreds of thousands moved to work in defense industries, clustered in seaports like Baltimore and Philadelphia, manufacturing centers like Detroit and Chicago, new aircraft assembly lines and shipyards in Los Angeles, the San Francisco Bay Area, and Seattle. All Americans were subject to wage and price controls and to food rationing, and high earners were subjected to near-confiscatory tax rates of 91 percent. The war moved Americans around and mixed them together more than in both the previous and the following three-quarters of a century.

These experiences, especially service in the military, brought Americans together in a process well described by Thomas Bruscino in *A Nation Forged in War: How World War II Taught Americans to Get Along*.[3] For almost all of the preceding three-quarters of a century the

United States had had only a small military, set apart from the rest of society, on duty in western frontier posts or in the far-off Philippines. Now the large majority of young American men were put into uniform, their hair was cut short, and their privacy, eliminated. Some were in territorially defined units, with members from one part of the country, but most were in units with men from all over the country. This became a cliché in the World War II movies, with units that had a guy from the South, a factory kid from Detroit or Pittsburgh, a farm boy from the Great Plains, and a loudmouthed guy—ethnicity not spelled out, but probably Irish or Italian or Jewish—from Brooklyn. The inclusion of Brooklyn was demographically valid; in 1940, 2 percent of all Americans lived there. The movies always showed that however different the unlikely compatriots initially seemed and sounded, they all ended up getting along and looking out for one another as soldiers in combat usually do. The reality may not have been so idyllic as in the movies, but as was often the case, the movies of this era encapsulated even as they idealized the American experience. The universality of the military experience and the similar experience of working in wartime production, often overtime and under great stress, promoted a sense of fellow feeling and civic equality, the sense that no matter how high your income and how venerated your ancestors, you had to wait your turn in line and march in order just like everyone else. It made Americans more conformist, more comfortable with working in large organizations, as small cogs in very large machines.

As Bruscino notes, the one large group not mixed together in military service was black Americans (who were enrolled in segregated units). Even if blacks were not allowed to serve with whites, recruits were taken out of the segregated South, where 77 percent of blacks lived in 1940, as were the very large number of blacks who were recruited or volunteered to work in defense industries and as civilians in defense installations. Moreover, the fact that black servicemen risked death and disfigurement but were not treated equally at home made many whites uncomfortable and turned out to be a strong argument for the civil rights movement after the war.

World War II set many Americans in motion and opened up to many of them what seemed to be promised lands, places where they could pursue their dreams much more than in the places where they had grown up. It sparked two surges of migration, which lasted a generation or more after the war. One was the northward migration of one-third of American blacks from the segregated South to the big cities of the North. The other was the migration from the often bitterly cold climates of the North to the sunny, temperate climate of California.

AS noted earlier, in 1940 more than three out of four, 77 percent, of American blacks lived in the segregated South. In 1940 Mississippi's population was 49 percent black and South Carolina's was 43 percent black—near-majorities—while three other Deep South states, Louisiana, Alabama, and Georgia, had populations that were more than one-third black. Except for Maryland and Delaware, no northern state had a population more than 6 percent black, and most northern states had populations that were 1 percent or less black. "One-eighth of the whole population were colored slaves," Abraham Lincoln in his Second Inaugural noted of the nation before the Civil War, "not distributed generally over the Union, but localized in the southern part of it." Because of heavy immigration, the black population had declined from 14 percent of the total in 1860 (Lincoln evidently didn't like the sound of "one-seventh") to 10 percent in 1940, but it was still mostly "localized in the southern part of it." Three-quarters of a century had not made a great difference.

Of course some blacks had migrated northward during that period, just as some Scots-Irish came over before their 1763–75 surge and some Irish Catholics landed before the potato famine struck in 1845. The northward migration started as a trickle in the first years of the twentieth century, accelerated with the onset of World War I, and continued during the 1920s, then slowed down markedly in the

Depression of the 1930s, when few Americans left the security provided by the vegetable patch in a small farm for the sudden insecurity of life in the big city where banks were failing and cash was needed for food, shelter, and clothing. In the 1920s this became known as "the Great Migration," with the growth of identifiable black neighborhoods in the nation's two largest cities—Harlem in New York and Bronzeville in Chicago—and with the doubling of the long-established black community in North Philadelphia in the third largest. The popularity of jazz music and the allure of Harlem and Bronzeville nightlife inspired much literati journalism and some sociological investigation. But blacks remained vastly outnumbered by white ethnics in these northern cities, and demographically the Great Migration was a much smaller phenomenon than the migration that started in 1940 and ended in 1965. The percentage of blacks living outside the South increased from 10 percent in 1900 to 23 percent in 1940—a sizable and noticeable increase, but over forty years averaging only about one-half of 1 percent each year. The percentage of blacks living outside the South increased much more in the next generation, from 23 percent in 1940 to 47 percent in 1965—averaging over twenty-five years nearly 1 percent each year. It had double the impact of the Great Migration over just a little more than half the time.

Government played a prime role in spurring the great northward migration. The sharp increase in defense production, combined with the first effects of the military draft, created a huge demand for labor, skilled and unskilled. In the 1930s unemployment ranged up to 22 percent and never fell below 16 percent; it fell abruptly to 5 percent in 1942, the first full year after Pearl Harbor, and 1 percent to 2 percent through 1945. As "the arsenal of democracy"—war production chief and former General Motors president William Knudsen's term, appropriated without acknowledgment by Roosevelt—ramped up production, the total size of the workforce plus the military increased by 35 percent during the war, from 48 million to 65 million. The economy was transformed from one where workers were looking for jobs to one where employers were looking desperately for workers.

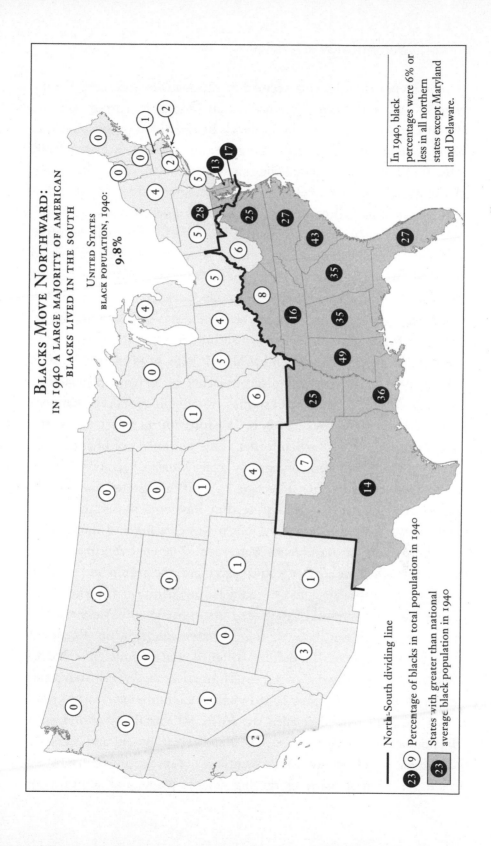

Blacks Move Northward:
IN 1940 A LARGE MAJORITY OF AMERICAN
BLACKS LIVED IN THE SOUTH

United States
Black population, 1940:
9.8%

In 1940, black percentages were 6% or less in all northern states except Maryland and Delaware.

—— North-South dividing line

⑨ Percentage of blacks in total population in 1940

❷❸ States with greater than national average black population in 1940

Suddenly the wall that seemed to block white and black Southerners from going north seemed to fall down. In spring 1941 A.
Philip Randolph, head of the all-black Brotherhood of Sleeping Car
Porters, demanded that blacks be given an equal chance at defense
jobs. Randolph had founded the porters' union in 1925, when none
of the railway unions accepted blacks as members. He built it with a
core of disciplined, literate members, rooted in every black neighborhood in American cities, who traveled around the country and acted
as "civil rights messengers on wheels."[4] Porters routinely circulated
black newspapers published in northern cities, especially the *Chicago
Defender* and the *Pittsburgh Courier*, to black readers in the South.[5] In
April 1941, before Pearl Harbor, the National Negro Council urged
Franklin Roosevelt to end racial discrimination in the federal government by executive order and Walter White, head of the NAACP,
asked union leaders to end discrimination by defense contractors.
When they got no positive response, Randolph proposed that tens
of thousands of Negroes march in Washington on July 1 unless the
administration issued such an order. This was an act of breathtaking
audacity: there had been controversy when Interior Secretary Harold
Ickes, former head of the Chicago NAACP, integrated the department's cafeteria a few years before. But Randolph sensed, correctly,
that the war gave him leverage, that it was creating vast numbers of
new jobs, and that once blacks were seen to be contributing equally
to the war effort and making equal sacrifices, the argument that they
should not be treated equally would be undermined. He knew also
that Roosevelt, mindful of the race riots in the World War I era, did
not want to risk the disorder that a march might bring. Roosevelt
tried to out-negotiate Randolph, but failed, and on June 25 issued an
executive order banning racial discrimination in defense industries
and creating a Fair Employment Practices Commission.

Historians have described the FEPC as toothless and indeed it
did not have sweeping legal powers. But its creation sent an unmistak-
able signal to defense industry executives and black Americans: blacks
could get hired at many of the big defense plants and shipyards of

the Northeast, the industrial Midwest, and the West Coast. Large firms like General Motors and leaders of the United Auto Workers union favored giving blacks a chance and during the course of the war some 1 million were hired. In the past southern plantation owners and community leaders, desperate to maintain their supply of cheap labor, had discouraged blacks from heading north, to the point of arresting blacks in the vicinity of train stations for vagrancy and putting them in jail.[6] Now the president of the United States, and a president of the Democratic Party, which virtually all southern whites supported, was weighing in against such practices and declaring them a detriment to the war effort. Moreover, as the war went on another development occurred that changed southern whites' attitudes and southern blacks' situation: the introduction in 1944 of the first practical mechanical cotton picker. A fieldworker could pick 20 pounds of cotton an hour; the mechanical cotton picker could pick 1,000 pounds an hour. The machine could do the work of fifty people and reduce the cost of picking cotton by more than 80 percent.[7] Southern planters who had worked for years to prevent blacks from moving now had a motive to buy them one-way train or bus tickets to the North. The demand for workers was plummeting in the South even as it boomed in the North. For the first time since Reconstruction large numbers of American blacks had the chance to live and work unconstrained by the rigid laws and practices of southern segregation. They were able to escape to what seemed in those hectic days to be a promised land.

BEFORE the war for most Americans California was an exotic land of palm trees and movie studios, religious cults and beaches, which they had never visited and expected never to actually see. Americans had been moving there at varying rates, but for many years only in small numbers since it had been acquired from Mexico in the Treaty of Guadalupe Hidalgo in 1848 and gold was found at Sutter's Mill near Sacramento in 1849. California then was almost entirely vacant, with brown rolling hills and barren plains, inhabited by a few thousand Mexicans and Indians and a scattering of Americans and foreigners. Even with the arrival of thousands of Forty Niners seeking gold (or, in many cases more profitably, providing food, clothing, and supplies to gold seekers), the 1850 Census reported only 92,000 people in California, with perhaps 34,000 more unreported in San Francisco, an instant city that sprang up in a single year, 1849 (the corresponding census records were destroyed by fire). Most of the rest of the population was up in gold country in the foothills of the Sierra Nevada; Los Angeles County had only 3,530 people; San Diego County, only 796. By one estimate the nonindigenous population of the state increased from 14,000 in 1848 to 225,000 in 1852.[8] For many years connections to the rest of the United States were limited. The Pony Express, operated for eighteen months in 1860 and 1861, reduced the time for passage of messages from the bulk of the country to ten days. The telegraph, completed in 1861, provided instantaneous but not always dependable communication. The iron rails of the transcontinental railroad, completed in 1869, linked California to the rest of the nation. But the line, financed by the government and milked of profits by its promoters, was chronically unprofitable, and into the twentieth century more goods were transported between California and the rest of the country by ship than on land.[9]

The state was peopled with an unusual variety: for most of the second half of the nineteenth century San Francisco had the largest foreign-born percentage of population of any large American city, and from the 1850s to the 1880s more than 10 percent of its population was Chinese-born, almost all of them men. Resentment at the Chinese men's willingness to work hard for low wages sparked creation of the San Francisco–based Workingmen's Party and ultimately led Congress to pass the aptly named Chinese Exclusion Act of 1882, which barred all Chinese immigration to the United States.[10] California in those years was a minor contributor to the American economy but a strategic military outpost, and indeed President James K. Polk had instructed the envoy he sent in 1848 to negotiate the treaty ending the Mexican War to make sure to obtain not only San Francisco Bay but also San Diego Harbor as ports for the U.S. Navy. In the late nineteenth and early twentieth centuries Californians in Congress, Julius Kahn of San Francisco and William Kettner of San Diego, worked successfully to establish hometown military bases.[11] With the buildup of the navy starting in Benjamin Harrison's administration in 1889 and symbolized by Theodore Roosevelt's dispatch of the Great White Fleet to sail around the world from December 1907 to February 1909, California emerged as the nation's military bastion on the Pacific, with California-built ships entering Manila Harbor in the Spanish-American War in 1898 and California-based troops fighting in the guerrilla conflict in the Philippines over the next four years.[12]

"California, Here I Come" is a song written for a long-forgotten Broadway musical from 1921 and one considered a state anthem by many ever since. Richard Nixon, a California native who carried California in six elections (and lost it once) but chose to live his last years in New York and New Jersey, ordered it played at slow tempo at his funeral. But it can also be said to be the theme song for one of the great migrations of American history, when California was the destination of one of the nation's greatest surges of internal migration a century after it was admitted to the Union as part of the Compromise of 1850.

California in the early twentieth century still seemed far removed from and only lightly connected with the rest of the nation. With faster-than-average population growth from 1850 to 1890 and average growth in the economically troubled 1890s, it still was home to only 2 percent of the nation's population in 1900. Another 3 percent lived in the other western states, so that 95 percent of all Americans lived between the Atlantic and the Great Plains. The first four decades of the twentieth century saw explosive growth in California, especially in the Los Angeles metropolitan area or, as it was becoming known, Southern California. The state's population expanded from 1.5 million to 6.9 million, with Southern California (Los Angeles, Orange, Riverside, and San Bernardino Counties) growing from 235,000 to 3.2 million, and the San Francisco Bay Area from 641,000 to 1.7 million. This growth came despite relatively few Ellis Island immigrants or their offspring making their way that far west, even in San Francisco where the Jewish community remained predominantly of German origin (like the Levi Strauss family) and the Italians predominantly from northern Italy (like Joe DiMaggio). Nor, despite California's geographical position directly west of the Confederate states, did many Southerners move there; the invisible wall between South and North seemed to extend southward to the Rio Grande somewhere in west Texas. The Americans moving to California in these years came mainly from the Great Plains states, the sons and daughters of large farm families who, with undependable rainfall and increasingly mechanized production, had had enough of farming and instead headed west, over the mostly inhospitable Rockies and into the golden land of California. Angelenos from the Great Plains were referred to offhandedly as Iowans, and Long Beach became known as "Iowa by the Sea"; the annual Iowa picnics in its Bixby Park drew 100,000 in the years around 1940 and were a must event for campaigning politicians.[13] This was the farthest westward migration of the Yankee diaspora, leavened by migrants from Germano-Scandinavian America. They brought with them a midwestern cheeriness and mostly Republican politics, but were also open to progressive and even populist causes. The midwestern newcomers of those decades did much to establish California's ethos and civic personality, as typified in many ways by an Illinois native and Iowa radio announcer who took a train west, wangled a screen test, and got a movie contract in 1937, Ronald Reagan.

This California in the first decades of the twentieth century was, as novelist Helen Hunt Jackson called it and as journalist Carey McWilliams subtitled one of his marvelous books on the state, "an island on the land." The San Francisco Bay Area and the Los Angeles Basin were still far from filled up; there were apricot orchards in the land that later became Silicon Valley, and Los Angeles County, with dairy farms and orange groves in between its mile-square grid streets, was the nation's number one county in agricultural production. Hollywood, a small suburb recently annexed by Los Angeles, became the center of what its creators called the motion picture industry almost precisely in 1915,[14] its mild weather and clear air making outdoor shooting possible almost every day of the year. Talking pictures were introduced in 1927, and in the Depression year of 1930 in a nation of 123 million, average movie attendance was 100 million weekly. Hollywood stars, Hollywood gossip columnists, and Hollywood fan magazines gave Americans a glamorous picture of life in Southern California. And so occasionally did major sports events, even though California had no major league baseball teams until 1957, including the 1932 Los Angeles Olympics and the epic but brief career of the racehorse Seabiscuit in 1937 and 1938.[15]

From all this Americans got the impression that California was an exotic place. "This is the California," John Gunther wrote in *Inside U.S.A.*, published just after World War II, "of petroleum, crazy religious cults, the citrus industry, towns based on rich rentiers like Santa Barbara and Pasadena, the movies, the weirdest architecture in the United States, refugees from Iowa, a steeply growing Negro population, and devotees of funny money."[16] The birthplace of the Pentecostal movement was a church on Azusa Street in Los Angeles in 1906, and Southern California's reputation as a center of religious cults was firmly established after national headlines screamed the news of Pentecostal radio evangelist Aimee Semple McPherson's disappearance from Venice Beach in May 1926. She turned up a month later in Mexico, just south of Douglas, Arizona, then resumed preaching at her Angelus Temple in the Echo Park neighborhood of Los Angeles. California also spawned odd-duck leftist political movements in a decade when extremist political ideologies seemed on the march abroad. Labor unions, led by the Communist Harry Bridges, staged a general strike in San Francisco in July 1934—the only general strike in American history.[17] That same year the elderly novelist Upton Sinclair ran as the Democratic candidate for governor on an End Poverty In California platform, calling for state economic planning, land colonies, and $50 monthly pensions for everyone over fifty years old. Conservative interests rallied and raised large sums for his Republican opponent, spent according to the recommendations of pioneer political consultants Clem Whitaker and Leone Baxter, and Sinclair lost by a 49 percent–38 percent margin; but the capture of a major party nomination by such a radical was a phenomenon not matched anywhere "back east," as Californians put it, except in Huey Long's Louisiana. Then there were the Townsend plan, sponsored by a Long Beach physician, for $200 monthly pensions to unemployed persons over sixty, to be financed by a national sales tax; and the Ham and Eggs movement, which called for paying everyone over sixty $25 every Monday. Ham and Eggs was endorsed by California unions and in 1938 helped elect Sheridan Downey as senator and Culbert Olson as governor, the state's only Democrat in that position between 1898 and 1958.[18] In 1940 California still contained only 5 percent of the nation's population and was connected to the rest of the country by western states that together held only another 5 percent. Some 90 percent of Americans still lived back east and only a small number seemed interested in moving to such a distant and exotic place. It was the nation's leading agricultural state and a major food producer, but had relatively little manufacturing; radio advertisements regularly noted that prices are "higher on the West Coast."

The war changed this, by sparking a demographically significant surge of migration into the Golden State, transforming California from a distant regional center to a national economic dynamo. In 1940 California produced 20 percent of the nation's oil at a time when the United States was the world's major oil exporter, and it was the home base of much of the nation's young aviation industry. The attack on Pearl Harbor seemed to put California on the front lines, and many feared an invasion. In February 1942 a Japanese submarine cruised off the coast of San Diego, surfaced near Santa Barbara, and fired on oil tanks there. There were fears that Japanese Americans and alien Japanese would commit acts of sabotage, despite scant evidence, and in March 1942 the army rounded up 112,000 of them in the three West Coast states and placed them in internment camps inland until January

1945. President Franklin Roosevelt signed the order, eagerly sought by California attorney general Earl Warren, who defeated liberal governor Culbert Olson in November 1942 in large part on this issue.[19]

California's military bases were greatly enlarged and filled with soldiers, airmen, and sailors headed to the Pacific theater. One million soldiers were processed at Camp Stoneman in the East Bay port of Pittsburg and 10,000 civilians worked across the Carquinez Strait at the Mare Island Shipyard in Vallejo and at Hunters Point in San Francisco; the navy mess hall at Treasure Island in San Francisco Bay could serve 6,000 sailors; air bases were built at Hamilton Field in Marin County and El Toro in Orange County; San Diego County was jammed with 125,000 soldiers, sailors, and Marines. Even more were working in new defense installations. The Kaiser Shipyard at Richmond in the East Bay, which could turn out a ship in four and a half days, employed 91,000 people at its peak; in Los Angeles County 230,000 were working at the Douglas, Lockheed, Vega, Northrop, and North American aviation factories, and Lockheed's cafeteria in Burbank served 60,000 meals a day; Henry J. Kaiser, whose construction firm had helped build Hoover Dam, set up the Richmond shipyard and built a steel mill in Fontana, east of Los Angeles, the only steel mill on the West Coast; the Consolidated Vultee Aircraft factory employed 48,000 in San Diego, which, Gunther wrote, "was easily the most crowded city in the United States."[20] In the Los Angeles Basin more than 100,000 defense workers commuted more than 50 miles each day.

During the war years the government brought to California more Americans than had ever set foot in the state before. Millions of servicemen were assigned to or passed through California during the war and many hundreds of thousands flocked in to work in the defense industries. During the war years Los Angeles County's population rose from 2.8 million to 3.4 million and the San Francisco Bay Area increased from 1.7 million to 2.2 million. The state's black population more than doubled in the war years, with migrants primarily from Louisiana and Texas; white Southerners arrived as well, and in greater numbers than the Okies who had abandoned their Dust Bowl farms in the 1930s for the lush irrigated fields of the Central Valley. Midwesterners from the prairie and Great Plains states made their way west to join others from the area, like Ronald Reagan and John Wayne, who had made the same trek to work in the motion picture industry.

⸺

DURING the war and in the immediate postwar years the North offered southern blacks a life where they would not be restricted by laws and mores enforcing a rigid system of racial segregation and providing everyday reminders of their inferior status. Blacks' newspapers and the black magazine *Ebony* were particularly influential in shaping southern black opinion. The circulation of the *Chicago Defender*, which referred to northward migration as "the exodus," rose to 230,000 in the 1920s, the large majority of its subscribers living outside of Chicago; the *Pittsburgh Courier* was selling 277,000 copies in the 1940s. *Ebony*, founded in 1947, quickly sold 400,000 copies a month.[21] They portrayed an abusive South and an inviting North, where blacks were treated as equals, where black men were not referred to as "boy" or "uncle," where the taboo that they could enter whites' homes only by the back door was unheard of. Blacks could shake hands with whites in the North, they could ride with them in the front of buses, they could wait in lines without being shunted to the back, and they could eat at restaurants with whites and carouse in nightclubs with them, too. They would be free as well from the constant threat of violence, violence that was sanctioned by those who ruled the community, if they failed to live up to the unwritten code. The North was depicted as a promised land, one that was now ready for settlement, where black men and women could find jobs and be treated with a dignity they had never experienced before. Black migrants to the North before 1940 had been relatively well educated and the new migrants on average tended to be, too. But there was also work for those with little education and few skills. Black newspaper editors and leaders of black organizations encouraged northward migration and saw it as the only way for blacks to escape the southern system of segregation.

With the spread of the mechanical cotton picker reducing the demand for black labor in the rural South and with the onset of postwar prosperity and the continued lure of a promised land in the North, where segregation was unknown, the black northward flow continued and at times grew even larger for the next two decades after the war. Patterns of migration tended to follow the railroads. From Mississippi blacks headed straight north on the Illinois Central or the parallel U.S. 51 to Chicago. From Alabama blacks headed up the Louisville & Nashville to Detroit. From coastal South Carolina, North Carolina, and Virginia blacks headed up the Atlantic Coast Line to Philadelphia and New York. Much of this was a chain migration, with the first pioneers joined by relatives and friends or acquaintances from their old home area. "For a time, in the late 1950s and early 1960s," writes journalist Nicholas Lemann, "it seemed as if the whole black society of Clarksdale and the Mississippi Delta had transferred itself to Chicago. Everybody was either living in Chicago, or going back and forth to Chicago, or occasionally visiting Chicago. Certain venues in Chicago were known to be gathering places for Clarksdalians—taverns on the South Side, kitchenette apartment buildings, weekly-rate residential hotels on the Near West Side. Children would be sent up for the summer to stay with relatives and get jobs that paid much better than chopping cotton on the plantations back home."[22] This was in very large part a movement of young people who saw continued menace and lack of opportunity in the South, where they had grown up. One-quarter of southern blacks between ages twenty and twenty-four migrated north in the 1940s and another one-quarter went north in the 1950s. More than one-third of young blacks in the Cotton Belt states—South Carolina, Georgia, Alabama, Mississippi—headed north in the 1940s.[23] Chicago's black population increased from 278,000 in 1940 to 492,000 in 1950 and 813,000 in 1960. New York's black population increased from 458,000 in 1940 to 748,000 in 1950 and 1,088,000 in 1960. The ten largest cities in

1940, all in the North, had a total black population of 1,646,000; by 1960, the black population in these cities was 4,205,000. The vast numbers of southern blacks moving in transformed the racial balance in many central cities. By 1970, nearly three-quarters of the residents of Washington, D.C., were black. There were black near-majorities in Detroit and Baltimore, and one-third or more of the residents of Cleveland, Chicago, and Philadelphia were black, as were one-quarter of the residents of New York City.[24] The northern cities became new homelands for southern-raised blacks who had mostly lived in rural areas or small towns.

But the promised land was not ready to deliver on all the promises it seemed to offer. Northern whites did not want to impose a system of legal segregation like the South's. They were willing to see blacks among people generally in stores and shops, in movie theaters, even in restaurants, though not so much in swimming pools or parks. A riot broke out in Detroit in June 1943 over a black-white altercation on Belle Isle, the Frederick Law Olmsted–designed park on a large island in the Detroit River. Rioting went on for three days, with twenty-five blacks and nine whites killed, until federal troops were sent in and restored order. But most of all, "Whites did not want blacks next door," as historians Stephan Thernstrom and Abigail Thernstrom write. "Even before the Great Migration, when the African-American population was too small to seem truly threatening, a color line had to be drawn."[25] The uncomfortable fact is that housing was effectively segregated in northern cities, even more than in much of the South where residential proximity of whites and blacks did not mean that their children would have to attend school together or that the adults would have social relations as equals with their neighbors. Since little housing had been constructed anywhere in the United States in the 1930s (with the prominent exception of Washington, D.C.) and construction ceased in the war years, this meant that in wartime blacks were jammed into the relatively small neighborhoods where they had been living before the 1940s. The larger black ghettoes—Bronzeville, Harlem, North Philadelphia—

were jammed, but the overcrowding was even greater in Detroit's Paradise Valley, just a few blocks wide, and similar neighborhoods in Cleveland and other northern industrial cities as well as in Los Angeles and the San Francisco Bay Area.

This confinement to small ghettoes ended after the war. Postwar prosperity and government-guarantee mortgage programs generated new housing construction, and whites quickly moved out to the remaining vacant areas within the city limits and across the line to the suburbs beyond. Blacks rapidly moved out of the enclaves to which they had been confined during the war. Identifiably ethnic neighborhoods had been the norm in northern cities at least since the surge of Irish Catholic migration started in the 1840s. But ethnic separation was seldom as stark as the racial patterns that resulted from the decisions of blacks to move outward and the decisions of most whites to move out. "Neighborhood change" became a vivid and real fact of life in northern cities, though seldom commented on in the press, and it was rapid. Chicago's West Side neighborhood of Lawndale, a fairly typical area, was 13 percent black in 1950 and 91 percent black in 1960.[26] I saw the process firsthand in Detroit in the 1950s when my father would take me with him to the hospital for Saturday rounds and would point out neighborhoods—whole square miles—that had changed from all white to almost all black within the past year.

Whites' attitudes had institutional sanction. The Federal Housing Administration limited loans to all-white neighborhoods and newspaper Classified sections had different listings for "Homes, White" and "Homes, Colored." The appearance of a few black home owners or renters in a neighborhood was usually greeted with hostility or even violence and often resulted in panic selling by whites. These practices continued despite the U.S. Supreme Court's 1948 decision ruling that racial covenants on title deeds prohibiting sales to blacks could not be enforced in court and despite passage in New York of a state law banning racial discrimination in housing sales in 1957. After California passed a similar law in 1963, it was voted down in a referendum in 1964 with 65 percent of the vote. Not until passage of the federal fair housing law in 1968 did this kind of racial discrimination start to diminish. An examination of the 1960 Census returns for census tracts (containing usually several thousand people) in large northern metropolitan areas shows dozens of tracts in central cities and most tracts in suburbs with exactly zero black residents; by way of comparison the 2010 Census shows very few such tracts in metropolitan areas except those where blacks are a very low percentage of the total population.[27] A recent biography of Chicago mayor Richard J. Daley, first elected in 1955 and mayor until his death in 1976, argues that Daley could have integrated Chicago's neighborhoods if he had had the will to do so.[28] The authors are too young to have memories of the 1950s and 1960s; anyone who grew up in such cities in those times and was paying attention knows that nothing short of martial law could have produced enduring neighborhood racial integration then.

As black neighborhoods grew and spread across the cities—south and west from Chicago's Loop, across all of Harlem and edging outward from Bedford-Stuyvesant and the South Bronx, north and west of Center City Philadelphia, eastward and northwest in Detroit, east from downtown Cleveland—black institutions grew. Northward migrants were somewhat better educated and more ambitious than southern blacks generally;[29] many were young and some considerable number had been in the military, and they had guidance from the educated elites—W. E. B. DuBois's "talented tenth"—the editors of the black newspapers, black doctors and lawyers, and the leaders of the local NAACP, which was building a mass membership after World War II. As in the South, black businesses were relatively rare; the few major black-owned businesses, like Madame C. J. Walker's hair-straightening company and the firm that published *Ebony* magazine, were the exception rather than the rule. "The business infrastructure," writes historian James Gregory, had a southern air, with "barbecue stands and grocery stores emphasizing Southern food ways; insurance companies and funeral clubs based in Atlanta, Durham and other Southern cities and employing business practices familiar to Southerners. In addition, Southerners had introduced styles of music, dance, socializing and worship that over time became standard features of Cleveland and Detroit community life."[30] Newcomers tended to seek jobs in large organizations that increasingly did not discriminate by race: in the big manufacturing firms with their pro-integration industrial unions and the federal, state, and city governments. In many ways blacks' entrepreneurial impulses were channeled into churches. Black preachers had been natural community leaders in the South, and they were in the North as well. Unlike Catholic priests, who could count on the attendance of most Catholics in their geographical parishes, the black preachers had to attract a congregation with articulate and fiery preaching and with first-rate choral music. A prime example is the Reverend C. L. Franklin of Detroit's New Bethel Baptist Church, whose services attracted a congregation of thousands and were broadcast nationally over the radio; getting her start in the choir was his daughter, the singer Aretha Franklin. The churches, writes Gregory, "were gateway institutions that led to other commitments." They "provided much of the impetus behind the distinctive community-building ideology of the period. They were a principal source of the atmosphere of welcome that greeted migrants, of the call to service that the old settlers answered and of the 'we are building the promised land' story that [black] newspapers trumpeted."[31]

The northward migrants did not break all their ties with what they often still regarded as home: people returned for holidays, for the summer. These visits often brought rude and even tragic reminders of the difference between northern and southern mores. When a Lowndes County, Alabama, migrant to Detroit on a return visit forgot to say "Yes, sir," a white storekeeper said, "Don't think just because you've been up North you can forget you were raised here."[32] Emmett Till, a fourteen-year-old raised in Chicago, visited relatives in Mississippi in 1955 and there reportedly "wolf-whistled" at a white woman. He was murdered by two white men who, when tried for the crime, watched the proceedings contemptuously and were quickly acquitted by the inevitably all-white jury.[33] But this case proved to be a turning point. It received wide coverage not only in black media but also in

national media, in which the trial was portrayed as a travesty; in the
courtroom was Charles C. Diggs Jr., in his first year as the third black
member of Congress.

⌒⟋

"*THE* war has brought to final conclusion," wrote Carey McWilliams in 1946, "th[e] insular phase of the development of California
as a state and Southern California as a region." He predicted that
"California will now begin to outgrow some of its eccentric social
mannerisms, contradictory attitudes and narcissistic tendencies."[34]
McWilliams proved more prescient than the experts who predicted
that the bulk of servicemen and defense workers would return home
and leave California after the war ended. They had some reason
to: in the eighteen months after the surrender of the Japanese the
number of defense industry jobs in Los Angeles fell from 300,000
to 78,000. "How will [California] find jobs and residence for them
all?" asked John Gunther in 1947.[35] But California did. In the decade
following the war Los Angeles was the fastest-growing major metropolitan region in the United States. In the years around 1947 it
was generating one out of every eight jobs in the nation and building one out of eleven new houses. The key was not big business—
the auto companies built West Coast assembly plants at the edge of
urban settlement only in the 1950s and 1960s—but small operators.
In her book *The Economy of Cities* Jane Jacobs described what happened. "The new enterprises started in corners of old loft buildings,
in Quonset huts and in backyard garages. But they multiplied swiftly,
mostly by the breakaway method. And many grew rapidly. They
poured forth furnaces, sliding doors, mechanical saws, shoes, bath-
ing suits, underwear, china, furniture, cameras, hand tools, hospital
equipment, scientific instruments, engineering services and hundreds
of other things."[36] Why did they stay? Southern California native
James Q. Wilson explains, "The important thing to know about
Southern California is that the people who live there, who grew up

there, love it. Not just the way one has an attachment to a hometown, any hometown, but the way people love the realization that they have found the right mode of life."

One thing that attracted people to California, especially to Southern California, was the climate. Coastal California between the Pacific and the mountains that seal it off from the Central Valley and the Mojave Desert has what has been called a Mediterranean climate, but it is actually even more pleasant, not too hot in the summer (the thermometer rarely reaches 80° in the Bay Area and 90° in the Los Angeles Basin) and almost never freezing in the winter. The 90 percent of Americans who lived east of the Rockies in 1940 all had to deal with months of unpleasant weather every year: months of gray skies, winters with snow and blustery winds in the North; scalding, pervasive, and humid summers in the South; frequent rain almost everywhere. Winter clothing was often skimpy and quickly became sodden with snow; air-conditioning had been developed but was uncommon even in public buildings and usually available only in movie theaters. The rich few could avoid the worst of their local climes, with Southerners and city dwellers heading to resorts and cottages in the North in the summer, and urban Northerners riding the train to Florida for a few precious weeks in the winter. But for the rest of the country, to whom those means of escape were unavailable, it was unpleasant to be outdoors during much of the year and insufferable to be indoors during the summer.

Those who passed through California during the war years found something different, a place where it was comfortable to be outdoors except on the few rainy days and when a Santa Ana wind blew in from the desert. To Carey McWilliams, who came by train to Los Angeles from Denver in early 1922 after dropping out of college, "the absence of snow was quite shocking" as he arrived "in the land of giant geraniums, poppies, oranges and perpetual sunshine that was even then beginning to be widely advertised as a kind of far western paradise facing the Pacific."[37] McWilliams's delight was shared by millions a quarter century later. At a time when postwar veterans were raising large families in 1,000-square-foot houses California's climate meant you could have double that living space and more, because your backyard was almost always comfortable. Kids could play outside all year, and without having to put on snowsuits; the family could eat lunch and dinner on the patio out back; you could sit on the porch and read or listen to the ball game on the radio (major league baseball arrived in California in 1957). You almost never were too hot to function at normal levels and you never had to put on winter coats and leggings or to shovel snow. Coastal California's climate seemed a miracle to the newcomers who, like Ronald Reagan, were always delighted to return when they had to go back east. If California had a distinctive visual and climatological allure, its culture was not shockingly unfamiliar, but as plainly and unaffectedly American as the 1930s and 1940s movies. The atmosphere was friendly, the civic leaders boosterish, the old-timers welcoming. The avenues and boulevards of the Los Angeles Basin may have been lined with palm trees, but they were laid out largely in the mile-square grids reminiscent of the Midwest until they reached the mountains or the ocean. The state's governors in the postwar years were familiar types, the Protestant Republicans Earl Warren and Goodwin Knight and the Catholic Democrat Pat Brown, hearty and cheerful individuals with a determination to build freeways, enormous university and community college systems, and a water system that could serve millions of future Californians. California in the war years attracted famous foreigners—authors Aldous Huxley and Christopher Isherwood from Britain and Thomas Mann and Erich Maria Remarque from Germany; musicians Igor Stravinsky, Jascha Heifetz, and Artur Rubinstein—and the San Francisco business and cultural elite stayed aloof from those outside its ranks. But the overall tone was quintessentially American, free of regional accents and seemingly unaware of the gulfs between Northern and Southern, between Ellis Islanders and *Mayflower* descendants that were defining aspects of the lives of so many Americans in the rest of the country.

In the immediate postwar years it became clear that America

would not fall back into a depression and that California's dynamic economy could not only generate jobs for wartime workers determined to stay but for hundreds of thousands and even millions who suddenly were determined to move in. Between 1950 and 1965 an average of 272,000 Americans per year migrated to California, and very few chose to head back east. The population of California increased from 6.9 million in 1940 to 10.6 million in 1950, 15.7 million in 1960, and (rounded off) 20.0 million in 1970, nearly tripling in thirty years. In those three decades California accounted for 18 percent of the population increase of the entire nation, and in 1963, or so the Census Bureau estimated, California passed New York and became the nation's largest state. This was reflected in the apportionment of members of the House of Representatives mandated by the Constitution after each decennial census: California got twenty-three congressional districts from the census results in 1940, thirty in 1950, thirty-eight in 1960, and forty-three in 1970—a larger increase than any other state has achieved in a similar period since the membership of the House was set at 435 after the 1910 Census.

Where did these postwar migrants to California come from? From all over the United States, but primarily from the Midwest and especially the Great Plains states.[38] The nation saw a more or less constant rural-to-urban, farm-to-factory migration from the 1880s through the 1960s, accelerated in war years—many servicemen never returned to their struggling family farms—then diminished in years of economic recession and depression. For those who grew up west of the Mississippi River, there were relatively few local metropolitan magnets; metro Kansas City and Denver never grew much more than the national average. From there west, the next concentration of population was in California. The new Californians were mostly midwestern, with little in the way of ethnic identification, exemplars of "fundamentalist Protestant individualism."[39]

California's huge population increase made it increasingly important politically, and for a long period it seemed to become a leading political indicator, ahead of national trends. It voted for Harry

Truman, the upset winner in 1948, and twice for Dwight Eisenhower in the 1950s. It swept in Pat Brown and Democratic legislative majorities in 1958, a harbinger of the Democratic victories of the 1960s, though it voted very narrowly for its native son Richard Nixon in his exceedingly close race against John Kennedy. It voted by a wide margin for Lyndon Johnson in 1964—though in Southern California the race was closer than in most Northern metropolitan areas, a sign of a potential conservative resurgence that in fact occurred when Ronald Reagan swept Pat Brown out of office in a landslide in 1966 and when Richard Nixon, rejected when he came back and ran for governor in 1966, was elected president in 1968.

IN the years to come blacks in the North followed closely the successes and the setbacks of the civil rights movement in the South. They also became increasingly involved in local politics, protesting exclusion from housing and recreation areas.[40] As has been the case with other low-income urban migrants, there was some overlap between community activists and those involved in the black neighborhoods' organized crime, the numbers racket.[41] This was a lottery: pay a small amount, as little as a penny, pick a three-digit number, and get paid off at a rate of 600–1 if your number is the same as a random number, for example the last three digits of the amount of money bet at a racetrack, selected daily. The payoff left plenty of profit for numbers operators except on days that had a popular three-digit number like *666*. Numbers operators were important people in the ghettoes, with many contacts; the story goes that if a black apartment dweller was robbed in 1940s Detroit, he told the numbers operator and got his property back within twenty-four hours. The sociologists St. Clair Drake and Horace R. Cayton in their 1945 book *Black Metropolis: A Study of Negro Life in a Northern City* emphasize the importance of the numbers operators as community leaders and contrast the lower-class "shadies" who patronized them with the lower-class "respectables" who did not.[42] Black politicians had to navigate between these segments, often promising support to city hall leaders in return for non-enforcement of gambling laws in the ghettoes.

This dynamic was notable in Chicago, where the successful black politicians had close ties to political machines. The first black congressman elected in the twentieth century was a Republican, Oscar De Priest, a real estate operator who specialized in buying houses from whites and selling them to blacks. He had the support of Republican mayor William Hale Thompson when he was first elected in a heavily Republican district, though with a lower-than-usual percentage, in 1928. Thompson successfully sponsored an amendment barring racial discrimination in the Civilian Conservation Corps. But the New Deal was popular among blacks and they left the party of Lincoln for the party of Franklin Roosevelt; in 1934 De Priest was defeated by Arthur Mitchell, a black lawyer who had himself switched from the Republican to the Democratic Party. After Mitchell retired in 1942, the seat was won by William Dawson, also a successful lawyer and party switcher. He was a loyal and influential supporter of machine Democratic mayor Ed Kelly but broke with his successor, Martin Kennelly, reportedly because police were cracking down on the numbers game and helped unseat him by providing key support in the 1955 Democratic primary to Richard J. Daley.[43]

The next two blacks elected to Congress had professional backgrounds of importance in black communities: one was a preacher; the other, part of a family funeral home firm. The large black community in New York's Harlem did not elect a black for many years because the state legislature did not revise the congressional districting plan, based on the 1910 Census when Harlem had a much smaller population, until the 1944 election. At that point the Harlem district elected the Reverend Adam Clayton Powell, pastor of Harlem's Abyssinian Baptist Church, an eloquent orator, who became a controversial figure in his twenty-six years in Congress. In the 1950s he filed Powell amendments banning racial discrimination in federal aid programs; other liberal Democrats criticized these as killer amendments, since it made southern Democrats reluctant to support the legislation; and Powell endorsed Republican Dwight Eisenhower for reelection in 1956. At the time Powell was the second-ranking member of the Education and Labor Committee, but the chairman, a North Carolina Democrat, refused to call on him to ask questions; as chairman from 1961 he was the sponsor of much Great Society legislation. Involvement in a lawsuit prevented him from returning to his district except on Sundays, and in 1966 a majority of members voted to exclude him from the House; he filed a lawsuit and was successful in the Supreme Court, which said the House could expel but not exclude members. But Charles Rangel beat him in the Democratic primary in 1970.

Dawson, the silent machine supporter, and Powell, the flamboyant maverick, were joined by a third black member, Charles C. Diggs Jr. from Detroit, after the 1954 election. Diggs's father had started the House of Diggs mortuary firm and was elected to the state senate in the 1930s and 1940s, but was forced out for ethics violations. However, he was not through with politics, engineering his son's election to the state senate in 1950 at age twenty-eight. Detroit's congressional districts, drawn after the 1930 Census and not redrawn till 1964, extended from the Detroit River northward to the city limit of Eight Mile Road, cutting across the boundaries of ethnic and racial neighborhoods. As blacks moved out from the narrow confines of Paradise Valley, by 1954 they constituted a majority in the 13th district, which also included the city's richest precincts. So a district that had been politically marginal, voting Republican in 1938 and 1946, became heavily Democratic, and Charles Diggs Jr. easily beat the incumbent Democrat in the 1954 primary. In his first year in Congress he showed courage in attending the Mississippi trial of Emmett Till's killers; but in 1978 he was convicted of accepting kickbacks from staffers' salaries; he resigned in 1980.

In many respects blacks made great progress during the years of the Great Migration. Northward migrants, according to James Gregory, "were self-selected for ambition and apt to be inspired throughout their working lives by evidence and self-mythology of their own success,"[44] and for good reason. Black life expectancy rose from 53.1 years in 1940 to 63.6 years in 1960. Black men's earnings in real dollars rose 75 percent in the 1940s and 45 percent in the 1950s, leaving them with incomes almost two and one half times higher; and black women's earnings rose almost as much.[45] Home ownership among blacks increased from 23 percent to 38 percent in the same period. The lion's share of these gains was accrued in the North.

But the northward migration also posed problems—for the blacks who moved and for others in the metropolitan areas where they thronged. The distinctive culture of southern blacks, particularly that of those who were rural sharecroppers, was in some ways poorly suited to life in the large cities of the North. Novelist Richard Wright described the problem in the 1940s. "Perhaps never before in history has a more utterly unprepared folk wanted to go to the city; we were barely born as a folk when we headed for the tall and sprawling centers of steel and stone. We, who were landless upon the land; we, who barely managed to live in family groups; we, who needed the ritual and guidance of institutions to hold our atomized lives together in lines of purpose; we, who had known only relationships to people and not relationships to things; we, who had our personalities blasted with two hundred years of slavery and had been turned loose to shift for ourselves—we were such a folk as this when we moved into a world that was destined to test all we were, that threw us into the scales of competition to whet our mettle."[46]

The daunting challenge of adjustment could be seen in housing. In the South, blacks tended to live in ramshackle housing that they either did not own or which they could not easily afford to upgrade or renovate. The South's mild winters made such shelter acceptable or at least tolerable. The northern climate was less forgiving. Structures were more solid but also more often in need of repair and reconstruction, and the neighborhoods in which black migrants were confined typically had housing built decades earlier. But migrant renters did not have much incentive to keep up their houses or apartments, and in New York City rent control laws disincentivized landlords to do so.

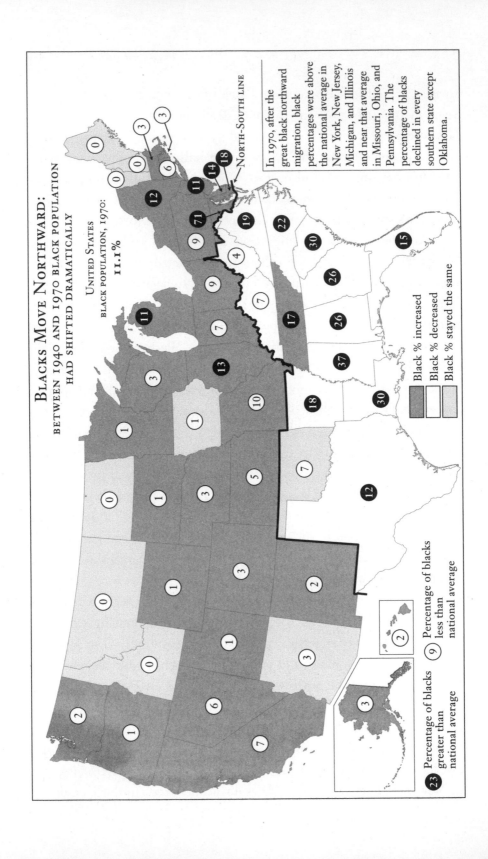

Blacks Move Northward:
between 1940 and 1970 black population had shifted dramatically

United States
black population, 1970:
11.1%

North-South line

In 1970, after the great black northward migration, black percentages were above the national average in New York, New Jersey, Michigan, and Illinois and near that average in Missouri, Ohio, and Pennsylvania. The percentage of blacks declined in every southern state except Oklahoma.

Black % increased
Black % decreased
Black % stayed the same

23 Percentage of blacks greater than national average

9 Percentage of blacks less than national average

And home-owning migrants were not adept at upkeep either. Anyone familiar with the big cities of the 1950s and 1960s, even those sympathetic to blacks, could not help noticing the dilapidated condition of housing in neighborhoods that had become all-black a few years before, and could not help contrasting it with the tidy and meticulous condition of housing in heavily Polish, German, Italian, and Jewish neighborhoods where home owners benefited from old-country traditions quite different from those of the segregated South. Detroit's Paradise Valley did not look at all like paradise, and indeed much of it was torn down to make way for the Walter P. Chrysler Freeway.

Family structure, not strong among southern blacks, became weaker in the North. Sociologist Hortense Powdermaker described the southern black family as "matriarchal and elastic" and wrote that "the personnel of these matriarchal families is variable and even casual," including illegitimate children.[47] In 1960 67 percent of black children nationally lived in two-parent families, well below the 91 percent figure for whites; one-quarter of black families in metropolitan New York that year were headed by women.[48] One might have expected the percentage of two-parent families to rise during the years that blacks' incomes had risen so slowly. But in 1965 Daniel Patrick Moynihan, then assistant secretary of Labor, took a look at the numbers and found something quite different. In a report published as a large paperback pamphlet and titled "The Negro Family: The Case for National Action," Moynihan noted that the percentage of black families headed by women had risen from 18 percent to 21 percent in the 1950s and that the percentage of black births to unwed mothers had risen from 17 percent in 1940 (when three-quarters of blacks lived in the South) to 24 percent in 1963 (when nearly half of blacks lived in the North). He noted as well a "startling increase" in welfare dependency in a time of economic growth.[49] Connected to these developments, he suggested, was another puzzling trend. "From 1951 to 1963, the level of Negro male unemployment was on a long-run rising trend, while at the same time following the short-run ups and downs of the business cycle."[50]

THE California dream shone brightly during the first two postwar decades. The state's high cost of living was reduced to national levels while incomes rose far above; the state's older-than-average population became younger than average as veterans with young families moved in; home owning and the two-car family became the norm. It was a very different environment from that encountered by those who moved from farms to densely populated cities like New York and Chicago, with their high-rise office buildings, apartment buildings, and subways. In Southern California newcomers bought single-family homes, usually small bungalows, where they carefully tended their lawns and exhibited their cars, necessary in a metropolis where the electric Red Car interurban system was torn down and freeways were built in the 1940s and 1950s. White middle-class Midwesterners spread all over the Los Angeles Basin, converting orange groves to subdivisions in the San Fernando Valley, southern Los Angeles County, the string of suburbs east of Los Angeles, and southeast into Orange County, where the population increased from 130,000 in 1940 to 216,000 in 1950, then 703,000 in 1960, double that (1,420,000) in 1970, and 1,932,000 in 1980. In the San Francisco Bay Area similar in-migrant spread took place in the interstices between mountains and bay, spreading most rapidly in the south end of San Francisco Bay in the orchard country around San Jose, where the municipal government struggled to maintain an accurate street map, and in the towns to the northwest of there along El Camino Real— Cupertino, Sunnyvale, Mountain View, Palo Alto, Menlo Park—that would become famous as Silicon Valley. This postwar California nurtured "a strong, socially reinforced commitment to property," while "low-density, single-family homes, a lack of public transportation, the absence of ethnic neighborhoods and the use of cars combined to prevent the formation of street corner gangs," which were common in the cramped cities of the Northeast and industrial Midwest.[51]

But by the middle 1960s, it was becoming apparent that all was not well with paradise. The inversion of air over the Los Angeles

Basin—a condition noticed by mariner Richard Henry Dana in 1838 when he saw smoke from Indian fires hover low rather than dissipate skyward—combined with vast population increase resulted in the health hazard and aesthetic disaster of smog. The skies over prewar Los Angeles were almost always blue and the mountains bounding the basin gloriously visible; by the middle 1960s, the air was usually a murky gray-green and the mountains were mostly invisible. State politicians and regulators responded with limits on emissions in the 1950s, but smog continued to increase and reached a peak around 1970.[52] By the late 1960s, most of coastal California seemed filled up. The land with the golden climate between the ocean and the mountains in the Los Angeles Basin and the San Fernando Valley and in the interstices between coastal mountains and the water in the San Francisco Bay Area had been platted and planted with subdivisions. Strict environmental regulations, promulgated by the California Coastal Commission, created by voter approval of a Proposition 20 in 1972, and by local zoning authorities, prevented the building of much new housing, and as a result housing prices in coastal California—for long not that much different from the national average—started to zoom up toward the stratosphere.

In the meantime the promise of California dimmed as the seeming beneficiaries of its liberal public policies suddenly showed ingratitude and disdain. The state had built a wondrous university system, but on the historic Berkeley campus of the University of California, student rebels in 1964 launched a free speech movement (their initial grievance was the refusal of university authorities to allow students to set up tables to enlist supporters for Lyndon Johnson's presidential campaign). Protests, rallies, and occupations of Berkeley parks continued sporadically through 1969, as students threatened with the military draft focused their protests on the Vietnam War. In 1965, a year after passage of the great federal civil rights act and in the summer after passage of the Voting Rights Act, blacks rioted in the Watts district of Los Angeles, looting and burning.

For the aging GI generation migrants, the California dream

seemed to be turning into a nightmare. As James Q. Wilson described it at the time, "The very virtues they have and practice are, in their eyes, conspicuously absent from society as a whole."[53] They wanted "limited government, personal responsibility, 'basic' education, a resurgence of patriotism, an end to 'chiseling' and a more restrained Supreme Court." They opposed "those who would legalize marijuana, abortions, and pornography and tolerate or encourage draft resistance, all in the name of personal freedom, and who would support court-ordered school busing, bans on gun ownership, affirmative action, and racial quotas, all in the name of rationalizing and perfecting society."[54] These attitudes produced something in the nature of a political upheaval in 1966, when Ronald Reagan defeated incumbent governor Pat Brown by a 58 percent–42 percent margin. Brown had defeated two Republican heavyweights, senator William Knowland in 1958 and former vice president Richard Nixon in 1962, and had pushed through the Democratic legislature an ambitious water project, major freeway construction, and expansion of the university and community college systems. His liberal Democrats seemed to have embodied Californians' attitudes as had the progressive Republicans who had held the governorship most of the half century between the election of Hiram Johnson in 1910 and the Democratic breakthrough in 1958. Reagan represented a sharp break with that tradition. Although he did not succeed in holding down spending and tax rates as much as he wished, and also signed a liberalized abortion law he later regretted, he did demonstrate that the reassertion of traditional values was a viable political strategy in a major state, and his success as governor made him a plausible presidential candidate briefly in 1968, more seriously in 1976, and as a landslide winner in 1980.

THE breakdown of family structure in the northern black communities had consequences that turned what had seemed a promised land into something like the opposite for many. The 1950s and early 1960s were years that liberals a half century later would view with nostalgia as a time when unskilled young men could emerge from high school or military service and in the large northern cities get a well-paying and steady job as a low-skill assembly line worker. And indeed many northward black migrants did get and hold such jobs and achieve a degree of earned success and economic prosperity unimaginable for most of their forebears. But, as Moynihan noted in his report, unemployment levels relative to the national average were rising for blacks even in years of booming economic growth; many were not getting or holding such jobs, much less achieving climbing the occupational ladder. At the same time black women were less likely to wait until marriage to have children or to be able to enlist the services of a husband to help raise them. Moynihan, who hoped that the antipoverty programs being developed just as he was writing could reverse the trend, found himself denounced for "blaming the victim" by many liberals who were quite confident that increased welfare and government aid could ameliorate the condition of black Americans. But these critics seemed to avoid what now came to seem the obvious conclusion that northward migrants and the children they raised in the North who were reaching adulthood were being conditioned by the availability of unemployment insurance and welfare assistance, particularly Aid to Families with Dependent Children. Many men were shunning employment and marriage and many women were raising their children alone as best they could without fathers. Federal policy allowed states to set the level of unemployment and welfare benefits. Southern states from the beginning of those programs have set benefits low, and in the pre–mechanical cotton-picker South the possibility that "desperate black men in Depression years could usually find someone to take them on as a farmhand"[55] provided a safety net, however flimsy, that was less available in the postwar South and not available in the postwar North. Northern states, especially New York, the largest state and among the richest states in the two decades after the war, set unemployment and welfare benefits high. Over the years northward migrants and their offspring fell into a trap baited by generous benefits provided by many northern states rather than southern ones. Even as large numbers of blacks became medium and high earners, and as the median incomes of black married-couple families rose to 87 percent of those of whites in 1995,[56] the percentage of black children not in two-parent families roughly tripled from the 24 percent that alarmed Moynihan. The percentage of black men unemployed at some point in the year rose from Moynihan's 29 percent figure for 1963. Welfare dependency roughly tripled in the ten years between 1965 and 1975, then plateaued for nearly two decades, before falling with the success of welfare reform laws in Wisconsin and other states and the passage of a national Welfare Reform Act in 1996.

ALSO roughly tripling between 1965 and 1975 and plateauing for the next two decades was the national rate of violent crime,[57] and much of this shocking increase was due to very high crime rates among the offspring of black northward migrants. Although there is dispute about crime rates in the segregated South, overall southern states have long tended to have high rates of violent crime. According to Nicholas Lemann, in the 1930s, "most of the murders were black-on-black,"[58] and according to legal scholar William Stuntz, southern law enforcement officers traditionally paid little attention to black-on-black crime.[59]

Since national crime statistics are compilations of local crime statistics, there is reason to doubt that black-on-black crime was fully reported and prosecuted in the pre-1940 South, although we can be sure that black-on-white crime was vigorously prosecuted, and that suspected incidences resulted in lynchings. There is reason to believe that southern police and prosecutors were in many cases complacent about black-on-black crime, leaving it to be handled by black ministers, professionals, and other community leaders. We do know with more certainty that the black northward migrants were less likely to commit crimes than blacks raised in the North and that black crime rates in the big cities in the North did not spike sharply upward in the 1940s or early 1950s. Indeed nationally crime rates were very low in the 1930s and 1940s and inched up only slowly in the 1950s; in that decade the main crime problem treated in media was juvenile delinquency, and offenders were typically depicted as white kids.

We know as well that relationships between the police and black residents in northern cities were certainly tense. Police forces were virtually all white, with new recruits very often the sons, nephews, and cousins of serving officers; policemen were used to upholding the law in a way acceptable to the mores of Irish, Italian, and Jewish neighborhoods and before the great northward migration had little contact with blacks. Certainly northern urban police had a difficult time reading the body language of black youths, while young black men had reason to dislike and mistrust police officers but much less reason to fear them than blacks feared their counterparts in the South. "Young men kill when the governments and laws that tell them to do otherwise seem unstable or otherwise unable to command loyalty,"[60] writes Stuntz. He argues further that "[f]or the most part, urban crime in immigrant-dominated cities was governed by local politics, not the state and national kind. Voters who lived in or near crime-ridden streets mattered; the relevant government officials had to listen to those voters in order to keep their jobs. Black Americans have never enjoyed that power."[61]

Relations became more tense as crime rates began to increase in black neighborhoods. In one fairly typical northern city, Philadelphia, the homicide rate among whites increased from 1.8 per 100,000 in population in the early 1950s to 2.8 per 100,000 in the middle 1970s. The homicide rate among blacks increased "more than two and one-half times in the same period, to 64.2 per 100,000, or fully 23 times higher than the white rate."[62] Whites who fled neighborhoods when blacks moved in often said they did so because blacks were more likely to commit crimes. Though this was true, the difference seems not to have been huge in the first decade after the war, when white flight was most prevalent. In the second decade after the war, when the black crime wave became more pronounced, scholars and liberal analysts said that much of the change was a statistical artifact; crime among blacks had just not been reported to the police before, but now it was. As noted, that was probably true in the South, but not so much in the North; these analysts were reluctant to believe that members of a group that had been treated badly could behave badly themselves. By the decade between 1965 and 1975, it became impossible to deny that blacks, almost entirely young black males, accounted for a hugely disproportionate share of violent crime. Since the 1950s, about 30 percent of people arrested and about 45 percent of prison inmates nationally have been black. One might argue that some part of this divergence has been due to racial discrimination. But a criminologist sympathetic to claims of discrimination nonetheless concluded in 1995, "For nearly a decade there has been a near consensus among scholars and policy analysts that most of the black punishment disproportions result not from racial bias or discrimination within the system but from patterns of black offending and blacks' criminal records."[63]

The demands and policy prescriptions of black politicians and black voters arguably exacerbated these problems. In the early 1960s black leaders in northern cities, focused on some genuine excesses by police officers and knowing that many white policemen held blacks in contempt, began demanding less aggressive policing and established civilian review boards to examine cases of alleged police brutality. Mayors, prosecutors, and judges, responding not just to black pressure but to the feelings of voters generally that black Americans had been maltreated, adjusted police tactics and hired more blacks as police officers. Even as crime rates were rising sharply, the prison population actually declined in the late 1960s, and in 1966 a Gallup poll showed that for the first and only time in our history a plurality of Americans opposed capital punishment. American voters have never elected a president who opposed it in all cases. This mood among most voters soon passed, as crime rates rose higher still and large parts of central cities became acutely dangerous. But the black mayors who started to be elected—Carl Stokes in Cleveland and Richard Hatcher in Gary in

1967, Coleman Young in Detroit in 1973, Marion Barry in Washington in 1978—continued to pursue such policies, as did mayors elected with heavy black support, like John Lindsay in New York in 1965. The riots that broke out in central cities in the second half of the 1960s—in Los Angeles in 1965, Newark and Detroit in 1967, Washington and many other cities in 1968—strengthened the demand from black voters and from many white elites for such policies as well.

Similarly, there was a move toward much more generous welfare provision, led by Lindsay's welfare commissioner who announced that there would be no checking the eligibility of welfare applicants—he was dubbed "Come and Get It Ginsberg" by conservative critics. The result was a growing black underclass, consisting of male criminals and unmarried mothers raising children who in large numbers became male criminals and unmarried mothers raising children. The chief victims of all this, it was clear, were black Americans. Whites for the most part were able to move into growing and safe suburbs or into the remaining all-white neighborhoods in central cities (the west side of Cleveland, for example, remained almost entirely white, while the east side, separated by the gorge of the Cuyahoga River, became almost entirely black, with blacks moving later to close east side suburbs rather than west of the river). Blacks were the great majority of victims of black criminals, including black home owners who saw the value of their houses fall or remain stagnant because of high rates of crime while white home owners accumulated significant wealth from increasing housing values: crime operated as a confiscatory wealth tax on middle-class and working-class blacks. Welfare dependency and crime rates eventually fell sharply in the 1990s, thanks to welfare and crime-control policies that were initiated by politicians—such as the welfare reforms of Governor Tommy Thompson of Wisconsin and the policing reforms of Mayor Rudolph Giuliani of New York City and imitated and adapted by many others, most of them Republicans but many Democrats as well. Through all this, black voters since 1964, when Republican presidential nominee Barry Goldwater voted against the Civil Rights Act, have voted about 90 percent Democratic in most elections, and black elected officials with a few exceptions have championed generous welfare and soft crime-control policies.

This transformation went on even as the civil rights movement was transforming the South. The NAACP Legal Defense Fund's litigation strategy, devised by Thurgood Marshall, aimed at ending segregated schools that were supposedly "separate but equal" by challenging first segregation in segregated state graduate schools, for which there were no black equivalents and which resulted in the *Brown v. Board of Education* decision in 1954 declaring all school segregation illegal, followed by *Brown II* in 1955 calling for desegregation "with all deliberate speed." In 1956 a young minister in Montgomery, Alabama, named Martin Luther King Jr. led a boycott of the city's buses after Rosa Parks was evicted from a bus for refusing to give up her seat to a white. King understood, as few politicians did, that if Northerners were forced to see the means by which segregation was upheld, they would come to regard it as intolerable, as indeed became the case, and Congress passed civil rights acts in 1957 and 1960. But progress was slow as Virginia in 1959 employed "massive resistance," shutting one county's schools rather than admit blacks; as "freedom buses" that blacks were riding were stormed and burned in 1960; as governors of Alabama and Mississippi "stood in the schoolhouse door" in showboating attempts to prevent black students from enrolling at their state universities in 1963 and 1964. Finally there were breakthroughs that integrated important parts of southern life. The Civil Rights Act of 1964 effectively opened up most public accommodations and workplaces to blacks within a few years. The Voting Rights Act of 1965 effectively opened the voting rolls to blacks; by 1968 they were close to a proportionate part of the electorate in every southern state but Mississippi, which followed by 1972. The Supreme Court's *Green v. New Kent County* in 1968 finally compelled widespread rather than token integration of southern public schools, though in some heavily black areas whites formed private academies and enrolled their children in them.

The result of all this was that the North came to seem more

unattractive to blacks and the South less unattractive. The percentage of blacks living in the South had declined from 77 percent in 1940 to 53 percent in 1965—and has stayed within one or two percentage points of that ever since. Net northward black migration declined to about zero just as the Civil Rights Act of 1964 and the Voting Rights Act of 1965 took effect. This was not because blacks could expect to enjoy electoral majorities in the South; by 1970, Mississippi's black percentage had declined to 37 percent and South Carolina's and Louisiana's to 30 percent. Blacks, voting about 90 percent Democratic from 1964 on, could expect to be a more dominant force politically in large northern states where they made up just about 10 percent of the electorate but where much larger percentages of whites were willing to vote for liberal Democrats and where elected officials of both parties were more likely to favor policies they supported than were white Democrats, much less Republicans, in the South. In any case the great northward migration of blacks mostly from the rural South to the large cities of the North ended abruptly, without announcement and without much notice, in 1965, just after the passage of national civil rights legislation and at the same time as the outbreak of black riots in northern cities.

DOMESTIC migration to California, after three decades of enormous flow, tapered off sharply in the 1970s, sank far below that of many other western and southeastern states in the 1980s, and turned into domestic outflow in the 1990s. The two Olympic games held in Los Angeles are, almost, bookends to the period of major internal migration to California—California, here I come—which started a few years after the 1932 Olympics and ended a few years after the 1984 Olympics. California's total population had risen by 3.7 million in the 1940s, 5.1 million in the 1950s, and 4.2 million in the 1960s; in the 1970s it rose by only 3.7 million, the same as in the 1940s, but from a much higher base. In percentage terms the slowdown in California's growth was even more vivid: from 53 percent in the 1940s, 48 percent in the 1950s, and 27 percent in the 1960s to 19 percent in the 1970s. The difference owed something to the end of the postwar baby boom, but by far the more important factor was the decline of internal migration—which for the 1970s was not entirely captured by these figures, since that was the first decade of the surge of Hispanic and Asian immigration—the subject of the next chapter—into California.

The dearth of new and comfortable housing in coastal California was only one respect in which California's comparative advantage in climate—discovered by the GIs, sailors, and defense workers in World War II—no longer attracted many migrants to the state. By the 1970s, there was not only less space in comfortable California; it was becoming more comfortable to live in the rest of the country. After a generation of postwar prosperity, middle-income Americans had come to live in larger houses, more like 2,000 square feet than 1,000, and didn't need the outdoor space to spread out in; suburban lots in California came to be smaller than in suburbs back east. In the South and in the North summertime air-conditioning made life bearable and even productive; in the North winter clothing was far improved, and it was possible to walk around in comfort in −10° weather in Minnesota or Michigan. The prevalence of garages and electric garage doors meant that you could pretty much avoid bad weather altogether, at least if your destination had indoor or covered parking lots. You didn't need to move to California to be comfortable most of the year. You could live pretty comfortably anywhere your volition took you.

After the vast migration to California petered out in the 1970s, in the 1980s, as immigration to the United States vastly increased, it very nearly disappeared from the Golden State. In the five years from 1985 to 1990, after the shining success of the 1984 Los Angeles Olympics, net domestic migration to California was only 173,000—one-sixth the number moving to Florida (1,071,000) and significantly lower than the net domestic migration to Georgia (302,000), North Carolina (282,000), Virginia (227,000), and Washington (216,000) and only microscopically ahead of Nevada (172,000). The defense builddown of the early 1990s was followed by an exodus from California: laid-off aerospace employees, hard put to afford coastal California, headed back east or north to the Pacific Northwest or Idaho. In the two decades following 1990 there was more domestic outmigration from California than from any other state but New York. "California, Here I Come" had become, for Americans, as dated a song as the theme songs of the Scots-Irish *drang nach* southwest "Shenandoah" and "Oh! Susanna."

THE difficulties blacks faced in the North should not obscure the great progress many black Americans have made in the years since the middle 1960s. America now has a thriving black middle class and a growing number of black entrepreneurs and role models; in the first decade of the twenty-first century we had two black secretaries of state and in 2008 and 2012 we elected a black president of the United States. Blacks have moved in significant numbers to affluent suburbs, not only in mostly black areas like Prince George's County, Maryland, outside Washington, and DeKalb County, Georgia, outside Atlanta, but also into mostly white suburbs in every metropolitan area with a significant black population. But the black northward great migration ended quite abruptly around the year 1965. Northward migration by blacks has been minimal since then, and between 1990 and 2010 there was net black migration from North to South, as blacks left metropolitan areas like Los Angeles, where they were heavily outnumbered by Latinos, and moved to metropolitan areas like Atlanta, where they could find an agreeable southern culture and plenty of economic opportunity. The passage of the 1964 Civil Rights Act was quickly, and to most Americans surprisingly, followed by widespread compliance by white Southerners of its ban on racial discrimination in public accommodations and employment. The passage of the Voting Rights Act in 1965 was followed by an almost instantaneous entry of southern blacks into the electorate (it took a few years longer in Alabama and Mississippi and some isolated rural pockets elsewhere). All of this, plus the increasing availability of air-conditioning, made the South more attractive to blacks. At the same time, the North seemed to be getting less attractive. Black complaints against white policing and discrimination were being stoutly resisted by white voters, and residential segregation was still largely effective, to become less so only slowly over the next decades. The late-1960s riots gave voice to a certain anger among many blacks; more practically, they resulted in the destruction of many black neighborhoods and businesses, which are still visible in the burnt-out houses and commercial establishments in much of Detroit, to take an extreme example. Many millions of blacks have achieved success in both the North and the South and encounter only occasional unpleasant behavior in going about their daily lives; for them, and for blacks who have done less well, the mass impulse to move has been largely absent now for nearly five decades, as it has been for most blacks during most of American history.

6. MIGRATIONS OF CHOICE

A GENERATION out from World War II, the two surges of migration set in motion by the war were dwindling. The northward migration of southern blacks ended abruptly in 1965, as civil rights and air-conditioning were making the South more attractive while riots and high rates of crime and welfare dependency were making the northern cities less attractive. The surge of migration to California continued into the 1970s, but at a far lower rate. The promised lands were turning out to be problematic, and fewer and fewer people were impelled to move.

American migration patterns were also changing in other respects at about this time. A comparison of American states' growth rates in the three decades from 1940 to 1970 and the four decades from 1970 to 2010 shows sharply different patterns, with a discontinuity coming almost precisely at 1970. The nation's overall population growth rate was almost identical in the two periods, 54 percent in 1940–70 and 53 percent in 1970–2010. But the areas of above-average and below-average growth were distinctly different.

Growth in the quarter century after World War II was driven by the same factors as in the war. The war brought Americans to California and made the dream of moving there a reality for many, and in 1940–70 the population of California almost tripled. There was robust growth as well in sparsely populated states: in Florida (the lowest-population southern state in 1940) and in very lightly populated Arizona and Nevada, the population more than tripled in those

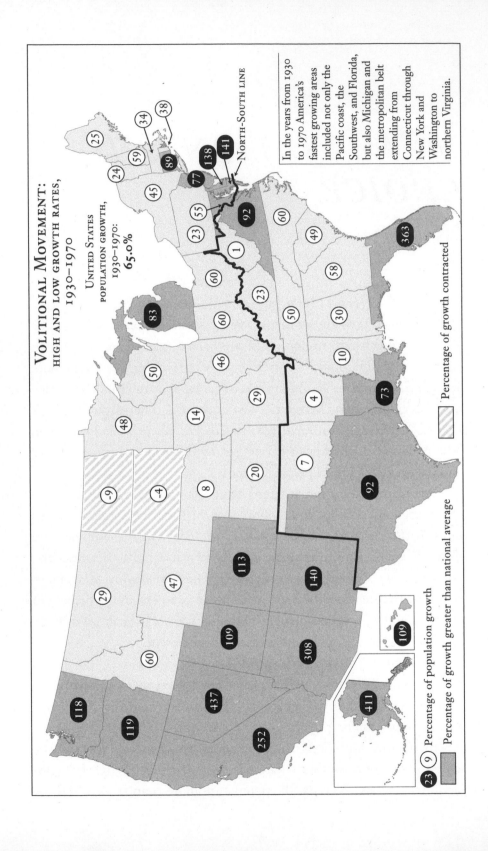

VOLITIONAL MOVEMENT:
HIGH AND LOW GROWTH RATES,
1930–1970

UNITED STATES
POPULATION GROWTH,
1930–1970:
65.0%

NORTH-SOUTH LINE

In the years from 1930 to 1970 America's fastest growing areas included not only the Pacific coast, the Southwest, and Florida, but also Michigan and the metropolitan belt extending from Connecticut through New York and Washington to northern Virginia.

23 Percentage of population growth

9 Percentage of population growth

Percentage of growth greater than national average

Percentage of growth contracted

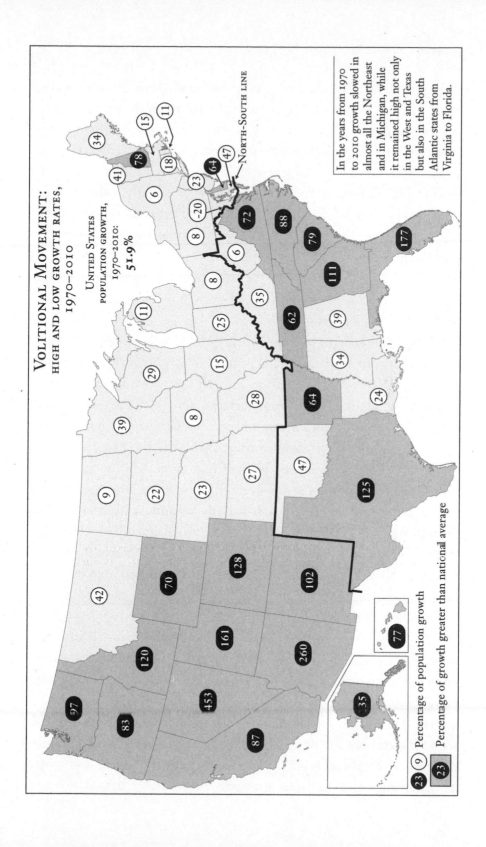

VOLITIONAL MOVEMENT:
HIGH AND LOW GROWTH RATES,
1970–2010

UNITED STATES
POPULATION GROWTH,
1970–2010:
51.9%

NORTH-SOUTH LINE

In the years from 1970 to 2010 growth slowed in almost all the Northeast and in Michigan, while it remained high not only in the West and Texas but also in the South Atlantic states from Virginia to Florida.

Percentage of population growth

Percentage of growth greater than national average

thirty years; and in Colorado, Utah, and New Mexico, it almost doubled. The war also drew blacks from the rural South, which resulted in zero population growth over three decades in Mississippi and Arkansas and significant population loss in rural Black Belt counties settled by southern grandees, from Virginia to Louisiana and east Texas. The Carolinas and Georgia grew at slightly below-average rates, as blacks left for the North but textile firms moved operations from expensive New England to the Piedmont region, where they hired only or mostly whites; the picture was similar in Tennessee. In contrast, the mechanization of the coal industry led to outmigration and population losses or very limited growth in West Virginia, Kentucky, and western Pennsylvania.

The American victory in World War II was largely attributed to the leaders of the nation's "big units"—big government, big business, and big labor—and 1940–70 growth was above average in areas where these big units were headquartered. One such area was a swath of territory from Boston through New York City and Philadelphia to Washington, which was dubbed Megalopolis by the French sociologist Jean Gottmann in a 1961 book of that name. On the map of the states, this region shows above-average growth in Connecticut, New Jersey, Delaware, and Maryland, plus in Virginia with its suburban growth outside Washington, D.C., and its many military installations there and in the Hampton Roads area around Norfolk. In addition, the New York City metropolitan area achieved above-average growth, with big population gains in suburban Nassau and Suffolk Counties on Long Island.

Similarly, there was above-average population growth in 1940–70 in Michigan, headquarters of the large auto-manufacturing companies, and growth at average levels in Ohio and Indiana, with their large manufacturing base also heavily oriented toward autos. This was in contrast to lower-than-average population growth in midwestern states farther west, where farm counties were losing population. But even there, metro Chicago, metro Milwaukee, and metro Minneapolis–St. Paul were growing above the national average.

Great Plains states without such large metro areas—Iowa, Nebraska, the Dakotas—grew hardly at all or lost population, as many people there left for California. And Texas, headquarters of much of the oil industry, also gained population above the national average, while oil-producing Louisiana, despite the exodus of many blacks, gained at the national average. The widespread switch from coal to oil in home heating and some industrial processes is evidenced by population decline in the Appalachian coal country and population gain in the oil patch of Texas and Louisiana.

The persistence of wartime population movements for more than two decades after the war made many expect that these patterns would continue indefinitely. But something like the opposite happened. In a few years around 1970 movements shifted abruptly to patterns that persisted for the next four decades. A map of states showing population growth percentages for 1970–2010 looks quite different from a map of growth percentages in 1940–70.

In the later time period, growth in California, while robust and with a large base, increased in percentage terms less than in Texas, where population more than doubled, and in Florida, where it came close to tripling. Growth in Megalopolis plummeted far below the national average, with New York City and its close-in suburbs losing more than 1 million people in the 1970–80 decade alone, while the exodus of both blacks and whites from the South has ended. Every southern state except West Virginia and Louisiana had higher percentage growth than every midwestern state as well as every northeastern state except Maryland (which gets an outflow of blacks from the District of Columbia) and the tax havens of Delaware (no state sales tax) and New Hampshire (no state sales or income tax). Michigan, which formerly grew much more than average, all but ceased to grow, losing population in the 1980–90 and 2000–10 decades, while percentage growth dropped to single digits in Ohio, Pennsylvania, and New York State and to 15 percent in Illinois. The big metropolitan areas of the Northeast and Midwest, except for Washington, were transformed from growth leaders to growth laggers, with percentage growth well below most Great Plains states, much less than those in the Rocky Mountain states, which except for Montana exceed the national average. Growth on the Atlantic coast has not ceased, however, but has moved southward, with Virginia, North Carolina, South Carolina, and Georgia, as well as Florida, growing well above average, as has the tax haven (no income tax) of Tennessee.

These different patterns result from two surges of migration, neither foreseen by demographic experts. One was immigration from Latin America, primarily Mexico, and various parts of Asia, triggered by the Immigration Act of 1965, which reversed the restrictive Immigration Law of 1924 in important respects. The four decades between passages of these laws saw the lowest levels of international migration as a percentage of preexisting population in American history: immigration totaled 17.2 million in the twenty-five years between 1900 and 1924 and 7.6 million in the forty-one years between 1925 and 1965. The other can be called volitional migration, which consists primarily of movement from high-tax states to low-tax states but also of movements to culturally congenial communities. In some sense this is a complement to immigration. Metropolitan areas with the highest levels of immigration—Los Angeles, New York, San Francisco, Chicago, Miami—during this period also started to experience domestic outflow, as Americans moved elsewhere. This, however, was not true of all high-immigration areas: metro Phoenix, Houston, Dallas, and Atlanta and several smaller metro areas in the South and West, areas generally with lower tax rates, continued to receive domestic inflow as large as or larger than immigration inflow during this period.

THERE was little migration from Latin America generally and from Mexico specifically before the 1960s. When the United States purchased Louisiana in 1803, it technically bordered the colony of New Spain, but the boundary was not determined until the Adams-Onís Treaty of 1819, just two years before Mexico became independent in

1821. Even after that it was less of a border than an imaginary line in an open space very sparsely populated by Indians and out of the effective control of both Washington and Mexico City—witness the relative ease with which Americans moved into part of the Mexican state of Coahuila y Tejas and established it as a separate Republic of Texas in 1836. Texas was annexed by the United States in 1845, but without any clear determination of the location of its southern border. Mexico claimed it was the Nueces River; U.S. president James K. Polk claimed the Rio Grande farther south and ordered American troops there; when they were fired on, he persuaded Congress to declare war on Mexico. The Treaty of Guadalupe Hidalgo in 1848 set the boundary as the Rio Grande and then a line westward through desert and mountain, which at Polk's insistence met the Pacific several miles south of San Diego Harbor. In 1853 the United States obtained the Gadsden Purchase, moving part of the line farther south and obtaining the land that now includes Tucson and the south side of Phoenix. Well into the twentieth century this arid land was open country. The Rio Grande was lightly settled on both sides of the border, and Apache and other Indians ran across the only lightly drawn "line in the sand" from the river west to the ocean.[1]

Migration across the line was occasional, multidirectional, and mostly unrecorded; the U.S. government has no figures for immigration from Mexico between 1886 and 1893. Spanish-speaking people lived north of the line, in San Antonio and most of south Texas, and hundreds of miles north, around Santa Fe, New Mexico. English-speaking people, like Mitt Romney's Mormon ancestors, moved south of the line. But this was mostly empty land, with the vast majority of Americans far to the east and the vast majority of Mexicans far to the south. Mexico City had a longer history, an older university, and through most of the nineteenth century a much larger population than any American city (in the twenty-first century its metropolitan population is, depending on how the metropolitan boundaries are defined, larger than that of metro New York or metro Los Angeles), and many Mexicans farther south spoke Indian languages such as Zapotec or Maya more than Spanish, much less English. Mexico never produced as many as 1,000 immigrants to the United States by official count until 1904 or as many as 10,000 until 1909. The Mexican Revolution, which broke out in 1910 and resulted in violent disorder, produced migrant flow to the United States that is reckoned at 700,000, but many of these travelers returned or moved back and forth.[2] After the Mexican leader Pancho Villa crossed the border and killed Americans in Columbus, New Mexico, in 1916, the U.S. Army under Gen. John Pershing was sent into Mexico in a punitive expedition that was less successful at quelling Villa's forces than in training American forces for the fighting in Europe two years later.[3]

Until well into the 1920s border enforcement was lax to nonexistent. Lloyd Bentsen Sr., who settled in the Lower Rio Grande Valley after World War I and became a large landholder and citrus and cotton producer, reported that people just went back and forth when they wanted.[4] After the stock market crash of 1929, the American government deported many Mexicans, and the flow of immigration from Mexico stopped in the 1930s, as the American economy languished and as the rule by successive presidents of the contradictorily named Party of the Institutional Revolution (PRI) beginning in 1929 brought stability and economic growth to Mexico. The Mexican population in the United States declined from about 600,000 to 400,000 during the 1930s.

The PRI policies—trade barriers, constructing factories and resort centers, confiscating foreign oil holdings and converting them into the Pemex government monopoly, setting up landless farmers in *ejidos* (collective farms)—resulted in 6 percent average annual economic growth between 1946 and 1970.[5] It also resulted in a massive movement from rural Mexico to the cities, with 20 percent of the nation's population in metro Mexico City. Immigration to the United States was still limited, averaging 43,000 annually from 1955 to 1969; immigration from the rest of Latin America averaged 32,000 annually. Many more participated in the bracero program, which allowed farmers in California and other western states to temporarily bring in

Mexicans and other Latin Americans in harvest season. At its peak, in 1957, 192,000 were admitted,[6] but the program was ended in 1964 at the urging of liberals, including Cesar Chavez, head of the United Farm Workers Union, who also sought to drive Mexican illegal immigrants out of the country.

There was little hint in these numbers that Latin immigration would increase very substantially starting around 1970. "If you look at present immigration figures from the Western Hemisphere," testified Attorney General Nicholas Katzenbach in hearings on the immigration bill pending in 1965, "there is not much pressure to come to the United States from these countries. There are in a relative sense not many people who want to come."[7] But as with the Scots-Irish in 1763, Irish Catholics and Germans in 1845, and Ellis Islanders in 1890, extrapolations from previous immigration figures turned out to be utterly misleading. An examination of other statistics—the high birth rates in Mexico and other Latin countries in the years up through the 1980s—and foresight about the slowdown of economic growth and recurrent peso devaluations in Mexico, as the PRI system became more corrupt and the statist economy less flexible, would have counseled against taking the recent past as a forecast of the future. In fact Latin immigration more than doubled from 75,000 in the 1955–69 period to 150,000 annually in the 1970s and doubled once again to more than 300,000 annually from 1980 to 2007.

The initial immigrants were, like those leaving the *ejidos* for Mexico City or Monterrey or for the rapidly growing border cities of Juarez, Mexicali, and Tijuana, young men seeking work. The border was not an unbreachable barrier and proved easy to cross, at checkpoints clogged with traffic or through the shallow Rio Grande or the line-in-the-sand desert. Latin immigrants came in large numbers first to major cities with existing Spanish-speaking clusters—Los Angeles most often, Houston, New York, Chicago, Miami. Los Angeles's vibrant economic growth was more important in making it a prime destination than its proximity to the border, for many immigrants there came from more than 1,000 miles away in Mexico. Relatively few sought the farmworker jobs Cesar Chavez sought to reserve for American citizens and legal immigrants. Instead Latin immigrants worked in construction, as janitors, in landscaping and grass cutting, parking cars, in garment and apparel factories, in restaurants and hotels, in textile mills and meatpacking factories, in retail stores and as messengers, driving trucks or tractors, and as maids and baby-sitters. They compensated for low levels of education, particularly among Mexicans, by a willingness to work hard and without complaint, as they had at home.

AMERICA in 1970 in many ways eerily resembled the America that won World War II. Government was still large, with a hefty share of spending devoted to defense industries. Big businesses seemed to dominate the private sector economy, as John Kenneth Galbraith preached in a late-1960s bestseller, *The New Industrial State.* The companies at the top of the Fortune 500 list of industrial corporations in 1970 were pretty much the same companies as in the first Fortune 500 in 1955, and the list would not have looked much different in 1945 if Fortune had compiled one then. Falling off the list since 1955 were two meatpacking firms (Swift, Armour), Bethlehem Steel, Kraft Foods, and Boeing; added to it were Ford (not a publicly held company yet in 1955), IBM, and three conglomerates (ITT, LTV, GTE). Large labor unions still represented hundreds of thousands of workers in industrial firms, and one of the biggest news stories of the year was the United Auto Workers' multiweek strike against General Motors, which resulted in a contract permitting workers to retire and start receiving a pension after thirty years on the job. The northward surge of southern blacks was over, but it had remade the big central cities of the North; the westward surge to California was still on, tamped down a bit by a lagging economy. Eight of the ten largest metropolitan areas in 1940 had grown faster than, or in 1970 almost as fast as, the national population. The two in California, Los Angeles and San

Francisco, had more than doubled in population between 1940 and 1970, but there were still above-average or just-about-average population percentage increases in metro New York, Chicago, Philadelphia, Detroit, St. Louis, and Cleveland. Only Boston and Pittsburgh lagged behind the national pace. If anything, the heft of these metro areas had only increased. In 1940 they had 28 percent of the nation's population; in 1970 they had 30 percent.

It seemed natural that the largest metropolitan areas should be the focus of growth, because in a nation whose economy seemed dominated by the big units—big government, big business, big labor—that is where most of the large corporations were headquartered and performed most of their major operations. The ten largest metro areas of 1940 were the same as those in 1970, except that Cleveland, with fewer prominent corporate headquarters than most others, fell off the list and was replaced by Washington, D.C., the seat of big government. Dozens of major corporations deemed it necessary to have their headquarters (or their chairman's office, in the case of General Motors) in New York City or its suburbs, to be in touch with Wall Street financial markets and the big New York banks, along with the leading advertising, media, and broadcasting firms. In three decades with minimal immigration, it came to seem natural that Americans would move into these large metro areas to seek their fortunes and make their livings. If, as Galbraith taught, big corporations could endlessly generate sales and profits by clever advertising and so would inevitably become a larger and larger part of the economy, it only made sense to join their ranks or hitch a ride on their growth.

Galbraith's book turned out to be a reasonable depiction of the recent past but a poor guide to the emerging future. In the high-inflation, low-growth economy of the 1970s it was becoming increasingly obvious that large corporate managements were complacent and inefficient, and techniques were developed to replace them with more competent leaders who could wring greater value out of corporate assets. One technique was the leveraged buyout employed by private equity firms, which took companies out of public securities markets and used debt, often in the form of so-called junk bonds, to finance their turnarounds. Not all LBOs were successful, of course, but on balance they vastly improved, and it turned out that junk bonds were often a good investment. Another technique was to reinvent the corporation from inside. Jack Welch in his twenty years as CEO of General Electric did this brilliantly, shedding low-performing units and investing in high-return fields, systematically weeding out low-performing employees and rewarding executives who produced good returns. Not all large corporations were so rejuvenated. The Big Three auto companies, as they were called, General Motors, Ford, and Chrysler, were burdened with United Auto Workers contracts that reduced workplace flexibility and piled huge retiree pensions and health care benefits on companies that were not innovating and growing as fast as competitors. Foreign manufacturers, roped into building plants in the United States to avoid protectionist laws, located none of them in Michigan except for a Ford-Mazda joint venture, despite the fact that it had the largest concentration of subcontractors and automotive engineers in the nation. Rather, they headed south, to Ohio and Indiana, but even more often to Tennessee, South Carolina, Alabama, and Mississippi, states where unions were weak and they could avoid the burdens of UAW contracts. They have paid wages comparable to those at the Big Three but have avoided the lavish UAW benefits and, freed from thousands of pages of work rules in union contracts, were able to use flexible management techniques and to innovate constantly.

But all this was largely unforeseen at the beginning of the 1970s. Those in charge of state and local governments believed that the economy would continue to grow at rates like those of the postwar quarter century, that the corporate and union order would remain in place. They therefore assumed that the wise and compassionate thing to do was to appropriate an increasing share of this inevitable economic activity and spend it on alleviating poverty. State and city income taxes were seen by many as the best means to hitch a ride on the tailgates of the big corporations. In the 1960s and early 1970s state and local income tax rates were increased by Republicans, including Governors Nelson Rockefeller of New York, Francis Sargent of Massachusetts, and even Ronald Reagan of California, and by New York City mayor John Lindsay. Large states without income taxes hastened to adopt them, whether their governors were Democrats (Pennsylvania in 1971, Ohio in 1972, New Jersey in 1976) or Republicans (Michigan in 1967, Illinois in 1969). Public employee unions, granted bargaining rights by Mayor Robert Wagner in New York in 1958 and by Governor Gaylord Nelson in Wisconsin in 1959, were gathering strength in these years, violating or skirting bans on strikes and wresting wage increases and generous benefit packages first from city governments and then from states. The National Education Association was shedding its long-standing status as a professional organization and moving toward becoming an aggressive union in competition with the American Federation of Teachers. This move toward public sector unionization, even as private sector unions were losing members, added to the costs being imposed by these states' and cities' generous welfare benefits and created a constituency, financed by involuntary transfers from taxpayers, for more pay and benefits and less accountability in education and other public services.

The politicians and advocates who supported these changes believed that they were in the vanguard and that less enlightened states would inevitably follow. But not all states did. In the South most states avoided major tax rate increases and held down spending; most blocked the emergence of public employee unions. Florida, which got one-third of its sales tax revenues from out-of-staters, had a constitutional provision banning an income tax, and Texas and Tennessee remained determined to have none either. Nevada, with gambling revenue, and Wyoming, with mineral revenue, had no state income tax; neither did Alaska after 1982, when North Slope oil revenue was starting to flow in. Washington State had no income tax, while its neighbor Oregon had no state sales tax. In the Northeast New Hampshire, after pitched battles, stuck to the policy, backed strongly by *Manchester Union Leader* publisher William Loeb, of having no state income or sales tax. Loeb himself lived in Massachusetts, a high-tax state in the 1970s and 1980s; there was an outflow of migration from "Taxachusetts" to New Hampshire that slowed after referenda and Republican governors of Massachusetts reduced tax rates in the 1990s.

High tax rates typically raised less in revenue than projected, but, more important, the increased spending in high-tax states did not produce the visible positive results that were promised. Black neighborhoods in central cities continued to be plagued by high rates of crime and welfare dependency, as one generation of single mothers raised children who too often became criminals or welfare dependents themselves. Crime and welfare dependency roughly tripled nationally between 1965 and 1975 and then plateaued at high levels, with a spike upward due to the crack cocaine epidemic of the late 1980s and early 1990s. This resulted in the emptying out and even abandonment of many central city neighborhoods, which were shunned and avoided by law-abiding citizens. The chief victims were law-abiding black residents. Latin immigrants tended to shun these neighborhoods as well. Latins tended to settle in what had been low-income predominantly white neighborhoods, geographically separate from black ghettoes. The result has been a flight of businesses and people from the high-tax states to low-tax alternatives.

The ten largest metropolitan areas of 1940 grew 65 percent between 1940 and 1970, above the national average of 54 percent. Between 1970 and 2010 these metropolitan areas grew by only 24 percent, well below the national average of 52 percent. That percentage was buoyed upward by above-average growth, especially in Los Angeles and also in San Francisco, reflecting heavy immigration and continued domestic migration, though much smaller than previously, in the 1970s and 1980s. But starting in 1990, even as immigrants continued arriving, there was domestic migration out of California, and those two metro areas grew at a rate under the national average between 1990 and 2010—the first time since the gold rush they have done so. None of the other eight metro areas on the list grew more than 20 percent in this period and three—Detroit, Cleveland, and Pittsburgh—lost population between 1990 and 2010. Pittsburgh, the one metro area with more deaths than births at the end of this period, had fewer people in its metropolitan area in 2010 than in 1940. The trend can be illustrated by comparing the growth of two states with very different policies over the forty years after 1970. In 1970 Michigan had 9 million people. In 2010, forty years later, it had 10 million. In 1970 Texas had 11 million people. In 2010 it had 25 million people.

FOR eight decades American law discouraged immigration from Asia. This reflected popular attitudes. A vast influx of Chinese men poured into California for three decades after the gold rush in 1848, and Chinese provided much of the labor for the construction of the transcontinental railroad, completed in 1869. Chinese were 9 percent of the population of California in the 1870 and 1880 Censuses. Their presence in San Francisco's tightly packed Chinatown and their willingness to work hard for low wages aroused white workers' ire and sparked the creation of Dennis Kearney's Workingmen's Party, which demanded an end to Chinese immigration. Congress responded by passing the aptly named Chinese Exclusion Act of 1882, which barred further immigration, and in time the Chinese population mostly died out.[8]

But the demand for labor on the sparsely populated West Coast continued, and between 1884 and 1906 some 300,000 Japanese migrated to Hawaii and California to work as agricultural laborers. Even though many were sojourners who returned to Japan, California politicians demanded a Japanese Exclusion Act. The Japanese government protested bitterly, and Theodore Roosevelt negotiated the so-called Gentleman's Agreement of 1907, in which Japan agreed to bar emigration of male laborers and the United States agreed to allow family unification.[9] Japanese emigration was then directed to Brazil, which now has more than twice as many citizens of Japanese descent as the United States. The 1924 immigration act cut off all immigration from Asia, except from the Philippines, which was U.S. territory, although Filipinos were ineligible for U.S. citizenship. These harsh measures reflected widespread American attitudes that Asians were sinister, even inhuman, attitudes expressed most vividly in anti-Japanese rhetoric in World War II.

By 1965, when President Lyndon Johnson was pressing Congress to pass immigration legislation, only 1 percent of people in the United States were classified as Asian, and they were concentrated largely in Hawaii, with its many Japanese-, Chinese-, and Filipino-Americans, in enclaves in the San Francisco Bay Area and the Los Angeles Basin, and in tiny Chinatowns in other large cities.

The immigration bill provided for quotas of 20,000 immigrants annually from every country, which meant opening up the border to many more Asians than had emigrated since 1882 or 1907. But the expectation was that most immigration would come from Europe, as had always been the case; the main constituencies favoring the bill were Jewish and Italian organizations, still aggrieved over the cutoff of Ellis Islander immigration in the law passed in 1924. Attorney General Robert Kennedy, testifying on the legislation in 1964, predicted that the "Asia-Pacific triangle" would produce "approximately 5,000 [immigrants], after which immigration from that source would virtually disappear."[10] Once again experts and conventional wisdom failed to anticipate the surge of migration that was about to occur.

In the nineteenth century nations whose economies were growing rapidly, like Britain and Japan, also generated a large number of emigrants who settled in other countries. High birth rates and falling death rates generated a labor surplus in these countries, and emigrants settled in countries that were also growing but had labor shortages—the United States especially, but also Canada, Australia, New Zealand, Argentina, and Brazil. In time a combination of lower birth rates and continuing economic growth reduced the incentive to leave, in Britain and Germany in the 1890s, in Japan in the 1920s. Not many people in the late 1960s supposed that the nations of East Asia and South Asia would either cease to grow demographically or grow economically in like manner. The great Swedish sociologist Gunnar

Myrdal, whose 1944 book *An American Dilemma* showed great pre-science in diagnosing America's racial problems and pointing the way toward solutions, published a massive volume in 1968, *Asian Drama: An Inquiry into the Poverty of Nations.* He forecast that Asian nations were trapped in a mire of overpopulation and poverty from which there was no escape even on the far horizon. It proved to be as bad a prophecy as Galbraith's vision of big government, big business, and big labor growing ever bigger in America. Over the next four decades, at varying paces, most of the Asian nations would experience vigorous economic growth. But even as their birth rates fell, they also gener-ated a surplus supply of labor that, as was the case with Britain, Ger-many, and Japan, would seek opportunity elsewhere, particularly in the United States. The Philippines, a U.S. colony and commonwealth from 1898 to 1946 (although occupied by the Japanese from 1942 to 1945), was long the country that produced the most immigrants; it was not until the 2000s that its number of immigrants was overtaken, only slightly, by the number of immigrants from India and China. Filipinos had long been stewards on U.S. Navy vessels and in that capacity were waiters at the White House Mess; Filipino immigrants tended to be relatively low skill, with an increasing number of Filipina nurses over the years. Nearly half of Filipino immigrants headed to California, especially the San Francisco Bay Area, where they have been concentrated in modest-income suburbs such as Daly City just south of San Francisco, in Vallejo, and the industrial towns across the Carquinez Strait in Contra Costa County and in Fremont in the East Bay. The next most frequent Filipino destinations were Hawaii and metro New York.

The two nations in which the United States fought in order to save them from Communism, Korea and Vietnam, contributed relatively few immigrants in the 1960s—hence Robert Kennedy's prediction—but immigration stepped up in the 1970s to 27,000 annu-ally from South Korea and 18,000 annually from Vietnam, the latter consisting mostly of refugees who managed to escape as the Commu-nists took over South Vietnam in 1975. Korean immigration stepped up to 34,000 annually in the 1980s, but then dropped off to about half that figure, as Korea's economy headed rapidly toward first-world status and the dictatorial government gave way to a vigorous electoral democracy. Korean immigrants tended to come over with relatively low skills but fierce work habits and entrepreneurial spirits, setting up the vibrant Koreatown commercial district in a declining neighborhood in Los Angeles (pillaged by black rioters in 1992) and establishing iconic grocery stores with beautifully polished and symmetrical displays of fruit in New York City. Los Angeles and then New York were their most common destinations, but they also had a presence in metro Washington and Chicago. Korean parents became known for their fierce devotion to education and their insistence that their children get top grades; they tended to buy or rent the cheapest homes in the best school districts. Despite the commercial concentration in Koreatown, they tended to move out to suburbs like Torrance on the ocean or the San Gabriel Valley, outside the Los Angeles Unified school district with its largely Hispanic student body and low academic standards. In the New York metro area Koreans are most heavily concentrated in the bucolic suburbs of Bergen County, New Jersey, across the George Washington Bridge from upper Manhattan.

While Korean immigration numbers declined in the middle 1980s, Vietnamese kept arriving at the rate of 40,000 annually in the 1980s and 1990s, with a decline to 27,000 annually in the 2000s. The Vietnamese, from a more tropical climate, tended to avoid northern cities. Their largest migration was to Los Angeles, centered in the Vietnamese communities in Westminster, Garden Grove, and Fountain Valley in Orange County, with a secondary group in the San Gabriel Valley (again, not in the heavily Hispanic Santa Ana Unified or Los Angeles Unified school districts). Their second-largest migration was to Texas, to Houston and the fishing communities on the Gulf coast and to the east.

Immigration from Laos and Cambodia spiked upward in the 1980s, to 15,000 and 11,000 annually. Many of these appear to have been low-skill refugees, especially the Hmong people, who, attracted by offers of aid from local church and charitable groups, settled in large numbers in the Minneapolis–St. Paul area and adjacent parts of Minnesota and Wisconsin and also in significant numbers in the Central Valley of California. The largest concentrations of Cambodians are in the old textile mill town of Lowell, Massachusetts, and in Long Beach, California. But immigration from these countries declined to small numbers after 1990.

America's historical record on Chinese immigration is not an admirable one. The Chinese Exclusion Act was passed in 1882 and was modified in 1943, in wartime when China was a valued ally, to allow a grand total of 60 Chinese to enter. Immigration from China proper was blocked for years after the Communist takeover, and Chinese immigrants in the 1960s amounted to about 10,000 annually from Taiwan, 2,500 from Hong Kong, and an undetermined number of ethnic overseas Chinese from other Asian countries, including the Philippines, Malaysia, and Thailand. Immigration from China and Taiwan rose to 20,000 annually in the 1970s (almost all from Taiwan) and 39,000 annually in the 1980s (with a somewhat higher proportion from China presumably, as Deng's reforms). The 1990s saw 42,000 coming annually from China and 10,000 from Taiwan, which having reached an economic level similar to South Korea's was producing fewer immigrants. In the 2000s immigration from China zoomed to 59,000 annually, while from Taiwan it fell to 8,000 annually and from Hong King to 4,000 annually. Most Chinese immigrants, whether from Taiwan or the mainland, have headed to three metropolitan areas: Los Angeles, San Francisco, and New York. Increasingly in the 1990s and 2000s, Chinese immigrants have come with high skill levels, often with advanced degrees in math and science earned in American universities. There are large concentrations of Chinese residents in the middle-income, relatively family-oriented neighborhoods of Richmond and Sunset in San Francisco and in suburbs on the Peninsula heading south to Silicon Valley; in the San Gabriel Valley east of Los Angeles and in Flushing and adjacent neighborhoods in New York's borough of Queens. San Francisco's population is now

21 percent Chinese, and Cupertino, site of the headquarters of Apple, is 23 percent Chinese. Chinese form near-majorities of many cities in the San Gabriel Valley—Monterey Park, San Marino (long the home of much of Los Angeles's WASP elite), Alhambra, Arcadia, San Gabriel, Rosemead, Temple City. Another cluster lies farther east, along the hills, in Rowland Heights, Hacienda Heights, Walnut, and Diamond Bar. New York's giant borough of Queens, with more than 2 million people, is 6 percent Chinese, and after the 2010 Census the legislature drew a new congressional district there with a population that was 38 percent Asian. Earlier Chinese immigrants with relatively low skills have struggled to make sure their children are well educated, and more recent high-skill immigrants typically enroll their children in America's elite high schools, public and private, and secure their admission to highly selective colleges and universities. The metro areas with the biggest concentrations of Chinese after San Francisco, Los Angeles, and New York are places with concentrations of high-tech and life sciences technology—Boston, Washington, Chicago.

A similar pattern seems to have emerged with immigrants from India. They were few in number at first: 3,000 annually in the 1960s, then 17,000 annually in the 1970s. Even in the 1980s, when Indian immigration reached 26,000 annually (plus 6,000 from Pakistan and 1,500 from Bangladesh), they were far outnumbered by immigrants from the Philippines, Vietnam, Taiwan, and South Korea. But the Indian numbers kept increasing, to 38,000 annually in the 1990s and 59,000 annually in the 2000s. That last number was slightly larger than the numbers from China or the Philippines, and more than twice as many as the numbers from Vietnam or South Korea. Many early Indian immigrants made their livings as many Koreans and Vietnamese had, finding particular retail or service niches and working hard with all members of the family joining in to achieve success. An example is the Gujaratis known as Patels (by far their most popular surname) who came to dominate the management of bargain motels along interstate highways in the South, despite the lack of any tradition of hotel management back home. In addition, many Indian immigrants are medical doctors, happy staff at hospitals in blue-collar portions of metropolitan areas, while American-born physicians gravitate to prestigious hospitals attached to universities or on fashionable sides of town. And India has been increasingly producing scientists at the cutting edge in computer and life sciences technologies. The largest concentration of Indian immigrants is in metro New York, not so much in New York City as in central New Jersey, Middlesex County, and along the U.S. 1 corridor with its high concentration of pharmaceutical and life sciences businesses. The next-highest concentration is in Silicon Valley, with smaller concentrations around Washington and Chicago.

Overall, Asian immigration since the 1965 immigration act opened the doors has slowly changed from being a movement of people with low levels of education and high levels of aspiration, for their children if not so much for themselves, into gritty cities and struggling suburbs, into a movement of people with increasingly high levels of education and very high levels of competence, concentrated in the most innovative and high-skill centers of American society. While Asian migration has slowed during the great recession and afterward, it is poised to resume at high rates—and higher still if U.S. immigration law is revised to allow, along the lines of Canada's and Australia's immigration laws, the admission of significantly larger numbers of high-skill immigrants.

LATIN immigration accelerated only somewhat in the 1970s, then took off in the 1980s to reach high levels with some year-to-year fluctuations continuing in the 1990s and 2000s until the onset of the recession in 2007. The number of green cards issued to Latin immigrants averaged about 100,000 annually in the 1960s; 150,000 annually in the economically troubled 1970s; and more than 300,000 annually in the mostly booming years in the next three decades. In addition, there was a flow of illegal immigrants that of course was not

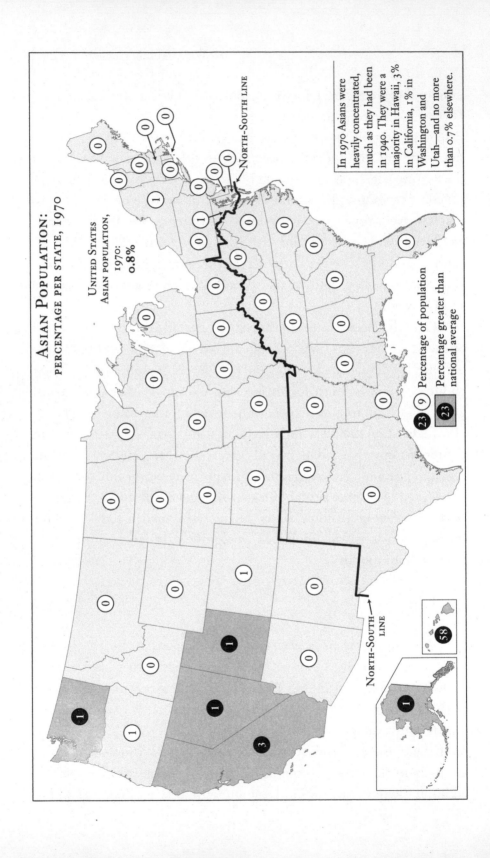

ASIAN POPULATION:
PERCENTAGE PER STATE, 1970

UNITED STATES
ASIAN POPULATION,
1970:
0.8%

NORTH-SOUTH LINE

NORTH-SOUTH → LINE

In 1970 Asians were
heavily concentrated,
much as they had been
in 1940. They were a
majority in Hawaii, 3%
in California, 1% in
Washington and
Utah—and no more
than 0.7% elsewhere.

23 9 Percentage of population

23 Percentage greater than
national average

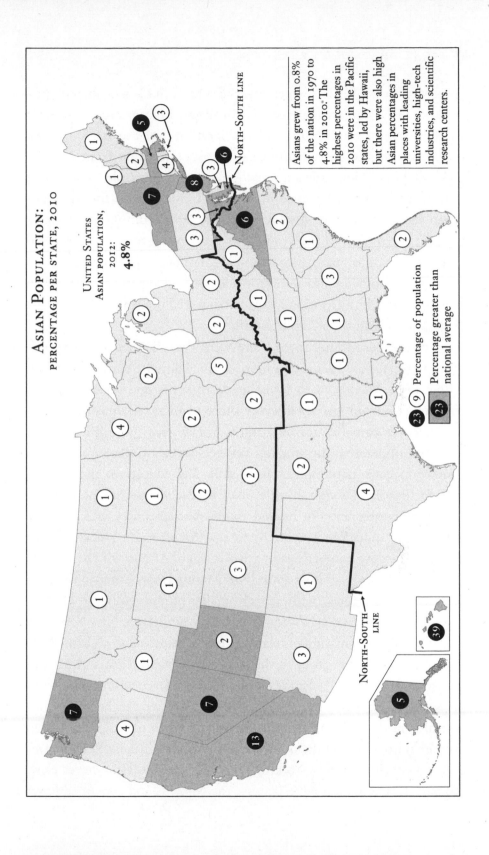

ASIAN POPULATION:
PERCENTAGE PER STATE, 2010

UNITED STATES
ASIAN POPULATION,
2012:
4.8%

NORTH-SOUTH LINE

Asians grew from 0.8%
of the nation in 1970 to
4.8% in 2010.* The
highest percentages in
2010 were in the Pacific
states, led by Hawaii,
but there were also high
Asian percentages in
places with leading
universities, high-tech
industries, and scientific
research centers.

23 9 Percentage of population

23 Percentage greater than
national average

NORTH-SOUTH
LINE

precisely measured, but which was the subject of Census Bureau estimates. They suggest that total Latin illegal immigration was about
half as large as total Latin legal immigration over the years. In both
cases the largest portion of Latin immigrants came from Mexico.
The fact that Mexico has a 2,200-mile-long penetrable border with
the United States of course made illegal entry easier for Mexicans
than those from more distant countries. Illegal immigration seems
to have accelerated in the 1980s. The 1986 immigration law provided
for legalization of many illegals and the number of green cards issued
in response spiked upward in 1990 and 1991 and again in 1996, when
the Clinton administration instituted a special program to encourage
legalization (and voter registration).

In the 1960s and 1970s there were two distinct and very different streams of Latin migration to the United States. About half
came from Mexico, with lower levels of skills and education than
immigrants from just about every other country. About one-fifth to
one-quarter came from Cuba, and U.S. law gave those fleeing Fidel
Castro's oppressive dictatorship refugee status. Cuban immigrants
tended to have quite high levels of skills and education, and by defi-
nition there is no significant Cuban illegal immigrant population.
Most Mexicans initially headed to the border states of California
and Texas, and more specifically to Los Angeles and Houston, with
the next-largest number heading to Chicago. Almost all the Cubans
headed to Florida, almost entirely to Miami-Dade County (the official name since 1999), with a much smaller number going to Hudson
County, New Jersey, across the river from Manhattan. New York City
itself was the destination of relatively few Mexicans and Cubans. New
York's largest Latin group at that time was Puerto Ricans, American
citizens by law since 1917; they arrived in very large numbers between
1949 and 1961, when income levels in Puerto Rico reached one-third
of those in the mainland United States and when net migration from
the island to the mainland fell suddenly to zero. Thus the *West Side
Story* scenario of a New York that was half Puerto Rican never came
to pass (and could not have, because the whole island contained fewer

than half the city's population). In the 1960s and 1970s the largest sources of immigrants to New York were the Dominican Republic and Jamaica, with Dominicans heading mainly to upper Manhattan and the Bronx, and Jamaicans and other black immigrants from small Caribbean islands, mainly to Brooklyn. The giant surge of Latin migration to the United States began in the 1980s, as low-inflation economic growth replaced the stagflation—high inflation and sluggish growth—of the 1970s. Earlier Latin migration had set in motion the process of chain migration, in which the first migrants, usually young men, would establish a beachhead in a large metropolitan area, get jobs and send remittances home, and then bring others, including women and children, from their villages or city neighborhoods. The prosperous economy of the 1980s created construction jobs and an expanding affluent class with the wherewithal to pay for personal services—for household servants, waiters and dishwashers, valet parkers, repairmen, carpenters and plumbers, workers in hotels and restaurants and theme parks.

The primary destination for Mexicans in the 1980s and 1990s was Los Angeles. At the beginning of this period it was still attracting domestic migrants, though in lesser numbers than in previous years, but it also had a large existing Mexican community, with entry neighborhoods in East Los Angeles, in the Pico-Union neighborhood in Los Angeles, and in Santa Ana in Orange County. Los Angeles's proximity to the Mexican border was an additional advantage, though many migrants came up on chains extending far into the Mexican cordillera. Los Angeles in the 1980s was an engine of growth in the American economy, with major defense and aerospace industries, an active banking sector, and the entertainment industry. Los Angeles had a reputation for being tolerant of minorities and California had high-spending welfare and social service programs. Los Angeles had symbolic attractions as well, as the second-largest American metro area, as the beloved home of President Reagan, as the site of the 1984 Olympics, which proved to be successful (at least from an American point of view, since the withdrawal of the Soviets allowed Americans to win a lion's share of medals). Ironically, the Olympic year probably marked the point at which more Latins than Americans were moving into California: destinations of secondary popularity for Mexicans were Houston and, well behind, Chicago; well behind that were Dallas and other western metro areas—San Francisco, Phoenix, Seattle, Denver, Las Vegas.

Latins from other countries tended to head farther east. Cubans still came, in reduced numbers, almost exclusively to Miami and Hudson County, New Jersey. Puerto Ricans, who had headed exclusively to New York three and four decades before, now moved to old factory towns in the Northeast and to metro Orlando, with its huge number of hospitality jobs. But Dominicans still tended to head to upper Manhattan and the Bronx and industrial clusters in northern New Jersey, with smaller numbers heading to northeast Massachusetts and Providence, Rhode Island. Salvadorans headed primarily to the Maryland and Virginia suburbs of Washington, to the Long Island suburbs east of New York City, and in smaller numbers to Los Angeles. Guatemalans fanned out in many directions, to small towns like Georgetown, Delaware, with chicken-processing plants; to small factory and farming towns in north Georgia and Alabama; and to meatpacking plants in Nebraska. Hondurans gravitated to parts of metro New York and Miami but also to small towns in North Carolina. Nicaraguans, in contrast, headed almost entirely to Miami.

It is a fact little known among Americans that almost all of South America lies east of the continental United States; the Pacific coast of Chile is east of the Atlantic coast of Florida, and Latin immigrants from South America have headed mostly to the East Coast of the United States. The most numerous have been Colombians, with about 12,000 arriving annually in the 1980s and 1990s, and 23,000 annually in the 2000s. Almost all of them have gone to metro New York or metro Miami. Ecuadorans, in contrast, have headed almost entirely to metro New York, settling in Queens near Kennedy Airport or fanning out to suburbs in all directions. Their numbers, like those of Colombians, increased in the 2000s, to 10,000 annually. Peruvians have come in slightly larger numbers, up to 13,000 annually in the 2000s, with the large majority in metro New York, smaller clusters in metro Miami and Washington, and almost none heading anywhere else. Brazil, with nearly 200 million people, sent only 11,000 annually to the United States in the 2000s, and that flow reversed entirely when Brazil's economy boomed after recession hit the United States. Brazilians are most numerous in the Ironbound district of Newark and the small New Jersey towns nearby; in Framingham and Somerville, Massachusetts; and in metro Miami.

The Latin immigration that has taken place since the 1965 immigration act has certainly not been what its framers expected. In the 1960s and 1970s nearly one-quarter of Latin immigrants were Cuban, relatively upscale or high skill, and, by their own choice, largely confined to a single metropolitan area, indeed a single county, Miami. They came with, and in many cases cherished, an easily understandable political grievance against the vicious Castro regime in Cuba, but otherwise they have been an unproblematic addition to the American population.

The Mexican immigrants who began arriving in vast numbers in the 1980s have been more downscale. On average they have come with lower levels of education and lower skill levels than immigrants from any other country, with illegals probably having even lower levels than legal immigrants. One reason is that Mexicans with high levels of education and skills have generally been able to live very comfortably in Mexico; another reason is that the existence of a long border over land or across the narrow and shallow Rio Grande (its waters are drawn down for irrigation on both sides of the border) means that crossing the border, legally or illegally, is relatively easy. Mexicans comprised fewer than half of Latin immigrants in the 1960s and 1970s but about 60 percent of a very much larger number of Latin immigrants in the 1980s and 1990s. Mexican immigrants have been very hardworking, and relatively few have attached themselves to American welfare state protections. But they have also had difficulty assimilating as rapidly as immigrants in the Ellis Island period. The existence of very large, predominantly Mexican neighborhoods in Los Angeles, Houston, and Miami and of employers and supervisors able to speak or willing to learn Spanish have made it unnecessary or impractical for many immigrants to master English. Plus the so-called bilingual education and poor instruction in public schools with very large numbers of Latin immigrant children have made it more difficult than it should be for their children to learn English. In addition many elite policymakers have regarded assimilation as a form of oppression rather than a means of liberation to live a full American life.

Not all the trends are negative or discouraging, however. The number of legal Mexican immigrants fell after 2000, and they now amount to less than half the total of Latin immigrants. Moreover, the people being legalized are less likely to be newcomers seeking work and more likely to be relatives of immigrants who have become U.S. citizens: extended family reunification.

All the available statistics suggest a sharp decline in the number of newly arriving illegal immigrants as well. The great recession of 2007–2009 altered the position of Mexican immigrants sharply. Many had been encouraged by policies encouraging "minority" home ownership to buy homes in the United States. The result was a rash of mortgage loans granted to non-creditworthy buyers and quickly off-loaded by lenders onto the government-sponsored enterprises Fannie Mae and Freddie Mac, to be securitized and sold to financial institutions all over the world as AAA-rated investments. Lenders employed Spanish-speaking salesmen and cut every corner available; day laborers with cash income and no W-2 forms were imputed to have incomes of $100,000 and granted $350,000 mortgages on houses far out in the desert. The assumption was that housing values would always increase and that the eventual holders of the securitized mortgages could bear a few foreclosures. Of course, all these assumptions proved false when housing values started plunging in 2006. That led to the deep recession beginning in 2007 and the financial crisis of 2008. Most of the foreclosures cascading through the 2007–2010 period were in just four states, California, Nevada, Arizona, and

Florida, all states with very high levels of Latin immigration. And the foreclosure rates were highest in those parts of those states with the most Latin immigration—the Inland Empire and Central Valley of California, Las Vegas, Phoenix, Orlando, and Miami. My estimate is that Latins of immigrant stock accounted for about one-third of all foreclosures during this period. Their dream of owning a comfortable home in America, their dream of accumulating wealth from its ever-increasing value—those dreams were dashed, just as the virtual shutdown of the construction industry in these areas also shattered their dreams of continuing to work hard and make their way ahead in their new country.

At the same time, stronger border enforcement was making it more difficult to go back and forth to and from Mexico. The effect was felt in California's Central Valley, where many Mexican immigrants, legal and illegal, could find seasonal work in harvesting crops but not year-long steady jobs. The result is that in the 2000s the Central Valley had above-average population growth and above-average unemployment rates at the same time—something that seldom happens when people are free to move. In addition, technological progress and state laws were making it more difficult for illegals to find jobs. The E-Verify system, to match job applicants with Social Security numbers, was developed and vastly improved in the 2000s, and some states, notably Arizona, required employers to use it. Some large national employers, like McDonald's, decided to use it voluntarily, to prevent the embarrassment of being sued for hiring illegals. These measures probably did more to discourage illegal immigrants than Arizona's much more controversial SB1070 law requiring police officers to notify immigration authorities of persons whom they stopped for other reasons who could not produce proof of citizenship or legal residence.

It is against this background that we should assess the Census Bureau estimate that the number of illegal immigrants in the United States was reduced from 12.5 million in 2008 to 11.5 million in 2009. Notably, the percentage decrease was larger in Arizona than in states not requiring E-Verify and without SB1070-type laws. The

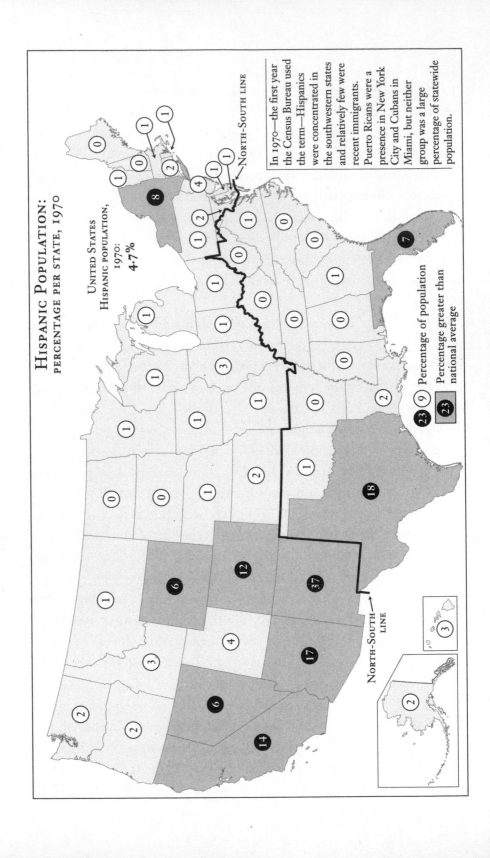

HISPANIC POPULATION:
PERCENTAGE PER STATE, 1970

UNITED STATES
HISPANIC POPULATION,
1970:
4.7%

In 1970—the first year
the Census Bureau used
the term—Hispanics
were concentrated in
the southwestern states
and relatively few were
recent immigrants.
Puerto Ricans were a
presence in New York
City and Cubans in
Miami, but neither
group was a large
percentage of statewide
population.

NORTH-SOUTH LINE

NORTH-SOUTH
LINE

23 9 Percentage of population

23 Percentage greater than
national average

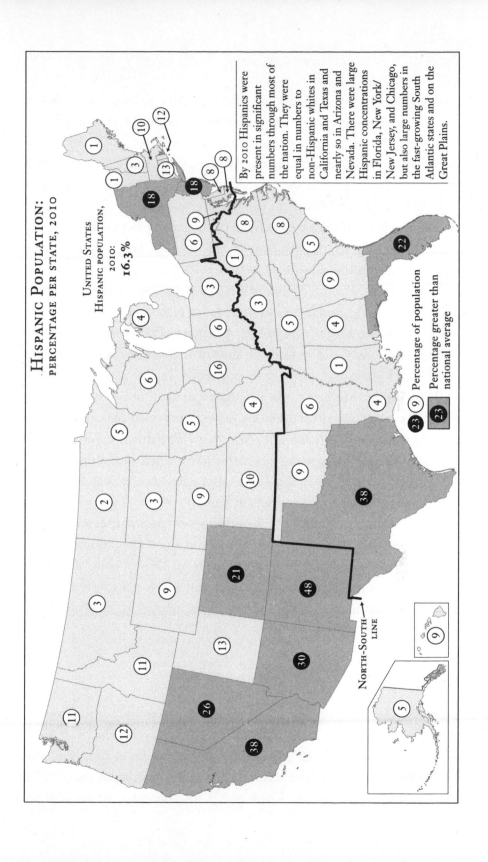

HISPANIC POPULATION:
PERCENTAGE PER STATE, 2010

UNITED STATES
HISPANIC POPULATION,
2010:
16.3%

By 2010 Hispanics were present in significant numbers through most of the nation. They were equal in numbers to non-Hispanic whites in California and Texas and nearly so in Arizona and Nevada. There were large Hispanic concentrations in Florida, New York/New Jersey, and Chicago, but also large numbers in the fast-growing South Atlantic states and on the Great Plains.

23 Percentage of population

23 Percentage greater than national average

NORTH-SOUTH LINE

Pew Hispanic Center, in a report based on these figures and on other U.S. and Mexican government statistics, concluded in April 2012 that there was no net migration from Mexico into the United States between 2005 and 2010: as many Mexicans left the U.S. as entered it. Since there is no question that there was net immigration into the United States from Mexico in the pre-recession years of 2005–2007, that means there must have been net outmigration between 2007 and 2010. Later data are not available at this writing, but it seems likely that the net outflow continued between 2010 and 2012. These were years when the Mexican economy was growing faster than the American economy. Mexican birth rates had fallen close to U.S. levels by the early 1990s, the birth years of the age cohort likeliest to immigrate in the early 2010s, and indeed the flow of migration from Mexico to the United States did drop about 25 percent in the 2000s compared with the 1990s. Moreover, the searing experience of the avalanche of mortgage foreclosures on Mexican immigrants must have had strong reverberations on both sides of the border. The dream of owning an American house and getting rich off it had turned into a nightmare, and many Mexicans and other Latins may have turned away from that American dream to pursue others at home.

Just as few predicted the beginnings of past surges of migration, so few predicted when they would end—and they usually ended abruptly. The surge of Latin migration from the 1980s to 2007 has ended, as this is written, and it seems unlikely to this writer that it will resume again at anything like the same rate or in the same numbers ever again.

EVEN as Latin and Asian immigrants were streaming into many of America's great cities, Americans were streaming out. The most vivid example, although one largely ignored by the media of the time, was the flight out of New York City and its close-in suburbs during the 1970s. Census data for the 1970s and 1980s showed a net population loss of more than 1 million even as immigrants were moving in the very center of the Megalopolis that had been growing vigorously for the previous thirty years. The population of the city's five boroughs fell by 823,000, or 10 percent; the New York suburban counties of Nassau and Westchester, scenes of amazing growth in the early postwar years, saw their combined populations fall by 134,000, or 6 percent; the population of the five adjacent counties in northeast New Jersey (Essex, Bergen, Hudson, Union, and Passaic) fell by 236,000, or 7 percent. This was in vivid contrast to the years from 1940 to 1970, when the population of these same areas rose by 2,686,000, or 24 percent, even though tenement neighborhoods in Manhattan were shedding residents. Much of this shocking population loss can be attributed to public policies. The continuation of rent control, adopted during World War II but abandoned soon afterward almost everywhere else in the country, meant that landlords allowed buildings to deteriorate and had an incentive to empty them out. Even more damaging were policies of the state and city governments led by Governor Rockefeller and Mayor Lindsay—ever higher taxes to support rapidly increasing public spending and indebtedness, lax law enforcement, refusal to screen welfare applicants for eligibility. The city was also hurt by economic trends. The garment industry largely relocated out of New York City because of low-wage competition (the state's high minimum wage did not help) and the financial sector was sagging in a time of stagnant stock prices and economic activity.

Some of the population loss in New York and other central cities was inevitable. Like many other cities, New York's population peaked in 1950, when the postwar housing boom had barely begun and large families were crammed into small apartments and 1,000-square-foot houses. As the economy continued to grow and the baby boom continued, and with very little open land left within city limits, it was inevitable that many people would move beyond the city limits and the number of people per housing unit would decline as extended families thrust together by the wartime housing shortage moved out on their own. In addition, the migration of southern blacks to northern cities brought additional residents into proximity with unneighborly whites. The result was a slight decline in central city populations together with vigorous growth in the suburbs in the 1960s.

But in the 1970s something new was starting to take place. Rising crime and disintegrating family structure were making black neighborhoods much more dangerous places to live. Law-abiding and industrious blacks started moving out, leaving many neighborhoods abandoned or with far smaller populations. Similarly, the mostly Jewish, Irish, Italian, and Polish residents of the neighborhoods they moved to also tended to move out, to the suburbs or, in the case of many New Yorkers, to Florida. This pattern was evident in all the northern cities with large numbers of southern black migrants—New York, Chicago, Philadelphia, Detroit, Baltimore, Washington, Cleveland, St. Louis—which had relatively little population loss in the 1960s (New York even had a slight gain) but much greater percentage population loss in the 1970s.

This had bruising fiscal consequences for central city governments, which in the late 1960s took on responsibility for eliminating poverty or at least in some way aiding their poor residents. The cities were losing relatively affluent taxpayers and they were losing the commercial base that was dependent on their patronage. Downtown real estate development slowed in the huge office centers in New York, Chicago, and Washington and virtually ceased in cities including Philadelphia, Detroit, Baltimore, Cleveland, and St. Louis; and downtown department stores did far less business—all reducing property values and city revenues. The response in most cases was to tax this declining tax base at higher rates, even as city police forces were unable to reduce violent crime rates. Again New York in the 1970s was an exceptional case. In the 1960s the city government increasingly sold bonds to pay for current spending and in 1975, tottering at the brink of bankruptcy, was taken over by a state control board.

In the 1980s Latin and Asian immigrants started coming in very large numbers to New York, Chicago, and Washington, but they tended to avoid Philadelphia, Detroit, Baltimore, Cleveland, and

St. Louis, leaving large swaths of land there abandoned and empty; in Washington they headed directly to the Maryland and Virginia suburbs rather than to the central city, and in New York and Chicago they tended to move outward to suburbs in time. Instead of the old northern cities that had been the destinations of so many northward-bound blacks, immigrants headed to cities like Los Angeles, Houston and Dallas, Phoenix and Las Vegas, with significantly smaller neighborhoods in which the criminal underclass thrived.

The result was a mass internal migration out of most big northern metro areas to other parts of the country. In the four decades from 1970 to 2010, population growth was minimal in most of the northern states containing large metro areas: 6 percent in New York, 15 percent in Massachusetts, 8 percent in Pennsylvania, 8 percent in Ohio, 11 percent in Michigan, 15 percent in Illinois. It was somewhat higher, 23 percent, in predominantly suburban New Jersey, but leaving aside that exception, growth in these high-population, high-tax states was less than in any other state except tiny Rhode Island, coal-dependent West Virginia, and, out on the Great Plains, Iowa and North Dakota. These large states were being abandoned and left behind, mostly by white Americans, most of them more affluent than average, some large portion of them retirees, but also by many young people at the start of their adult lives. Where did they go?

The first answer is Florida, whose population nearly tripled, up 177 percent, in 1970–2010: the highest population growth percentage except for those in Nevada and Arizona, which started off from much lower bases. The state that had been the lowest-population southern state in the 1940 Census became the fourth-largest state nationally, just a bit behind New York, in the 2010 Census. In 1940, when air-conditioning was a novelty encountered only in movie theaters and large department stores, Florida had 1.9 million people. In 1970, when air-conditioning was becoming common in cars and almost universal in new apartments and houses in the South, Florida had 6.8 million people. In 2010, when the presence of air-conditioning was considered totally unremarkable, Florida had 18.8 million people.

But air-conditioning is not the only reason for its growth. Florida's state constitution prohibits the imposition of a state income tax and that provision is unlikely ever to be repealed, since one-third of revenues in this heavy tourism state are paid by non-residents; no politician wants to ask voters to pay more so that outsiders can pay less. Florida also has no state inheritance tax, a major draw for rich people from New York and other states with hefty inheritance levies. South Florida famously has a large population of Jews, many originally from New York; they were concentrated in the 1950s in Dade (now Miami-Dade) County, but since the heavy Cuban migration there, most of South Florida's Jews have moved north to Broward and Palm Beach Counties. Florida has drawn people not just from New York and the East Coast, however. The Gulf coast has drawn retirees and migrants from the Midwest, coming down I-65 and I-75 from Chicago and Detroit, while the northern counties of Florida, more culturally southern, have drawn migrants from the South. In the early postwar years it was thought that Florida could never prosper economically because it had almost no manufacturing. It still has a very small manufacturing sector, but otherwise it has developed a strong commercial and services economy. While Upstate New York cities like Buffalo and Rochester, once known for their steel and optics industries, have been losing population or stagnating, Florida cities such as Tampa, Orlando, and Jacksonville, which were not much more than small towns when World War II ended, have become metro areas with more than 1 million people each.

A second area that has seen a surge of domestic migration has been the South Atlantic states from metro Washington south to the Florida border. In the 1940–70 period only Virginia, swollen by military bases, grew faster than the national average. The migration of textile industries from New England to the South Atlantic had given them more robust growth despite the outmigration of blacks than the interior South, though they still lagged the nation. But in 1970–2010 all of these states grew faster than the national average, with population growth of 74 percent in Virginia, 88 percent in North Carolina,

79 percent in South Carolina, and 111 percent in Georgia. On a map it looks as if the population of the Northeast was moving steadily down Interstate 95 from the Middle Atlantic states and New England to the South Atlantic states and Florida; but some of the movement was from other parts of the country as well. The South Atlantic states all have relatively low taxes and very low levels of unionization. They also have diverse economies. Metro Washington has grown more than the national average since 1930, thanks to the vast and continuing growth of the federal government and of the contractors and lobbyists it generates. This also accounts for much of the robust growth in Virginia, which has been more rapid than in higher-tax Maryland. The District of Columbia, like other central cities with large black migrations, suffered significant population loss in the 1970s but revived and actually grew in the 2000s. North Carolina began the forty-year period with an economy centered on textiles, tobacco, and furniture manufacturing and, as those declined, developed a high-tech center around the Regional Triangle near Raleigh and a national banking center in Charlotte. South Carolina, thought in 1970 to be dependent on military bases, saw most of them close but, after its system of segregation was dismantled, developed major port and manufacturing facilities, attracting big employers like BMW and Boeing. In Georgia, Atlanta grew from a regional center to one of the nation's ten largest metro areas, with a highly diversified economy and a culture that has attracted both black and white Americans as well as an increasing number of immigrants. Indeed Georgia actually grew at a higher percentage pace than Florida in the years from 1990 to 2010.

Another southern state that has grown faster than the national average is Tennessee, not coincidentally the only southern state except for Florida and Texas with no state income tax, as mentioned earlier. Tennessee's growth has been most rapid in Nashville, which like Charlotte, Raleigh, and Richmond has become a metro area with more than 1 million people. These metro areas could be called mini-Atlantas, except that some of their residents might take that label as an insult. Each has a diversified economy (Nashville is the center of the country music business and has a large auto-manufacturing sector) and a style of life that has attracted internal migrants from all over the country. And not just whites. There has been a significant migration of blacks from California and various northern cities to metro Atlanta, which with Washington, D.C., has the largest black middle class occupying increasing swaths of suburban territory. The southern climate—not just the weather, but southern habits of courtesy and southern food—has made Atlanta an attractive destination for professionals, black and white, who could make a good living in any major metro area.

Which leads us to our third area of internal migration in 1970–2010, the Mountain West, not including the West Coast states of California, Oregon, and Washington. In 1970–2010 the population more than quintupled in Nevada, more than tripled in Arizona, and more than doubled in Utah, Idaho, Colorado, and New Mexico. All these states have benefited from low tax rates and much more business-friendly regulatory climates as compared to California, and many of those moving in come directly from the previously Golden State. Most of this population growth has been concentrated in big or growing metro areas: Las Vegas, Phoenix, Tucson, Salt Lake City, Boise, Denver, and Albuquerque. Internal migration has been the chief source of growth here, although there has also been substantial Latin immigration in Las Vegas, Phoenix, and Tucson and somewhat lower levels in Salt Lake City, Boise, and Denver. During decades of rapid growth, Las Vegas and Phoenix developed economies with unusually large construction and real estate sectors, and so suffered disproportionately when real estate prices crashed in 2007 (and in Las Vegas's case, when gaming revenues started to decline in 2006). Nevada and Arizona in 2007–2009 had the highest rates of mortgage foreclosure in the country. Domestic migration into Nevada essentially ceased in 2007 and was vastly reduced in Phoenix.

The fourth major growth center and destination of domestic migration has been Texas. In 1940–70 its population growth rate trailed far behind those of Florida and California and, at 75 percent, was above, but not far above, the national average of 54 percent. But in 1970–2010 Texas's population more than doubled, growing 125 percent, far above the national average of 53 percent. This spectacular boom was helped along by the oil price rises of the 1970s. Texas has remained the nation's largest oil-producing state and, even more important, it is the center of the oil services industry and the largest producer of petrochemicals and refinery products. But Texas is more than just the Oil Patch, as some call it. With no state income tax, with a very business-friendly regulatory climate, with very few labor unions, with no noxious tort bar thanks to laws championed by governors George W. Bush and Rick Perry, Texas has attracted corporate headquarters and one-person start-ups. It has major high-tech clusters in Dallas and Austin, it has the nation's largest medical center in Houston, and it has major military bases in San Antonio and Killeen and El Paso.

In 1970, when the big-unit economy of big government, big business, and big labor still seemed firmly established, it was assumed by many that Michigan was the model of the future, with a few large dominant companies, a heavily unionized workforce, high levels of taxation and government spending, and a commitment to government anti-poverty programs. Texas, which had none of these things, was said to be retrogressive, behind the times, in need of liberal reform, and destined in any case to imitate the successful Michigan model. The four decades that followed have disproved this thesis. The population figures tell the story. Michigan had 9 million people in 1970. It had 10 million people in 2010. Texas had 11 million people in 1970. It had 25 million people in 2010. While Michigan has had heavy domestic outmigration and very little immigrant growth, Texas has attracted both domestic migrants and immigrants in very large numbers, with the bulk from Mexico but also significant numbers from Vietnam, China, and Taiwan, who are most visible on the southwest side of metro Houston.

This pattern of balanced growth, from both domestic and immigrant migration, is apparent in many other inland metropolises, including Phoenix, Las Vegas, and Denver in the West and Atlanta,

Tampa, Orlando, Charlotte, Raleigh, Nashville, and Richmond in the South. It is in vivid contrast to the pattern in the nation's largest coastal metropolises, New York, Chicago (on the coast of Lake Michigan), Los Angeles, and San Francisco, which in the two decades from 1990 to 2010 saw substantial immigration but heavy domestic outmigration in equal or larger numbers. As a result, the coastal metropolises are increasingly polarized economically and culturally, with a large and highly visible group of affluent, highly educated, and almost entirely white people and a much larger group of low-income, low-education people, with large numbers of Hispanics and blacks. Missing are white middle-class people with families, priced out of high-end housing and not willing to live in neighborhoods where English appears to be the second language. In contrast, the inland metropolises have much more even income distributions and middle-class white families are able to find affordable housing in congenial neighborhoods.

Economics is clearly not the only factor at work here. The four decades from 1970 to 2010 saw an increasing tendency for Americans to move to places that they find culturally congenial, a trend that journalist Bill Bishop has called "the big sort."[11] And, as American political divisions increasingly reflected cultural attitudes, personal morals, and religious beliefs, from the *Roe v. Wade* decision legalizing abortion nationally in 1973 to the onset of the great recession in 2007, Americans have tended to move to neighborhoods and to states and metropolitan areas where their own political views are dominant. Young professionals who can choose where they will live gravitate toward the San Francisco Bay Area and like-minded places if their values and views are liberal, and toward the Dallas–Fort Worth Metroplex and other like-minded places if their values and views are conservative.

Bishop overstates this trend a bit by using as a political benchmark the 1976 presidential election. In that election both major parties nominated candidates who happened to come from historic heartlands of their parties at a time when voters in each of those heartlands were trending away from their historic party. Jimmy Carter's south Georgia still remembered General Sherman's march to the sea (though not as vividly as in 1960, when it cast the second-highest percentage for John Kennedy), but it would, after Carter's departure from politics, become solidly Republican. Gerald Ford's outstate Michigan was one of the birthplaces of the Republican Party but, in recoil from the Watergate scandal and the Vietnam War, had elected Democrats in two 1974 special congressional elections, including one from Ford's own Grand Rapids district. Nonetheless, Bishop's thesis is broadly correct. Just as the Yankee diaspora and the southern planters founded new provinces on virgin (or Indian) land congenial to their moral values and political views, so in the late twentieth and early twenty-first century did liberal and conservative Americans, in suburbs and exurbs, central city enclaves, and suburban gated communities. This coincides with the demise of universal media, such as the 1930s and 1940s movies and 1950s and 1960s television, which sought to appeal to all Americans regardless of religion, race, ethnic group, national origin, or age, and the rise of niche media, in which entertainment figures and political journalists alike sought to appeal just to one or two like-minded segments of the population, often by exhibiting hostility to others. The collective results of these decisions and trends can be seen on the political map, in which a decreasing number of counties and congressional districts are closely divided between the two parties and an increasing number cast large majorities for one party or the other.

Do these trends mean that the country, nearly seventy-six years after Pearl Harbor, is in danger of flying apart? Not any more so than at most points in American history, and much less so than at some. Much of American social science was developed in the two post–World War II decades, and many analysts assumed that the attitudes and behaviors of Americans in that period were typical of our whole history. This was a conformist and consensus-minded America, a nation that celebrated the normal and the average and scorned the eccentric and the deviant. Ethnic and regional differences seemed far less important than before the annealing experience of World War II. It was an America where large majorities had confidence in the nation's institutions and leaders. But was this period the norm in American history or was it an atypical midcentury moment?

The history of American migrations suggests strongly that this confidence was the exception rather than the rule. Since the earliest colonial days, cultural and economic differences between American migrants have been a centrifugal force in American life, tending to drive the colonies and then the states apart rather than pushing them together. The origins of the different colonies were diverse: four British folkways, as historian David Hackett Fischer describes them in *Albion's Seed*, while adding in his text that there were other folkways—Dutch, French, African—as well. Their record of unified action in the face of repeated British wars with France in the seventeenth and eighteenth centuries was dismal. Their coming together in Philadelphia in 1774, 1775, and 1776 was the result of the efforts of men of extraordinary talent and courage—and of the fact that the representatives of two of the largest colonies, Virginia and Massachusetts, each had their own set of grievances against the British government. Their first attempt at a national government, the Articles of Confederation, was a failure, and it was by no means clear that the Constitution written in 1787 and adopted in 1788 would fare any better. Without the steady leadership of and the prestige enjoyed by George Washington, the young republic might have fallen apart over differences regarding which side to back in the world war between revolutionary France and royal Britain, an issue on which Cavalier-settled Virginia and Calvinist-settled Massachusetts took opposite sides. Without the Constitution's explicit neutrality on religion—Article VI's prohibition on religious tests for federal office, the First Amendment's denial of congressional power regarding an establishment of religion—and its framework of limited government, many more divisive issues might have arisen that would have grievously split the nation.

The Union did actually fly apart as a result of differences between the Yankee diaspora and the southern planters over the status of slavery—an issue that under the Constitution the federal government could not avoid—in the lands obtained and settled in the southwestward migration of the Jacksonian Scots-Irish. The Union was saved but the rupture was not healed as over the next three generations the North and the South remained within the same national boundaries but lived largely apart from each other.

World War II had an opposite, annealing effect. It put 16 million Americans in the military and shuffled millions of others to defense plants and installations across the country. In the process it put the South and the North in touch with each other, united descendants of German and Irish immigrants hitherto leery of cooperation with the British, and welcomed the Ellis Islanders into full citizenship. It also set in motion two surges of migration to what seemed to be promised lands, of southern blacks to the big cities of the North and of the young GI generation as well as Great Plains retirees to California. Those surges lasted about one generation and were followed by migrations that almost no one anticipated, of immigrants from Latin America and Asia and of Americans fleeing high-tax states, many of them previously growth magnets, for low-tax environments.

The emergence of deep divisions over cultural issues in the four decades beginning around 1970 and the sharp slowdown in immigrant and internal migrations during the 2007–2009 recession and the years of sluggish economic growth that have followed have sharpened fears that we are flying apart. The volitional migrations of the 1970–2010 period provided many Americans with a chance to live and work in culturally congenial environments even as the federal legislation and court decisions replaced, or attempted to replace, local and state decision-making with national uniformity. A federal government that is not observant of the limits envisioned by the Framers can exacerbate and intensify already-existing cultural differences and widen already-existing cultural divisions. Migration to a congenial cultural community can make such differences easier to endure, as the migrations over those four decades seem to have done.

But preliminary data suggest that the years from the onset of the 2007–2009 recession may have seen the end, or at least a sharp curtailment of, the Latino immigrant and volitional internal surges of

migration that began in the 1970s and continued at full strength in
the largely prosperous quarter century from 1982 to 2007. We may
be at a flexpoint as we were, unknowingly, in the years around 1970,
when two surges of migration set in motion by World War II had
either ceased (the northward migration of southern blacks) or slowed
down (the westward migration to California). In those cases the economic motivations for migration remained largely in place, but the
cultural motivation—the drive to pursue dreams—seemed diminished. To American blacks the northern cities looked less like a dream
and the South, after passage of the civil rights acts, less of a nightmare. For others the smoggier and snobbier California of the 1970s
seems far less dreamlike than the sunny and friendly California of
the immediate postwar years. The striking decline of immigration
from Mexico resembles if not exceeds sudden drop-offs in immigration from other countries earlier in American history—the decline
of Irish and German immigration in the 1890s especially. The collapse of the U.S. housing market in 2007 was especially sharp in the
four "sand states"—California, Nevada, Arizona, Florida—and especially in counties with high Hispanic percentages. Public policy had
encouraged the granting of mortgages to Hispanics with low credit
ratings in the decade running up to 2007, and it is estimated that one-
third of home owners nationally suffering foreclosure in the two or
three years starting in 2007 were Hispanic. These were people whose
dreams were shattered, dreams of gaining six-figure affluence from
hard work at blue-collar jobs and ever-guaranteed housing value
increases. At the same time, Mexico had an economy growing more
rapidly than the United States and was becoming a majority middle-
class country. Like Ireland and Germany in the 1890s, it was less of
a nightmare and America, which suffered a major recession in the
1890s, no longer seemed to offer fulfillment of a dream.

Data suggest there was a much sharper drop in immigration by
Hispanics than by Asians and a much sharper drop in immigration
by low-skill workers than by those with high skills. The interesting
question is whether the United States will modify its immigration

law to resemble those of Canada and Australia, which favor high-skill immigration rather than, as America's 1965 act inadvertently tended to do, family reunification of relatively low-skill workers. The sources and character of future surges of immigration may very well depend on whether Congress and the president make a decision to change current law.

Volitional internal migration slowed down sharply in the 2007–2012 period and could certainly gain speed again if the economy begins growing at historically more normal rates. Americans remain alert to signals in labor markets and can respond to sharp increases in job creation, as is apparent from the two jurisdictions that showed the highest percentage population growth between 2010 and 2012 according to Census Bureau estimates: North Dakota, site of the Bakken Shale oil boom, and the District of Columbia, the seat of a government able to spend far more than it receives in revenues. When one looks at larger numbers, however, what is notable is the continued move during Barack Obama's presidency to George W. Bush's home state of Texas, which accounted for 18 percent of total national population gain in 2010–2012. Though growth has resumed in Arizona and domestic outflow from California is less than in the 2000–2010 decade, immigration to the West is also sharply down. The picture that may be emerging is that even as the cultural style-setters of the country remain New York and California, the impetus for economic and demographic growth may be concentrated increasingly in Texas and the South Atlantic states from Virginia to Florida—places considered economically as well as culturally backward when post–World War II economic and demographic growth started in the 1940s.

But anything here in the nature of prediction is offered with great tentativeness and in the knowledge that very few have accurately predicted either the beginnings or the endings of the great surges of American migration of the past. These surges of migration have peopled what most Americans consider the world's greatest nation and there is an inclination to look back on them with pride and even complacency. But each surge of migration also brought challenges and conflicts. Those who wanted to pursue their own particular American dreams often enough found themselves in conflict—and once in civil war—with those seeking to pursue quite different American dreams. Cultural variety and cultural conflict have been a part of the American polity from its beginnings, and we should not forget that there are dark sides aplenty in our heritage. But in considering current problems, it is helpful to recollect that the conflicts produced by the surges of migration that have come before resulted in much worse strains than those of the early twenty-first century, and that in the process of dealing with them, Americans have developed a capacity and a habit of accommodating and uniting into one nation citizens with very serious and deep differences. Americans have been doing that now for a very long time, going back to the Founding Fathers, with their formula of limited government, civic equality, and tolerance of religious and cultural diversity. It is our responsibility, as we contemplate unanticipated surges of migration of the future, to carry forward that tradition.

Notes

Preface: A Story for Our Time

1. Michael Barone, *Our Country: The Shaping of America from Roosevelt to Reagan* (New York: Macmillan Free Press, 1990).
2. Michael Barone, *The New Americans: How the Melting Pot Can Work Again* (Washington: Regnery, 2001).
3. Michael Barone, *Hard America, Soft America: Competition vs. Coddling and the Battle for America's Future* (New York: Crown Forum, 2004).
4. Michael Barone, *Our First Revolution: The Remarkable British Upheaval That Inspired America's Founding Fathers* (New York: Crown Forum, 2007).
5. David Hackett Fischer, *Albion's Seed: Four British Folkways in North America* (New York: Oxford University Press, 1989).
6. Walter A. McDougall, *Throes of Democracy: The American Civil War Era 1829–1877* (New York: HarperCollins, 2008), pp. xv–xvi.
7. Charles C. Mann, *1491: New Revelations of the Americas Before Columbus* (New York: Knopf, 2005).
8. Charles C. Mann, *1493: Uncovering the New World Columbus Created* (New York: Knopf, 2011).
9. Timothy J. Hatton and Jeffrey G. Williamson, *Global Migration and the World Economy* (Cambridge: MIT Press, 2005), p. 7.
10. James Belich, *Replenishing the Earth: The Settler Revolution and the Rise of the Anglo-World, 1783–1939* (Oxford: Oxford University Press, 2009), pp. 30–36.

1. The Fighting Scots-Irish

1. David Hackett Fischer, *Albion's Seed: Four British Folkways in North America* (New York: Oxford University Press, 1989), pp. 623–30.
2. James G. Leyburn, *The Scotch-Irish: A Social History* (Chapel Hill: University of North Carolina Press, 1967), pp. 140–63.
3. Fischer, *Albion's Seed*, p. 614; Leyburn, *The Scotch-Irish*, 142.
4. Fischer, *Albion's Seed*, p. 613.
5. Leyburn, *The Scotch-Irish*, p. 169; Fischer, *Albion's Seed*, p. 606.
6. Alan Taylor, *American Colonies: The Settling of North America* (New York: Viking, 2001), p. 317.

7. Leyburn, *The Scotch-Irish*, pp. 166–67; Fischer, *Albion's Seed*, pp. 605–06.

8. Fischer, *Albion's Seed*, p. 633; Leyburn, *The Scotch-Irish*, pp. 191–92.

9. Taylor, *American Colonies*, p. 322.

10. Larry Hoefling, *Chasing the Frontier: Scots-Irish in Early America* (Lincoln, NE: Universe, 2005), p. 17; Theodore Roosevelt, *The Winning of the West* (New York: Current Literature Publishing House, 1905), Part I, pp. 143–47.

11. Leyburn, *The Scotch-Irish*, pp. 258–60; Roosevelt, *Winning of the West*, vol. 1, pp. 147–59.

12. Hoefling, *Scots-Irish in Early America*, pp. 36–39; James Webb, *Born Fighting: How the Scotch-Irish Shaped America* (New York: Broadway Books, 2004), p. 155.

13. Webb, *Born Fighting*, pp. 159–60.

14. Leyburn, *The Scots-Irish*, pp. 196–200.

15. Fred Anderson, *Crucible of War: The Seven Years' War and the Fate of Empire in British North America* (New York: Vintage, 2001), p. 10.

16. Charles C. Mann, *1491: New Revelations of the Americas Before Columbus* (New York: Knopf, 2005), pp. 54–56, 86–90, 92–96, 97–101, 107–12.

17. Anderson, *Crucible of War*, pp. 9–20.

18. Dale Van Every, *Forth to the Wilderness: The First American Frontier, 1754–1774* (New York: William Morrow, 1961), p. 150; J. H. Elliott, *Spain, Europe & the Wider World 1500–1800* (New Haven: Yale University Press, 2009), p. 150.

19. Anderson, *Crucible of War*, pp. 16–24.

20. Taylor, *American Colonies*, p. 316.

21. Leyburn, *The Scotch-Irish*, pp. 203–07.

22. Ibid., pp. 210–17.

23. Hoefling, *Scots-Irish*, p. 56.

24. Leyburn, *The Scotch-Irish*, pp. 216–17.

25. Anderson, *Crucible of War*, pp. 37–52.

26. Ibid., pp. 55–73.

27. Leyburn, *The Scotch-Irish*, p. 298.

28. John F. Ross, *War on the Run: The Epic Story of Robert Rogers and the Conquest of America's First Frontier* (New York: Bantam, 2009).

29. Leyburn, *The Scotch-Irish*, p. 173.

30. Bernard Bailyn, *The Peopling of British North America: An Introduction* (New York: Knopf, 1986), p. 9; Leyburn, *The Scotch-Irish*, p. 157; Fischer, *Albion's Seed*, pp. 606–08; Steckel, p. 172.

31. Leyburn, *The Scotch-Irish*, p. 213.

32. Leyburn, *The Scotch-Irish*, p. 34.

33. Webb, *Born Fighting*, pp. 164–73.

34. Works Progress Administration, *Kentucky: A Guide to the Bluegrass State* (New York: Harcourt Brace, 1939), pp. 36–37; Hoefling, *Scots-Irish*, pp. 92–96; Roosevelt, *Winning of the West*, vol. 1, pp. 179–86.

35. WPA, *Guide to Tennessee*, 23rd ed. (Knoxville: University of Tennessee Press, 1986), pp. 45–46; Roosevelt, *Winning of the West*, vol. 1, pp. 215–43.
36. Hoefling, *Scots-Irish*, pp. 92–94.
37. Ibid., pp. 112–13, 117–21.
38. Taylor, *American Colonies*, p. 316.
39. Roger Finke and Rodney Stark, *The Churching of America 1776–1990: Winners and Losers in Our Religious Economy* (New Brunswick, NJ: Rutgers University Press, 1992), pp. 92–96.
40. Leyburn, *The Scotch-Irish*, pp. 301–305.
41. Ibid., p. 314.
42. Ibid., pp. 268–69.
43. Fischer, *Albion's Seed*, pp. 749, 751–53.
44. Leyburn, *The Scotch-Irish*, pp. 260–70.
45. Roosevelt, *Winning of the West*, vol. 1, p. 141.
46. Robert Remini, *Andrew Jackson, The Course of American Empire 1767–1821* (Baltimore: Johns Hopkins University Press, 1998), vol. 1, p. 169.
47. WPA *Guide to Tennessee*, pp. 45–46; Roosevelt, *Winning of the West*, vol. 1, pp. 215–43.
48. Webb, *Born Fighting*, pp. 187–88; Lynn Hudson Parsons, *The Birth of Modern Politics: Andrew Jackson, John Quincy Adams and the Election of 1828* (New York: Oxford University Press, 2011), pp. 8–11.
49. David J. Weber, *The Spanish Frontier in North America* (New Haven: Yale University Press, 1992), pp. 281–82, 292–93.
50. Remini, *Andrew Jackson*, vol. 1., pp. 145–48; Parsons, *The Birth of Modern Politics*, pp. 18–20.
51. Remini, *Andrew Jackson*, vol. 1, p. 429.
52. Marquis James, *The Life of Andrew Jackson Complete in One Volume* (Indianapolis: Bobbs-Merrill, 1938), pp. 145–48.
53. Remini, *Andrew Jackson*, vol. 1, pp. 165–75.
54. Parsons, *The Birth of Modern Politics*, pp. 25–30.
55. Marquis James, *The Raven: A Biography of Sam Houston* (Austin: University of Texas Press, 2008), pp. 3–23, 29–34.
56. Ibid., p. 29.
57. Remini, *Andrew Jackson*, vol. 1, pp. 187–233.
58. Ibid., pp. 231–32; Parsons, *The Birth of Modern Politics*, pp. 31–35.
59. Remini, *Andrew Jackson*, vol. 1, p. 232.
60. Daniel Walker Howe, *What Hath God Wrought* (New York: Oxford University Press, 2007), pp. 98–107; Parsons, *The Birth of Modern Politics*, pp. 46–54.
61. Howe, *What Hath God Wrought*, pp. 255–56.
62. Ibid., pp. 342–57; Sean Wilentz, *The Rise of American Democracy: Jefferson to Lincoln* (New York: Norton, 2005); Jean Edward Smith, *John Marshall:*

Definer of a Nation (New York: Henry Holt, 1996), pp. 516–18; Robert Remini, *Jackson*, vol. 2, pp. 276–77.

63. Remini, *Andrew Jackson*, vol. 2, pp. 277–79.
64. Howe, *What Hath God Wrought*, p. 357.
65. Howe, *What Hath God Wrought*, pp. 24–25.
66. Remini, *Andrew Jackson*, vol. 1, pp. 388–89.
67. James, *The Raven*, pp. 63–65.
68. Howe, *What Hath God Wrought*, pp. 658–70; Remini, *Andrew Jackson*, vol. 3, pp. 352–68; James, *The Raven*, pp. 186–257.
69. Howe, *What Hath God Wrought*, pp. 677–90; Robert Remini, *Jackson*, vol. 3, pp. 495–511; Robert Merry, *A Country of Vast Designs: James K. Polk, the Mexican War, and the Conquest of the American Continent* (New York: Simon & Schuster, 2009), pp. 67–144.

2. Yankees and Grandees

1. David Hackett Fischer, *Albion's Seed: Four British Folkways in America* (New York: Oxford University Press, 1989), pp. 16–17.
2. Walter Isaacson, *Benjamin Franklin: An American Life* (New York: Simon & Schuster, 2003), pp. 35–37.
3. Stephen A. Flanders, *Atlas of American Migration* (New York: Facts on File, 1998), p. 66.
4. See Michael Barone, *Our First Revolution: The Remarkable British Upheaval That Inspired America's Founding Fathers* (New York: Crown Forum, 2007).
5. Fred Anderson, *The War That Made America* (New York: Penguin, 2006), pp. 9–24.
6. Ibid., pp. 9–24.
7. Francis Jennings, *Empire of Fortune: Crowns, Colonies & Tribes in the Seven Years War in America* (New York: Norton, 1988), p. 452; Michael Kammen, *Colonial New York* (Millwood, N.Y.: k+o Press, 1975), pp. 114–16, 197–99, 310–36; James Thomas Flexner, *Mohawk Baronet: A Biography of Sir William Johnson* (Syracuse, NY: Syracuse University Press, 1979); Fintan O'Toole, *White Savage: William Johnson and the Invention of America* (New York: Farrar, Straus & Giroux, 2005); John Ferling, *Almost a Miracle: The American Victory in the War of Independence* (New York: Oxford University Press, 2007), pp. 201–202; Bernard Bailyn, *Voyagers to the West* (New York: Knopf, 1986), pp. 576–82.
8. John Ferling, *Almost a Miracle*, pp. 202–03, 346, 352–54.
9. Dumas Malone, *Jefferson the Virginian* (Boston: Little, Brown, 1948), pp. 413–14.
10. William Lee Miller, *Arguing About Slavery: The Great Battle in the United States Congress* (New York: Knopf, 1996), p. 17.
11. Dumas Malone, *Jefferson the President: Second Term, 1805–1809* (Boston: Little, Brown, 1974), pp. 544–47.

12. Ibid., p. 541.

13. Walter McDougall, *Freedom Just Around the Corner: A New American History 1585–1828* (New York: HarperCollins, 2004), pp. 318–19.

14. *Historical Statistics of the United States 1789–1970*, vol. 1, p. 518.

15. Daniel Walker Howe, *What Hath God Wrought: The Transformation of America, 1815–1848* (New York: Oxford University Press, 2007), pp. 125–32.

16. Lois Kimball Mathews, *The Expansion of New England: The Spread of New England Settlement and Institutions to the Mississippi River, 1620–1865* (Boston: Houghton Mifflin, 1909), pp. 139–47.

17. Ibid., pp. 139–47, quotation at p. 146.

18. Lester J. Cappon, ed., *Atlas of Early American History: The Revolutionary Era 1760–1790* (Princeton: Princeton University Press, 1976), pp. 62, 130; Mathews, *The Expansion of New England*, pp. 150–52.

19. Stewart H. Holbrook, *The Yankee Exodus* (Seattle: University of Washington Press, 1968), p. 17; Mathews, *The Expansion of New England*, pp. 155–57.

20. Works Progress Administration, *A Guide to New York State* (New York: Oxford University Press, 1940), pp. 66–67; George R. Stewart, *Names on the Land: A Historical Account of Place-Naming in the United States* (Boston: Houghton Mifflin, 1967), pp. 184–86.

21. McDougall, *Freedom Just Around the Corner*, p. 473.

22. http://en.wikipedia.org/wiki/William_Bingham.

23. Holbrook, *The Yankee Exodus*, pp. 17–18; Mathews, *The Expansion of New England*, pp. 154–55.

24. Mathews, *The Expansion of New England*, pp. 154–55.

25. Ibid., pp. 155–60.

26. Whitney Cross, *The Burned-over District: The Social and Intellectual History of Enthusiastic Religion in Western New York, 1800–1850* (Ithaca: Cornell University Press, 1950), pp. 6–7.

27. Quoted by Mathews, *The Expansion of New England*, pp. 168–69.

28. Ohio WPA Guide, pp. 217–23.

29. Robert William Fogel, *Without Consent or Contract* (New York: Norton, 1991), p. 335.

30. Mathews, *The Expansion of New England*, pp. 171–85.

31. Ohio WPA Guide, pp. 505, 404, 522, 407, 481, 236–37.

32. Holbrook, *The Yankee Exodus*, pp. 77–89, 91–96.

33. Ibid., pp. 62–64.

34. Donald L. Miller, *City of the Century: The Epic of Chicago and the Making of America* (New York: Simon & Schuster, 1996), pp. 66–104; Holbrook, *The Yankee Exodus*, pp. 68–74.

35. William Cronon, *Nature's Metropolis* (New York: Norton, 1991); James Belich, *Replenishing the Earth: The Settler Revolution and the Rise of the*

Anglo-World, 1783–1939 (Oxford: Oxford University Press, 2009), pp. 339–45; Holbrook, *The Yankee Exodus*, pp. 69–74.

36. Holbrook, *The Yankee Exodus*, pp. 64–76.
37. Ibid., pp. 118–28.
38. Ibid., p. 131.
39. George William Pierson, *Tocqueville in America* (Baltimore: Johns Hopkins University Press, 1996). By my count, Tocqueville spent 156 days in New England, New York, and the westward lands of the New England diaspora, as compared with 126 days in the rest of the United States and 4 days in Canada (then British North America).
40. Robert William Fogel and Stanley Engerman, *Time on the Cross: The Economics of American Negro Slavery* (New York: Norton, 1989 [originally published 1974]), p. 46.
41. Ibid., pp. 48–52.
42. See Ira Berlin, *The Making of African America* (New York: Viking, 2010), pp. 18, 25, 131–32, 136, 145–46.
43. David Hackett Fischer and James C. Kelly, *Bound Away: Virginia and the Westward Movement* (Charlottesville: University of Virginia Press, 2000), p. 229.
44. James Oakes, *The Ruling Class: A History of American Slaveholders* (New York: Norton, 1998), pp. 38, 52, 67.
45. William W. Freehling, *The Road to Disunion: Secessionists at Bay 1776–1854* (New York: Oxford University Press, 1990), p. 18.
46. Fogel, *Without Consent or Contract*, pp. 63–67, 93–96.
47. Fogel and Engerman, *Time on the Cross*, p. 201.
48. Oakes, *The Ruling Class*, pp. 38–40.
49. Ibid., p. 39.
50. Ibid., p. 67.
51. Ibid., pp. 82–87.
52. Ibid., pp. 52, 62–63.
53. Ibid., pp. 76–80.
54. Ibid., p. 77.
55. Gavin Wright, *Old South, New South: Revolutions in the Southern Economy Since the Civil War* (New York: Basic Books, 1986), pp. 25–26.
56. Oakes, *The Ruling Class*, pp. 43–45.
57. Cross, *The Burned-over District*, p. 81.
58. Richard L. Power, *Planting Corn Belt Culture: The Impress of Upland Southerner and Yankee in the Old Northwest* (Indianapolis: Indiana Historical Society, 1953), p. 6.
59. Thomas J. Morain, *Prairie Grass Roots: An Iowa Small Town in the Early Twentieth Century* (Ames: Iowa State University Press, 1988), p. 256.
60. Cross, *The Burned-over District*, p. 41.

61. Mathews, *The Expansion of New England*, pp. 166–68; Cross, *The Burned-over District*, pp. 8–9, 14.

62. http://www.shakermuseumandlibrary.org/mtlebanon.html.

63. Cross, *The Burned-over District*, pp. 32–43.

64. Ibid., pp. 79–81.

65. Ibid., pp. 9–11.

66. McDougall, *Freedom Just Around the Corner*, pp. 510–12, quotation at p. 511; Sean Wilentz, *The Rise of American Democracy: Jefferson to Lincoln* (New York: Norton, 2005), pp. 349–52, quotation at pp. 350–51; Howe, *What Hath God Wrought*, pp. 170–76, quotation at p. 170.

67. McDougall, *Freedom Just Around the Corner*, pp. 510, 512–13; Wilentz, *The Rise of American Democracy*, pp. 269–72; Howe, *What Hath God Wrought*, pp. 166–70, quotations at pp. 168, 169.

68. Holbrook, *The Yankee Exodus*, p. 79.

69. Gilbert H. Barnes, *The Antislavery Impulse 1830–1844* (New York: Harcourt Brace, 1964), pp. 64–73.

70. Holbrook, *The Yankee Exodus*, pp. 42–47.

71. McDougall, *Freedom Just Around the Corner*, p. 513; Howe, *What Hath God Wrought*, pp. 170–76; Barnes, *The Antislavery Impulse*, pp. 74–78.

72. Eugene Genovese, *The World the Slaveholders Made: Two Essays in Interpretation* (Middletown, CT: Wesleyan University Press, 1987), p. xv.

73. Freehling, *The Road to Disunion*, pp. 478–79.

74. Lee Benson, *The Concept of Jacksonian Democracy: New York as a Test Case* (New York: Atheneum, 1964).

75. Michael Holt, *The Rise and Fall of the American Whig Party* (New York: Oxford University Press, 1999), pp. 804–35.

76. Ibid., p. 838.

77. Ibid., pp. 835–66; William Gienapp, *The Origins of the Republican Party 1852–1856* (New York: Oxford University Press, 1987), pp. 103–21.

78. Holt, *The American Whig Party*, pp. 866–71; Gienapp, *The Origins of the Republican Party*, pp. 121–27.

79. Holt, *The American Whig Party*, pp. 871–77; Gienapp, *The Origins of the Republican Party*, pp. 129–33.

80. Holt, *The American Whig Party*, pp. 877–908; Gienapp, *The Origins of the Republican Party*, pp. 133–60.

81. Holt, *The American Whig Party*, pp. 909–50; Gienapp, *The Origins of the Republican Party*, pp. 166–303.

82. http://geoelections.free.fr/USA/elec_comtes/1856.htm.

83. Holbrook, *The Yankee Exodus*, pp. 187–207.

84. Richard B. Morris, *Encyclopedia of American History* (New York: Harper, 1953), p. 220.

85. http://geoelections.free.fr/USA/elec_comtes/1860.htm.

3. The Irish and Germans

1. *Historical Statistics of the United States, Colonial Times to 1970* (Washington: Bureau of the Census, 1975), vol. 1, pp. 105–08.
2. Kerby A. Miller, *Emigrants and Exiles: Ireland and the Irish Exodus to North America* (New York: Oxford University Press, 1985), pp. 280–86.
3. George Marlin, *The American Catholic Voter: 200 Years of Political Impact* (South Bend: St. Augustine's Press, 2004), p. 62.
4. *Encyclopedia Britannica*, 11th ed., vol. 19, p. 991.
5. R. F. Foster, *Modern Ireland: 1600–1972* (New York: Viking Penguin, 1988), p. 298.
6. Ibid., p. 301.
7. Ibid., pp. 298–302; Andrew Greeley, *That Most Distressful Nation: The Taming of the American Irish* (Chicago: Quadrangle Books, 1972), pp. 27–29.
8. Paul Bew, *Ireland: The Politics of Enmity 1789–2006* (Oxford: Oxford University Press, 2007), pp. 87–174.
9. Foster, *Modern Ireland*, p. 298.
10. Miller, *Emigrants and Exiles*, pp. 325–26.
11. Ibid., p. 292.
12. Ruth Dudley Edwards, *An Atlas of Irish History*, 3rd ed. (New York: Routledge, 2005), p. 214; John Bodnar, *The Transplanted: A History of Immigrants in Urban America* (Bloomington: Indiana University Press, 1985), p. 6.
13. Stephan Thernstrom, ed., *Harvard Encyclopedia of American Ethnic Groups* (Cambridge: Harvard University Press, 1980), p. 529.
14. Miller, *Emigrants and Exiles*, pp. 320–21.
15. Frank McCourt, "Scraps and Leftovers: A Meditation," in Michael Coffey and Terry Golway, eds., *The Irish in America* (New York: Hyperion, 1997), p. 41.
16. Thernstrom, *Harvard Encyclopedia*, pp. 530–31.
17. Steven P. Erie, *Rainbow's End: Irish-Americans and the Dilemmas of Urban Machine Politics, 1840–1985* (Berkeley: University of California Press, 1988), p. 26; Thernstrom, *Harvard Encyclopedia*, p. 532.
18. Thernstrom, *Harvard Encyclopedia*, p. 533.
19. Miller, *Emigrants and Exiles*, pp. 325–26.
20. Thomas Sowell, *Ethnic America: A History* (New York: Basic Books, 1981), p. 1.
21. Randolph Roth, *American Homicide* (Cambridge: Harvard University Press, 2009), p. 11.
22. Ibid., pp. 11, 84.
23. Ibid., p. 187.
24. Ibid., p. 198.
25. William J. Stuntz, *The Collapse of American Criminal Justice* (Cambridge: Harvard University Press, 2011), p. 17, table 1.

26. Roth, *American Homicide*, p. 390.

27. Ibid., p. 198.

28. Thernstrom, *Harvard Encyclopedia*, pp. 531–32.

29. Marlin, *The American Catholic Voter*, p. 62.

30. Miller, *Emigrants and Exiles*, p. 334.

31. Nathan Glazer and Daniel Patrick Moynihan, *Beyond the Melting Pot: The Negroes, Puerto Ricans, Jews, Italians, and Irish of New York City* (Cambridge: MIT Press, 1963), p. 232.

32. Ellen Skerrett, "Bricks and Mortar: Cornerstones of the Irish Presence," in Coffey and Golway, *The Irish in America*, p. 52.

33. Frederick M. Binder and David M. Reimers, *All the Nations Under Heaven: An Ethnic and Racial History of New York City* (New York: Columbia University Press, 1995), p. 69.

34. Coffey and Golway, *The Irish in America*, pp. 56–66; Thernstrom, *Harvard Encyclopedia*, pp. 534–35.

35. Coffey and Golway, *The Irish in America*, p. 67.

36. Glazer and Moynihan, *Beyond the Melting Pot*, p. 230.

37. Thernstrom, *Harvard Encyclopedia*, pp. 535–36.

38. Sean Wilentz, *Chants Democratic: New York City & the Rise of the American Working Class, 1788–1850* (New York: Oxford University Press, 1984), p. 327.

39. Ibid., p. 329.

40. Glazer and Moynihan, *Beyond the Melting Pot*, pp. 224–26.

41. Ibid., pp. 226, 227.

42. Ibid., p. 229.

43. Thernstrom, *Harvard Encyclopedia*, p. 533.

44. Marlin, *The American Catholic Voter*, pp. 83–86.

45. Hajo Holborn, *A History of Modern Germany 1840–1945* (Princeton: Princeton University Press, 1969), p. 39.

46. Ibid., p. 35.

47. Thomas Cieslik, David Felsen, and Akis Kalaitzidis, eds., *Immigration: A Documentary and Reference Guide* (Westport, CT: Greenwood Press, 2009), pp. 25–26.

48. Marlin, *The American Catholic Voter*, pp. 76–79.

49. Roth, *American Homicide*, pp. 389–90.

50. Stuntz, *The Collapse of American Criminal Justice*, p. 17, table 1.

51. Glazer and Moynihan, *Beyond the Melting Pot*, pp. 242–44.

52. Erie, *Rainbow's End*, pp. 1–66; Marlin, *The American Catholic Voter*, pp. 137–42.

53. Thernstrom, *Harvard Encyclopedia*, p. 539.

54. Glazer and Moynihan, *Beyond the Melting Pot*, p. 246.

55. Ibid., p. 287.

56. Hajo Holborn, *A History of Modern Germany 1840–1945* (Princeton: Princeton University Press, 1982), pp. 367–68.
57. Ibid., pp. 367–70.
58. John Milton Cooper, *The Warrior and the Priest* (Cambridge: Harvard University Press, 1983), p. 323.
59. http://historymatters.gmu.edu/d/5017.
60. David M. Kennedy, *Over Here: The First World War and American Society* (New York: Oxford University Press, 1980), pp. 24, 67.
61. Ibid., pp. 60–66.
62. Ibid., p. 68; Louis Auchincloss, *Woodrow Wilson* (New York: Viking, 2000), p. 67.
63. Kennedy, *Over Here*, pp. 60–66; Robert H. Ferrell, *Woodrow Wilson & World War I 1917–1921* (New York: Harper & Row, 1985), pp. 205–06.
64. Stephan Thernstrom, ed., *Harvard Encyclopedia of American Ethnic Groups* (Cambridge: Harvard University Press, 1980), p. 406.

4. Incomplete Conquest

1. J. R. Hicks, *The Theory of Wages* (London: Macmillan, 1932), p. 76, quoted in Michael J. Greenwood, *Research on Internal Migration in the United States: A Survey, Journal of Economic Literature*, vol. 13, no. 2 (June 1975), p. 397.
2. Stephan Thernstrom and Abigail Thernstrom, *America in Black and White* (New York: Simon & Schuster, 1997), p. 45, citing *Historical Statistics*, vol. 1, p. 422.
3. *Historical Statistics*, Tables A57–72, A172–94.
4. Gavin Wright, *Old South, New South: Revolutions in the Southern Economy Since the Civil War* (New York: Basic Books, 1986), pp. 7, 12.
5. Ira Berlin, *The Making of African America: The Four Great Migrations* (New York: Viking, 2010), pp. 18, 25, 131–32, 136, 145–46.
6. Thernstroms, *America*, p. 59.
7. John Dollard, *Caste and Class in a Southern Town* (Madison, University of Wisconsin Press, 1988). This is a reissue of the book first published in 1937 by Yale University Press, with a characteristically insightful foreword by Daniel Patrick Moynihan.
8. Vincent J. Cannato, *American Passage: The History of Ellis Island* (New York: HarperCollins, 2009), pp. 57–61.
9. Timothy J. Hatton and Jeffrey G. Williamson, *Global Migration and the World Economy: Two Centuries of Policy and Performance* (Cambridge: MIT Press, 2005), p. 57.
10. James Belich, *Replenishing the Earth: The Settler Revolution and the Rise of the Anglo-World, 1783–1939* (Oxford: Oxford University Press, 2009), p. 288.
11. Stephan Thernstrom, ed., *Harvard Encyclopedia of American Ethnic Groups* (Cambridge: Harvard University Press, 1980), pp. 545–47.

12. Thernstrom, *Encyclopedia*, p. 165.
13. Robert D. Putnam et al., *Making Democracy Work: Civic Traditions in Modern Italy*.
14. Thernstrom, *Encyclopedia*, p. 548.
15. Randolph Roth, *American Homicide* (Cambridge: Harvard University Press, 2009), pp. 389–94.
16. William J. Stuntz, *The Collapse of American Criminal Justice* (Cambridge: Harvard University Press, 2011), p. 18.
17. Thernstrom, *Encyclopedia*, pp. 261–65, 269–71.
18. Ibid., pp. 927–33.
19. Ibid., pp. 934–41.
20. Ibid., pp. 247–55.
21. Ibid., pp. 916–26.
22. Belich, *Replenishing*, p. 189.
23. Roth, *American Homicide*, p. 394.
24. For a vivid picture of pre–World War I Brody, see Joseph Roth's novel *The Radetzky March* (London: Granta Books, 2013).
25. Paul Johnson, *A History of the Jews* (New York: Harper Perennial, 1987), p. 339.
26. Michael Barone, *The New Americans: How the Melting Pot Can Work Again* (Washington: Regnery, 2001), pp. 212–15, and references cited.

5. Promised Lands

1. See Dan Morgan, *Rising in the West: The True Story of an "Okie" Family from the Great Depression Through the Reagan Years* (New York: Knopf, 1992), and Mark Arax and Rick Wartzman, *The King of California: J. G. Boswell and the Making of a Secret American Empire* (New York: Public Affairs, 2003). And of course the canonical work is John Steinbeck's novel *The Grapes of Wrath*.
2. Arthur Herman, *Freedom's Forge* (New York: Random House, 2012).
3. Thomas Bruscino, *A Nation Forged in War: How World War II Taught Americans to Get Along* (Knoxville: University of Tennessee Press, 2010).
4. Juan Williams, *Eyes on the Prize* (New York: Viking, 1987), p. 197; William H. Harris, "A. Philip Randolph, Black Workers and the Labor Movement," in Melvin Dubofsky and Warren Van Tine, eds., *Labor Leaders in America* (Urbana: University of Illinois Press, 1987), pp. 258–73; Herman, *Freedom's Forge*, pp. 258–62.
5. James N. Gregory, *The Southern Diaspora* (Chapel Hill: The University of North Carolina Press, 2005), p. 50.
6. Nicholas Lemann, *The Promised Land: The Great Black Migration and How It Changed America* (New York: Knopf, 1991), p. 16.
7. Ibid., p. 5.
8. David E. Lorey, *The U.S.–Mexican Border in the Twentieth Century* (Wilmington: Scholarly Resources, 1999), p. 32.

9. Richard White, *Railroaded: The Transcontinentals and the Making of Modern America* (New York: Norton, 2011).

10. Kevin Starr, *California, A History* (New York: Modern Library, 2005), pp. 120–26, 178.

11. On Kettner, see Kevin Starr, *The Dream Endures: California Enters the 1940s* (New York: Oxford University Press, 1997), pp. 110–14.

12. Starr, *California, A History*, pp. 219–20.

13. John Gunther, *Inside U.S.A.* (New York: Harper & Brothers, 1947), pp. 51–52.

14. Kevin Starr, *Inventing the Dream: California Through the Progressive Era* (New York: Oxford University Press, 1985), p. 313.

15. Laura Hillenbrand, *Seabiscuit: An American Legend* (New York: Random House, 2001).

16. Gunther, *Inside U.S.A.*, p. 4.

17. Kevin Starr, *Endangered Dreams: The Great Depression in California* (New York: Oxford University Press, 1996), pp. 111–20.

18. Gunther, *Inside U.S.A.*, pp. 52–54.

19. See Kevin Starr, *Embattled Dreams: California in War and Peace 1940–1950* (New York: Oxford University Press, 2002), pp. 34–65.

20. Gunther, *Inside U.S.A*, pp. 71, 55; Starr, *Embattled Dreams*, pp. 72–81, 123–26.

21. Gregory, *The Southern Diaspora*, pp. 47, 50–52, 126–27.

22. Lemann, *The Promised Land*, p. 95.

23. Stephan Thernstrom and Abigail Thernstrom, *America in Black and White* (New York: Simon & Schuster, 1997), p. 80.

24. Additional data: in 1940 eight large metropolitan areas (New York, Philadelphia, Chicago, Detroit, Cleveland, St. Louis, Los Angeles, San Francisco) had 1,003,000 southern-born blacks; in 1970 they had 2,154,000 southern-born blacks. Gregory, *The Southern Diaspora*, p. 117.

25. Thernstroms, *America in Black and White*, p. 59.

26. Lemann, *The Promised Land*, p. 81.

27. Neighborhood segregation was almost as complete in 1970 as in 1940. Gregory, *The Southern Diaspora*, p. 273.

28. Adam Cohen and Elizabeth Taylor, *American Pharaoh: Richard J. Daley and His Battle for Chicago* (New York: Little, Brown, 2000).

29. Ibid., pp. 31, 83, 108.

30. Ibid., p. 123.

31. Ibid., pp. 214, 216.

32. Ibid., p. 29.

33. Thernstroms, *America in Black and White*, p. 515.

34. Carey McWilliams, *Southern California* (Salt Lake City: Peregrine Smith Books, 1973), p. 373.

35. Gunther, *Inside U.S.A.*, p. 5.
36. Jane Jacobs, *The Economy of Cities* (New York: Random House, 1970), pp. 151–54, quotation at p. 152.
37. McWilliams, *Southern California*, pp. viii–ix.
38. James Q. Wilson, "A Guide to Reagan Country: The Political Culture of Southern California," *Commentary*, May 1967.
39. Ibid.
40. "The important fact about African Americans in the diaspora period is how quickly they developed political capacity and how consistently they practiced it and made it grow," Gregory, *The Southern Diaspora*, pp. 239–40.
41. Lemann, *The Promised Land*, p. 65.
42. Gregory, *The Southern Diaspora*, pp. 114–15.
43. Cohen and Taylor, *American Pharaoh*, pp. 96–97.
44. Gregory, *The Southern Diaspora*, p. 108.
45. Thernstroms, *Americans in Black and White*, note 47.
46. Lemann, *The Promised Land*, p. 52.
47. Hortense Powdermaker, *After Freedom: A Cultural Study in the Deep South* (New York: Russell & Russell, 1968), pp. 143, 146, quoted in Lemann, *The Promised Land*, p. 29.
48. Thernstroms, *America in Black and White*, pp. 237–38; Nathan Glazer and Daniel Patrick Moynihan, *Beyond the Melting Pot: The Negroes, Puerto Ricans, Jews, Italians, and Irish of New York City* (Cambridge: MIT Press, 1965), p. 5.
49. Daniel Patrick Moynihan, "The Negro Family: The Case for National Action" (Washington: Office of Policy Planning and Research, United States Department of Labor, March 1965), pp. 8, 11–14.
50. Ibid., p. 21.
51. Wilson, "A Guide to Reagan Country," article in *Commentary*.
52. Kevin Starr, *Golden Dreams: California in an Age of Abundance 1950–1963* (New York: Oxford University Press, 2009), pp. 259–62.
53. Wilson, "A Guide to Reagan Country," article in *Commentary*.
54. James Q. Wilson, "Reagan and the Republican Revival," *Commentary*, October 1980.
55. Thernstroms, *America in Black and White*, p. 83.
56. Ibid., pp. 186–87, 194–97, 200.
57. *Historical Statistics of the United States*, vol. 1, p. 413; Thernstroms, *America in Black and White*, p. 262.
58. Lemann, *The Promised Land*, p. 31.
59. Stuntz, *The Collapse of American Criminal Justice* (Cambridge: Harvard University Press, 2011), p. 143.
60. Ibid., p. 29, citing Roth, *American Homicide*, pp. 16–26, 469–74.
61. Stuntz, *The Collapse*, p. 39. Stuntz's chapter "Two Migrations," pp. 15–40, is full of good stuff on this.

62. Roger Lane, *Roots of Violence in Black Philadelphia, 1860–1900* (Cambridge: Harvard University Press, 1989), p. 170.
63. Michael Tonry, *Malign Neglect: Race, Crime and Punishment in America* (New York: Oxford University Press, 1995), p. 49, quoted in Thernstroms, *America in Black and White*, p. 602.

6. Migrations of Choice

 1. Rachel St. John, *Line in the Sand: A History of the U.S.-Mexico Border* (Princeton: Princeton University Press, 2011).
 2. David E. Lorey, *The U.S.-Mexican Border in the Twentieth Century* (Wilmington: Scholarly Resources, 1999), pp. 69–72.
 3. John S. D. Eisenhower, *Intervention! The United States and the Mexican Revolution, 1913–1917* (New York: Norton, 1993).
 4. Interview with Lloyd Bentsen Sr., Mission, Texas, 1986.
 5. Jonathan Kandell, *La Capital: The Biography of Mexico City* (New York: Random House, 1988), p. 495.
 6. Lorey, *U.S.-Mexican Border*, pp. 89–90.
 7. Nathan Glazer, ed., *Clamor at the Gates: The New American Immigration* (San Francisco: Institute for Contemporary Studies, 1985), p. 10.
 8. Roger Daniels, *Coming to America: A History of Immigration and Ethnicity in American Life* (New York: HarperCollins, 2002), pp. 238–41.
 9. Ibid., pp. 250–55.
10. Glazer, *Clamor at the Gates*, p. 7.
11. Bill Bishop, *The Big Sort: Why the Clustering of Like-Minded Americans Is Tearing Us Apart* (New York: Houghton Mifflin, 2009).

Acknowledgments

I would like to thank my bosses, Stephen G. Smith, editor of the *Washington Examiner*, and Arthur Brooks, president of the American Enterprise, for their forbearance and help in enabling me to write this book. My agents, Lynn Chu and Glen Hartley, provided great encouragement. I am indebted to many at Crown Forum, including Mary Choteborsky, Derek Reed, Campbell Wharton, Tina Constable, Mauro DiPreta, Meredith McGinnis, Rebecca Marsh, Michael Nagin, Barbara Sturman, Norman Watkins, and Robert Siek.

Index

A

abolitionism. *See* slavery, abolition of
Act of Union (1707), 16, 19
Act of Union (1801), 109, 110
Adams, John, 94
Adams, John Quincy, 42, 43, 94
Adams-Onis Treaty, 232
African Americans. *See* blacks; slavery
Aid to Families with Dependent
    Children, 217
air-conditioning, 224, 226, 261
Alabama, 37, 40, 41, 42, 222, 226
Alamo (Tex.), 44
Albion's Seed (Fischer), 2, 4, 5, 268
Almanac of American Politics, The
    (Barone), 1
American Dilemma, An (Myrdal), 243
American Indians
    as ancestors, 3
    diseases, 23, 52
    Jackson's views on, 39, 43
    Proclamation of 1763, 27
    relationship with colonists, 24
    and Ulstermen, 21
    of Upstate New York, 55–56
    See also specific tribes
American Revolution, 2, 31, 34, 183
Ames, Oakley, 74
Andros, Edmund, 54
Anglican Church of Ireland, 17
Argentina, 150, 242
Arizona, 227, 254, 255, 264, 270
Arkansas, 41, 230

Armour, Philip, 71
Arnold, Isaac N., 70
Asian Drama (Myrdal), 243
Asians, 11, 232, 241–49, 260
assimilation, 180, 253
Astor, John Jacob, 137
Atchison, David, 101
Atlanta (Ga.), 158, 263, 264
Auchincloss, Louis, 143
Austin, Stephen, 43
Australia, 163, 242
Austria-Hungary, 115, 118, 162, 163,
    169
auto industry, 230, 238

B

Bancroft, Frederic, 78
Barry, Marion, 221
Battle of Fallen Timbers, 51
Battle of Quebec, 54
Battle of the Boyne, 108
Baxter, Leone, 196
Beecher, Edward, 72
Beecher, Henry Ward, 86, 88
Beecher, Lyman, 85–87, 103
Belich, James, 163
Benjamin, Judah P., 173
Benson, Lee, 94
Benton, Jesse, 39
Benton, Thomas Hart, 39
Bentsen, Lloyd, Sr., 234
Berger, Victor, 140, 142
Berlin, Ira, 75

Berlin, Irving, 177
Bingham, William, 65
Binghamton (N.Y.), 66
Bishop, Bill, 11, 266, 267
Bismarck (N.D.), 140
Bismarck, Otto von, 115, 138
Black Metropolis (Drake and Cayton),
    208
blacks
    businesses, 202
    in Chicago, 201, 202, 209
    churches, 203
    crime rates, 218–20, 240, 260
    equal rights for, 154–56
    family structure, 213, 216, 218, 260
    housing, 200–202, 211, 213
    jobs, 190–91, 203, 217
    in military, 186
    in New York, 199, 200, 211
    northward migration, 187–91,
        198–204, 210–12, 217–18, 223,
        225, 270
    and numbers racket, 208
    percentage in North, 181
    politics, 209–10
    segregation, 148, 149, 156, 157, 160,
        187, 200, 222, 226
    shunning of North, 159–60
    in sports, 184
    upwardly mobile, 225
    See also slavery
Blagojevich, Rod, 170
Blair, Francis Preston, 46
Blair, Montgomery, 46
Blatnik, John, 170
Blessing, Patrick, 114
Blount, William, 36
Boone, Daniel, 33
Boston (Mass.), 134, 135, 147
bracero program, 234
Braddock, Edward, 26
Bradley, James, 87

Brandeis, Louis, 176
Brant, Joseph, 56
Brazil, 150, 241, 242, 253
Breckinridge, John, 102
breweries, 137
Bridges, Harry, 195
British Empire, 16–17
    See also England; Scotland; United
        Kingdom
Bronson, Arthur, 70
Bronzeville (Chicago), 188, 200
Brooklyn (N.Y.), 186
Brooks, Preston, 91
Brown, John, 101
Brown, Pat, 206, 208, 216
Brown v. Board of Education, 222
Bruscino, Thomas, 185, 186
Bryan, William Jennings, 48
Buchanan, James, 46, 91, 100, 101
Burlington (Iowa), 73
Burr, Aaron, 38–39
Bush, George W., 49, 50, 265
Bush, Samuel, 148
Butler, Andrew, 91
Butler, Charles, 70

C
Calhoun, John C., 44, 46, 91
California, 191–98, 204–8, 270
    acquisition of, 7, 45
    Chinese immigration, 192, 241
    climate, 205–6, 224
    exodus from, 225, 240
    Filipino immigration, 243
    foreclosures, 254
    housing, 214, 224
    Mexicans in, 255
    military bases, 193, 197
    movie industry, 195
    politics, 207–8, 216
    population growth, 193–94, 197,
        207, 214, 227, 236–37

religious cults, 195
slowdown in growth, 223–24
smog, 214–15
See also Los Angeles; San Francisco
Calvinism, 17, 54, 55, 82
Cambodia, 244
Canada, 17, 54, 163, 242
capital punishment, 220
Carroll, Charles, 119
Cass, Lewis, 44
Caste and Class in a Southern Town
    (Dollard), 160
Castro, Fidel, 250, 253
Catawba Indians, 26, 29
Cather, Willa, 169
Catholic Association, 109–10
Catholic Emancipation Act (1829),
    109
Catholics. See Irish Catholics; Roman
    Catholics
Cavaliers, 16
Cavour, Camillo, 165
Cayton, Horace R., 208
Cermak, Anton, 169
chain migration, 251
Chandler, William Wallace, 71
Charles I (king), 4, 52
Charleston (S.C.), 58
Charlotte (N.C.), 263
Chase, Salmon P., 87
Chavez, Cesar, 235, 236
Cherokee Indians, 33, 37, 39, 42–43
Chesapeake colonies, 4, 5, 16
Chicago (Ill.), 52, 70–72
    blacks in, 201, 202, 209
    Czechs in, 169
    Latin/Asian immigrants, 260
    Poles in, 170–71
Chicago Defender, 198
Chickasaw Indians, 37
Chinese Exclusion Act (1882), 192, 241,
    245

Chinese immigration, 192, 241, 243,
    245–46
Choctaw Indians, 37
Church of England, 4, 12, 17
Church of Ireland, 18
Church of Scotland, 17
Cincinnati (Ohio), 68, 87
cities, 111–12, 240, 259–60
Civil Rights Act (1964), 222, 223,
    225
civil rights movement, 222
Civil War (U.S.), 7–8, 147, 182, 183
    casualties, 154
    and internal migration, 45
    and Scots-Irish, 47–48
    to prevent a divided nation, 149
    as Yankee conquest, 103, 148
Clay, Henry, 44, 90, 94
Cleaveland, Moses, 67
Cleveland (Ohio), 201, 202, 203, 221,
    240
Cleveland, Grover, 48
Cobb, Ty, 184
colleges, 147–48
Collins brothers, 72
Colombians, 252
Colorado, 230, 264
Communism, 145, 243
Congress of Vienna, 118
Connecticut, 12
conservatives, 10, 11
Constitution (U.S.), 268
Conzen, Kathleen Neils, 144
Coolidge, Calvin, 99, 144, 180
Cornwallis, Lord, 31
corporations, 236, 237, 238, 265
cotton, 61–63, 78, 80, 89–90, 91, 148,
    149, 191, 199
Cravath, Erastus, 88
Crawford, James, 29
Crawford, Jane, 29
Creek Indians, 37, 39–41, 42

Creel, George, 142
crime rates, 114–15, 168, 218–20, 221,
    240, 260
Croatians, 170
Crocker, Charles, 74
Crockett, David, 40
Croker, Richard, 124
Cromwell, Oliver, 4
Cross, Whitney, 82
Cuba, 159, 250, 253
cultural diversity, 3, 11, 13, 268, 269
Cumberland Gap, 33, 34
Curley, James Michael, 134
Czechs, 9, 169

D

Daley, Richard J., 202, 209
Dallas County (Ala.), 81
Dana, Richard Henry, 215
Davie, William Richardson, 31
Davis, John W., 144
Dawson, William, 209, 210
Deere, John, 72
defense industries, 185, 190, 197, 204,
    236
Delaware, 4, 5, 11, 17
Democracy in America (de Tocqueville),
    74
Democratic Party, 95–97, 101–2, 122,
    124, 134
Denver (Colo.), 52, 264
Depression (1930s), 180, 184
De Priest, Oscar, 209
Des Plaines River, 70
De Tocqueville, Alexis, 74
Detroit (Mich.), 159, 200–203, 210, 213,
    221, 226, 240
Diggs, Charles C., Jr., 204, 210
DiMaggio, Joe, 184, 194
Dinwiddie, Robert, 26
disease, 3, 4, 23, 52, 161
Dobbs, Arthur, 26

Dodge, Grenville, 73–74
Dollard, John, 160
Dominicans, 251
Donegal, Marquis of, 27
Douglas, Stephen A., 46, 72, 101,
    102
Downey, Sheridan, 196
Drake, St. Clair, 208
DuBois, W. E. B., 202
Dunmore, Lord, 33
Durant, Thomas Clark, 74
Dwight, Timothy, 67

E

Ebony magazine, 198, 202
economy, 236, 237, 238, 242, 258,
    259
Economy of Cities, The (Jacobs), 204
Edwards, Jonathan, 66
Eisenhower, Dwight, 208, 210
Ellicott, Joseph, 65
Elliott, J. H., 24
Ellis Island immigration, 105
    characteristics of immigrants,
        178–79
    cutoff of, 242
    European, 8–9, 161–63
    first immigrant, 160
    Italian, 166
    map of foreign born in U.S. states,
        167
    percent of immigrants (1890s–1914),
        150
    rising importance of, 134
    See also specific immigrant groups
Emerson, Ralph Waldo, 103
Engerman, Stanley, 75, 76
England, 4, 5, 12, 16, 17, 19
English language, 254
Espionage Act (1917), 142
European immigration, 8–9, 161–82
    See also specific immigrant groups

F

Fair Employment Practices
  Commission, 190
Farmer-Labor Party, 140–41
Fenian movement, 133–34
Field, Marshall, 71
Filipinos, 243
Fillmore, Millard, 91, 97, 100
Finney, Charles Grandison, 84–85, 87,
  88, 103
First Amendment, 12, 82, 268
Fischer, David Hackett, 2, 4, 5, 18, 20,
  35, 53, 268
Fitzgerald, John F., 134
Five Nations of the Iroquois, 55
Flagler, Henry, 157
Florida, 39, 270
  acquisition of, 7
  cession of, 43
  Cuban immigration, 250
  foreclosures in, 254–55
  income tax ban, 239, 262
  influx from Northeast, 261, 262,
    263
  population growth, 227, 231, 261–62
  Seminoles in, 42
  Spanish title to, 36–37, 38
Fogel, Robert, 75, 76
Forbes, John, 26
foreclosures, 254–55, 258, 264, 270
Fort Duquesne, 26
Fort Mims, 39
Foster, R. F., 109, 110
1491/1493 (Mann), 3
France, 26, 117, 150
Franklin, Aretha, 203
Franklin, Benjamin, 53, 117
Franklin, C. L., 203
Franz Josef (emperor), 169, 174
Free Soil Party, 95–97, 100
Fremont, John C., 98, 100, 102
French and Indian War, 26, 107

G

Gadsden Purchase, 233
Galbraith, John Kenneth, 236, 237, 243
Garfield, James, 68
Garibaldi, Giuseppe, 163, 165
Gates, Horatio, 31
Gehrig, Lou, 184
General Electric, 238
General Motors, 191, 236, 238
Genovese, Eugene, 88
George III (king), 109
Georgia, 5, 37, 41, 42, 43, 60, 154, 263,
  266
German-Americans, 127–32, 136–46,
  149
  Jews, 138, 164, 172–76
  in New York, 127
  politics, 130, 140–41, 145–46
  population (1870), 128
  in rural communities, 129
  in World War I, 142–43, 183
German migration, 4, 115–18, 125–27,
  148, 150, 161, 164, 243
Gershwin, George, 177
Giddings, Joshua, 68
Giuliani, Rudolph, 221
Glorious Revolution, 2
Goethe, 118
gold, 42, 191–92
Goldsmith, Oliver, 7, 30
Goldwater, Barry, 221
Golway, Terry, 120
Gooch, William, 25
Goodrich, Grant, 70
Gorham, Nathaniel, 65
Gottmann, Jean, 230
Grady, Henry, 157
Grant, Ulysses S., 46, 103, 148, 155
Granville, Lord, 25
Grapes of Wrath, The (Steinbeck), 47,
  185
Great Britain. *See* United Kingdom

Great Society, 210
Great Wagon Road, 24, 25, 26, 28, 29
Greeley, Horace, 73, 96
green card, 247, 250
Greene, Cary, 61
Greene, Nathanael, 61
Green v. New Kent County, 222
Gregory, James, 202, 203, 210
Grinnell (Iowa), 73
Grinnell, Josiah, 73
Guatemalans, 252
Gujaratis, 246
Gunther, John, 195, 197, 204

H
Hammond, James Henry, 89–90
Hard America, Soft America (Barone), 1
Harding, Warren, 144, 180
Harlem (N.Y.), 188, 200, 202, 209
Harrison, William Henry, 44, 90
Hatcher, Richard, 220
Hatton, Timothy, 162
Hayes, Rutherford B., 155
Heifetz, Jascha, 206
Henderson, Richard, 33
Hill, James J., 157
Hispanics. *See* Latin American
    immigration; *ethnic groups and
    countries of origin*
Hitler, Adolf, 144, 180, 184
Hmong people, 244–45
Holborn, Hajo, 126
Hollywood (Cal.), 194–95
Holt, Michael, 95
Holy Roman Empire, 116, 118
Homestead Act, 103
homicide, 114–15, 133, 168, 218, 219
Hondurans, 252
Hopkins, Mark, 74
housing, 200–202, 211, 213, 214, 221,
    224, 254–55, 258, 270
Houston, Sam, 40, 44, 46, 155

Howe, Daniel Walker, 43, 86
Hubbard, Gurdon Saltonstall, 70
Hughes, John, 119–20, 122, 124
Humphrey, Hubert, 141
Huntington, Collis, 74
Huxley, Aldous, 206

I
Ickes, Harold, 190
Idaho, 264
Illegal immigration, 11, 235, 250, 253,
    254, 255
Illinois, 72–73, 159
Illinois College, 72
Immigration Act (1924), 9, 10, 232, 242
Immigration Act (1965), 232
immigration restrictions, 179–80, 242
indentured servitude, 5
India, 243, 246–47
Indiana, 69
Indianola (Miss.), 160
Indian Removal Act (1830), 42
Indians. *See* American Indians; *specific
    tribes*
Industrial Revolution, 112
internal migration, 45, 51–103,
    187–226, 261–67, 270
Iowa, 8, 52, 73, 194
Iowa College, 73
Ireland, 16, 106–7
Irish-Americans, 111–15, 132–36
    crime rates, 114–15, 133
    in New York City, 121–24, 134–35
    population (1870), 113
Irish Catholics
    church, 119–20, 163
    Fenian movement, 133–34
    migration, 7–8, 105–11, 112, 148,
        150, 161
    politics, 121–24
    restrictions against, 108–10
    in Ulster, 18

Irish Republican Army, 134
Iroquois Indians, 23–24, 26, 55, 65
Isacson, Leo, 177
Isherwood, Christopher, 206
Isolationism, 145
Italians, 9, 134, 150, 162–66, 168, 178
Italy, 163, 164–65

J
Jackson, Andrew, 7, 28, 30, 31, 33,
    35–36, 38–46, 48, 121, 122
Jackson, Andrew, Sr., 28–30
Jackson, Elizabeth, 28, 31
Jackson, Helen Hunt, 194
Jackson, Hugh, 31
Jackson, Robert, 31
Jacobs, Jane, 204
James, Henry, 178
James II (king), 54, 108
Japan, 241, 242, 243
Japanese Americans, 196
Jefferson, Thomas, 36, 38, 57, 58, 59
Jennings, Francis, 55
Jews, 12, 126, 171
    Eastern European, 150, 174, 176
    in Florida, 262
    German, 138, 164, 172–76
    in movie industry, 184
    in New York, 134, 173, 175, 177, 178
    Russian, 9, 163
Johnson, Andrew, 46, 154, 155
Johnson, Guy, 56
Johnson, Hiram, 216
Johnson, Lyndon, 208, 215, 242
Johnson, Sir William, 56, 65
Johnston, Gabriel, 25
junk bonds, 238
juvenile delinquency, 219

K
Kahn, Julius, 193
Kaiser, Henry J., 197

Kansas, 52, 101, 102
Kansas-Nebraska Act (1854), 95, 101,
    130
Katzenbach, Nicholas, 235
Kearney, Dennis, 241
Kelly, Ed, 209
Kelly, "Honest John," 124
Kennedy, David, 143
Kennedy, Edward, 123
Kennedy, John F., 111, 123, 136, 208, 267
Kennedy, Joseph P., 111, 123
Kennedy, Patrick, 111
Kennedy, Robert, 242, 243
Kentucky, 33, 36, 37, 38, 41, 42, 60
Kerner, Otto, 169
Kettner, William, 193
King, Martin Luther, Jr., 222
King, William R., 81
Knight, Goodwin, 206
Knowland, William, 216
Know-Nothing Party, 95–97, 130
Knudsen, William, 185, 188
Kogovsek, Ray, 170
Koreans, 243–44

L
labor, 163, 169, 176, 179, 188, 236, 238,
    241–43, 271
La Follette, Robert, 140, 142, 144, 145
La Guardia, Fiorello, 168, 178
land grants, 25
land speculation, 65
Lane Theological Seminary, 86–87
language, 164
Laos, 244
Lasker, Albert, 177
Last Hurrah, The (O'Connor), 134
Las Vegas (Nev.), 264
Latin American immigration, 11, 232,
    234, 235, 247, 250, 251, 255–57,
    260, 270
    See also countries of origin

Laud, William, 4, 52
Lausche, Frank, 170
Lawrence, Amos, 101
Lazarus, Emma, 164
Lehman brothers, 173
Lemann, Nicholas, 199, 218
leveraged buyout, 237–38
Lewis, Dixon H., 81
Lewis, John L., 48
liberals, 10, 11
lifestyle, 11, 264, 266
Lincoln, Abraham
    administration, 103
    election, 102, 130, 131
    Emancipation Proclamation, 91
    and/on "house divided," 101,
        149
    and Scots-Irish, 46–47
    and secession, 91, 124
    on slave population, 187
    son's education, 148
    and Stowe, 88
Lindbergh, Charles, 144
Lindsay, John, 221, 239, 259
Lippmann, Walter, 138
Loeb, William, 239
Logan, James, 21
London, Meyer, 177
Los Angeles (Cal.)
    agriculture, 194
    Chinese immigration, 245
    defense industry jobs, 204
    Koreans in, 244
    layout, 206
    Mexican immigration, 251
    movie industry, 195
    New England Yankees in, 52
    Olympics, 195, 223, 224, 251–52
    overcrowding, 201
    population growth, 193, 197, 236–37,
        240
    riots, 221

smog, 214–15
    Vietnamese in, 244
Louisbourg fortress, 26
Louisiana, 26, 27, 37, 38, 41, 232
Louisiana Purchase, 37, 60
Louis, Joe, 184
Lovejoy, Elijah, 72
Lovejoy, Owen, 72
Lowell, Francis Cabot, 80
Lower East Side (N.Y.), 175, 177, 178
Lowndes County (Ala.), 81
Lubell, Samuel, 145
Lueger, Karl, 174
lynching, 156, 218

M
Macomb, Alexander, 65
mafia, 168
Maine, 63
Mann, Charles C., 3
Mann, Thomas, 206
Mansfield, Lord, 57
market capitalism, 16, 19, 20
Marshall, John, 39, 43
Marshall, Thurgood, 222
Maryland, 4, 59, 261
Massachusetts, 12, 268
Mazzini, Giuseppe, 165
McCain, John, 49, 50
McCarthy, Joseph, 145
McCormack, John W., 123
McCormick, Cyrus, 71
McCourt, Frank, 112
McDougall, Walter, 2, 85
McPherson, Aimee Semple, 195
McWilliams, Carey, 194, 204, 205
media, 267
Medill, Joseph, 70
Megalopolis, 230, 231, 259
Mennonites, 116
Metternich, Klemens von (prince), 118,
    125, 126

Mexican immigration
  characteristics of immigrants,
    253–55
  decline of, 270
  illegal, 11, 235, 253, 254, 255
  job preferences of immigrants, 236
  to Los Angeles, 251
Mexican migration, 11, 232, 250, 258
Mexico, 43, 45, 233–34, 270
Mexico City (Mex.), 233
Michigan, 52, 69, 100, 230, 265, 267
Middle Passage, 159
migration
  of choice, 227–72
  European, 149, 161–82
  German, 7–8, 115–18, 125–27, 148,
    150, 161, 164
  internal, 45, 51–103, 187–226,
    261–67, 270
  Irish Catholic, 7–8, 105–15, 148, 150,
    161
  Mexican, 11, 232, 250, 258
  Scandinavian, 137, 139–42, 149, 161,
    162, 164
  Scots-Irish, 5, 6–7, 15–50
  slave and slaveholder, 75–78, 92
  surges, 2, 5, 9–12, 51, 105–6, 149–51,
    271–72
  See also specific migratory groups
military, 185–86, 193, 197
Miller, Donald, 70
Miller, Kerby, 110, 114
Miller, William, 84
Mills, Caleb, 69
Milwaukee (Wis.), 137, 138, 140
Minnesota, 8, 140, 149
Mississippi, 37, 38, 40, 41, 222, 226, 230
Mississippi River, 36, 37
Missouri Compromise, 95
Mitchell, Arthur, 209
Monroe, James, 41
Montgomery (Ala.), 222

Moore, Annie, 160
Morgan, Dan, 47
Mormon Church, 83
Morrill Act (1862), 103
Morris, Robert, 65
Morris, William O'Connor, 109
movies, 184, 186, 195
Moynihan, Daniel Patrick, 120, 121,
    123, 124, 135, 136, 213, 217, 218
Murphy, Charles F., 124, 134, 135
Myrdal, Gunnar, 242–43

N
Naples (Italy), 165
Nashville (Tenn.), 39, 263
Nassau (N.Y.), 259
Natchez (Miss.), 80
Natchez Trace, 38
Nation Forged in War, A (Bruscino), 185
Native Americans. *See* American
    Indians; *specific tribes*
Nelson, Gaylord, 239
Nevada, 227, 254, 264, 270
New Americans, The (Barone), 1
Newark (N.J.), 221
Newberry, Walter L., 70
New Deal, 135, 140, 141
New England, 4, 5, 16, 17, 63, 74
New England Yankees, 51–56, 74–75,
    82–83, 94, 98–99, 147
New Hampshire, 11
New Industrial State, The (Galbraith),
    236
New Jersey, 4, 5, 17, 247, 259
New Mexico, 230, 264
New Orleans (La.), 37, 38, 39, 40, 61,
    89, 152
New South, 157–58
New York City
  blacks in, 199, 200, 211
  Chinese immigration, 245
  corporations in, 237

New York City *(continued)*:
  finances, 260
  flight from, 258–59
  Germans in, 127
  Irish in, 121–24, 134–35
  Italians in, 166, 168, 169, 178
  Jews in, 134, 173, 175, 177, 178
  Koreans in, 244
  Latin/Asian immigration, 260–61
  politics, 121–24, 134, 135
  population, 230, 231
  Tammany Hall, 122, 123–24, 134,
    135
  welfare benefits, 217
  Yankee culture in, 147
New York State, 5, 51–52, 55, 65–67,
    83, 100
New Zealand, 242
Nicaraguans, 252
Nixon, Richard, 136, 193, 208, 216
North (U.S.), 149, 152–60, 181–83,
    198–204
North America, 3, 4, 19
North Carolina, 5, 25, 28, 37, 41, 42,
    59–60, 263
North Dakota, 8, 136, 140, 149
Northern Ireland, 5
Northwest Ordinance, 58, 67
Norway, 164

O
Oakes, James, 80
Obama, Barack, 93
Oberlin College, 87–88
Oberstar, James, 170
Ochs, Adolph S., 173
O'Connell, Daniel, 109, 110, 119,
    123–25, 134
O'Connor, Edwin, 134
Ogden, William B., 70–71
Ohio, 52, 67–68
Ohio River, 26, 36, 151

oil, 196, 231, 239, 265
Oklahoma, 47, 48, 185
Olson, Culbert, 196, 197
Olson, Floyd, 140
Olympic games, 223, 224
Omaha (Neb.), 52
Oneida County (N.Y.), 66, 83, 84
Onís, Ambassador, 42, 43
Oregon, 45
Our Country (Barone), 1
Our First Revolution (Barone), 1
Owens, Jesse, 184

P
Parkman, Francis, 54
Parks, Rosa, 222
partible inheritance, 20, 54
Passage to the Interior. *See* Second
    Middle Passage
Peabody, Endicott, 148
Peel, Robert, 110
Penn, William, 4, 5, 16, 21, 116
Pennsylvania, 4, 5, 16, 17, 21, 27, 36,
    37, 116
Perpich, Rudy, 170
Perry, Rick, 265
Pershing, John, 234
Phelps, Oliver, 65
Philadelphia (Pa.), 21, 28, 116, 134, 135,
    188, 200, 202, 219
Philippines, 193
Phoenix (Ariz.), 233, 264
Pierce, Franklin, 91, 94, 97
Pittsburgh (Pa.), 240–41
Pius IX (pope), 114
Poles, 9, 150, 163, 164, 170–71, 178
police, 219, 220
politics, 266–67
Polk, James K., 44–45, 47, 122, 192, 233
Polk, Sarah Childress, 47
Pony Express, 192
population growth rate, 53, 227–32, 237

Portugal, 150
potato famine, 106–7, 117, 125, 126
Powdermaker, Hortense, 213
Powell, Adam Clayton, 209–10
Presbyterianism, 17–18
prohibition, 95, 168
Protestantism, 7–8, 107, 114, 124
public employee unions, 239
Puerto Ricans, 250, 252
Pulitzer, Joseph, 129
Puritans, 16, 52, 82
Putnam, Robert, 165

Q
Quakers, 4, 16, 21, 26–27, 75
Queens (N.Y.), 246

R
railroads, 72, 74, 157, 162, 192, 199,
    241
Raleigh (N.C.), 263
Randolph, A. Philip, 190
Rangel, Charles, 210
Rayburn, Sam, 154
Reagan, Ronald, 194, 206, 208, 216, 239
Reconstruction, 147, 148, 156
Red Stick Creek Indians, 39–40
religion, 12, 52, 82, 83, 195, 268
Remarque, Erich Maria, 206
Remini, Robert, 40
Republican Party, 52, 96, 97, 100–103,
    130, 131, 134, 145, 148
Revolutionary War. *See* American
    Revolution
Richmond (Va.), 263
Rio Grande, 233, 235
riots, 200, 215, 221, 226
Rising in the West (Morgan), 47
Rockefeller, John D., 157
Rockefeller, Nelson, 239, 259
Roebling, John A., 137
Rogers, Robert, 27

Roman Catholics, 54, 105, 203
    See also Irish Catholics
Roosevelt, Franklin, 145, 190, 197
    and antilynching statute, 156
    education, 148
    Jewish support, 178
    New Deal, 135, 140, 141
    wartime mobilization, 185
Roosevelt, Theodore, 35, 156–57, 178,
    179, 193, 241
Rosenwald, Julius, 177
Rostenkowski, Dan, 171
Rostenkowski, Joe, 171
Roth, Randolph, 115, 133
Rowan, Matthew, 25–26
Rubinstein, Artur, 206
Ruppe, Philip, 170
Ruppert, Jacob, 137
Russians, 162, 163, 173–74
Ruth, Babe, 184

S
Sabath, Adolph, 169
St. Lawrence River, 26
St. Patrick's Cathedral (N.Y.), 120
Salvadorans, 252
San Francisco (Cal.)
    Bay Area migrant spread, 214
    Chinese immigration, 241, 245
    Filipino immigration, 243
    foreign-born population, 192
    overcrowding, 201
    population increases, 197, 236–37,
        240
    subdivisions, 215
Santa Anna, Antonio López de, 43–44
Sardinia, 165
Sargent, Francis, 239
Scammon, J. Young, 70
Scandinavians, 137, 139–42, 149, 161,
    162, 164
Schermann, Anton, 170–71

Schurz, Carl, 130–32, 138, 141
Scotland, 5, 16, 18, 19, 25, 107
Scots-Irish
  as "American," 47
  during and after Civil War, 47–48
  code of behavior, 17–18, 34–35
  land quest, 22, 24–25, 34–35
  map of settlement areas, 32
  migration to North America, 5, 6–7,
    15–50, 105, 107
  southwest movement, 23, 33, 41, 49,
    50
  typical migrants, 20
  in Ulster, 18, 108
Scott, Sir Walter, 28
Scott, Winfield, 45, 97
secession, 91, 124
secondary schools, 147–48
Second Middle Passage, 75–78
segregation, 148, 149, 156, 157, 160,
  187, 200, 222, 226
Seligman brothers, 173
Seminole Indians, 37, 42
Serbians, 170
Seward, William, 94, 97, 101, 120, 122
Shakers, 83
Shawnee Indians, 34
Sherman, William Tecumseh, 103, 154,
  266
shipping, 36
Sicily (Italy), 165, 168
Sinclair, Upton, 195, 196
Singer, Isaac Bashevis, 174
Skubitz, Joe, 170
slavery, 5, 7, 41, 57–63, 268
  abolition of, 52, 57–58, 59, 75, 87,
    124, 148
  conflicting visions of, 45–46
  in England, 17, 57
  expansion in South, 41
  in gang system, 80
  high concentrations of, 60

internal migration of planters and
  slaves, 75–78, 92
map of population in cotton-growing
  areas, 62, 93
migration after War of 1812, 75–78
Missouri Compromise, 95
percent of slave population (1860),
  79
southern slaveholders, 81, 88–90
in Texas, 43, 44
Thirteenth Amendment, 91
Slavs, 9, 169, 178
Slovaks, 169
Slovenians, 169–70
Smith, Al, 134, 135, 145
Smith, Joseph, 83–84
smog, 214–15
Snow, George Washington, 71
socialism, 138
South (U.S.), 148, 149, 151–60, 181–83
South America, 252
South Atlantic states, 262–63
South Carolina, 5, 25, 28, 37, 41, 42,
  58–59, 60, 91, 263
South Dakota, 8, 11, 149
Sowell, Thomas, 114
Spain, 36, 37, 38, 42, 43, 150
sports, 184
Stanford, Leland, 74
state capitals, 64
steamships, 69, 117, 133, 163
Steinbeck, John, 47, 185
Steinway, Henry, 137
Stokes, Carl, 220
Stone, Lucy, 88
Stowe, Harriet Beecher, 86, 88
Straus, Isidor, 173
Straus, Lazarus, 173
Strauss, Levi, 172
Stravinsky, Igor, 206
Stuntz, William, 168, 218, 219
suburbs, 200, 201

Sumner, Charles, 91
Swift, Gustavus, 71
Syracuse (N.Y.), 52

T
Taft, William Howard, 179
Taiwan, 245
Tammany Hall, 122, 123, 124, 134
Taney, Roger, 119
Tappan, Arthur, 85
Tappan, Lewis, 85, 86
Tarleton, Banastre, 31
taxation, 10–11, 36, 232, 238–40, 260, 262, 263, 264
Taylor, Zachary, 45, 90
technology, 184, 246, 247
Tecumseh, 39
temperance measures, 86, 124, 130
Tennessee, 33, 36, 37, 38, 39, 41, 42, 48, 60, 263
Texas, 7, 43, 44, 45, 231, 233, 264–65
Thernstrom, Abigail, 159, 200
Thernstrom, Stephan, 159, 200
Thirteenth Amendment, 91
Thome, James, 87
Thompson, Tommy, 221
Thompson, William Hale, 209
Tilden, Samuel J., 155
Till, Emmett, 203, 210
transportation, 6, 36
Transylvania Company, 33
Treaty of Fort Stanwix (1768), 56
Treaty of Guadalupe Hidalgo (1848), 45, 191, 233
Treaty of Paris (1783), 51
Treaty of Quebec (1763), 54
Treaty of Westphalia (1648), 116
Troup, George, 42
Truman, Harry, 207–8
Tucson (Ariz.), 233, 264
Turin (Italy), 165
Twain, Mark, 147

Tweed, William Marcy, 124
Tyler, John, 44, 45

U
Ulster (Ireland), 15, 17, 18, 21, 22, 25, 27, 107–8
Uncle Tom's Cabin (Stowe), 88
unemployment, 213, 217, 255
unions, 236, 238, 239, 263
United Auto Workers, 191, 236, 238
United Kingdom, 16, 26, 42, 108, 133, 161, 162, 163, 242, 243
United Mine Workers of America, 48
unwed mothers, 213, 221
Upstate New York. *See* New York State
urban areas. *See* cities; *specific cities*
Utah, 230, 264
utopian communities, 83

V
Van Buren, Martin, 44, 121, 122
Vermont, 63, 69
Vicar of Wakefield, The (Goldsmith), 7, 30
Victor Emmanuel (king), 165
Vietnamese, 243, 244
Villa, Pancho, 234
Villard, Henry, 137
violence, 168, 218, 220
Virginia, 4, 12, 41, 58, 59, 78, 222, 261, 262, 263, 268
Virginia Company, 5
volitional migration. *See* Migration, of choice
Voting Rights Act (1965), 222, 223, 225

W
wages, 149, 150, 158, 238
Wagner, Robert, 134, 135, 239
Wallace, Henry, 177
Wallace, Sir William, 7, 30
War of 1812, 39

Warren, Earl, 197, 206
Washington (D.C.), 221, 260, 263
Washington, Booker T., 157
Washington, George, 26, 172, 268
Watauga Association, 33
Wayne, Anthony, 51
Weatherford, William (Red Eagle), 39
Wedgwood, Josiah, 57
Weed, Thurlow, 94, 97
Welch, Jack, 238
Weld, Theodore Dwight, 87
welfare, 213, 217, 221, 240
Welfare Reform Act (1996), 218
Wentworth, John, 70
Westchester (N.Y.), 259
Western Reserve, 64, 67, 68
Whig Party, 90–91, 94–97, 100, 120,
    121
Whiskey Rebellion, 34, 36
Whitaker, Clem, 196
White, Hugh, 90
White, Walter, 190
White Stick Creek Indians, 39, 40
Whitney, Eli, 61

Wilberforce, William, 57
Wilentz, Sean, 85, 122
Wilkinson, James, 38
Wilkinson, Jemima, 83
William III (king), 108
Williamson, Jeffrey, 162
Wilson, James Q., 204, 216
Wilson, Woodrow, 142, 144, 157,
    179
Winthrop, John, 5
Wisconsin, 8, 73, 100, 145, 149
women's rights movement, 52, 75
Wood, Fernando, 124
Workingmen's Party, 192, 241
World War I, 142–43, 179, 183
World War II, 11, 183, 185–87, 230,
    242, 269
Wright, Gavin, 158
Wright, J. Stephen, 70, 72
Wright, Richard, 211

Y
Yankees. *See* New England Yankees
Young, Coleman, 221

About the Author

Michael Barone is senior political analyst for the *Washington Examiner* and resident fellow at the American Enterprise Institute. He is a contributor to Fox News Channel and has been a coauthor of *The Almanac of American Politics* since its first edition. This is his fifth non-Almanac book.

He grew up in Detroit and Birmingham, Michigan, and graduated from Harvard College and Yale Law School. He served as law clerk to a federal judge and vice president of a political polling firm and then turned to journalism, working for the *Washington Post*, *U.S. News & World Report*, and *Reader's Digest* and writing for many other publications. He lives in Washington, D.C.